First World War
and Army of Occupation
War Diary
France, Belgium and Germany

21 DIVISION
Divisional Troops
Divisional Signal Company
8 September 1915 - 22 June 1919

WO95/2145/1

The Naval & Military Press Ltd
www.nmarchive.com
Published in association with The National Archives

Published by

The Naval & Military Press Ltd

Unit 10 Ridgewood Industrial Park,

Uckfield, East Sussex,

TN22 5QE England

Tel: +44 (0) 1825 749494

www.naval-military-press.com

www.nmarchive.com

This diary has been reprinted in facsimile from the original. Any imperfections are inevitably reproduced and the quality may fall short of modern type and cartographic standards.

© **Crown Copyright**
Images reproduced by permission of The National Archives, London, England, 2015.

Contents

Document type	Place/Title	Date From	Date To
Heading	2145/1 Divisional Signal Company		
Heading	21st Division 21st Divl Signal Coy R.E. Sep 1915-Jun 1919		
War Diary	Witley Camp	08/09/1915	08/09/1915
War Diary	Havre	09/09/1915	10/09/1915
War Diary	Watten	11/09/1915	20/09/1915
War Diary	Watten	18/09/1915	20/09/1915
War Diary	Racquinghem	20/09/1915	21/09/1915
War Diary	Norrent Fontes	22/09/1915	22/09/1915
War Diary	Ferfay	22/09/1915	24/09/1915
War Diary	Noeux-Les-Mines	25/09/1915	25/09/1915
War Diary	Philosophe	25/09/1915	28/09/1915
War Diary	Bethune	29/09/1915	29/09/1915
War Diary	Liettres	30/09/1915	30/09/1915
Heading	21st Division 21st Signal Coy R.E. Vol 2 Oct 15		
War Diary	Liettres	01/10/1915	01/10/1915
War Diary	Morbecque	01/10/1915	01/10/1915
War Diary	Hondeghem	02/10/1915	06/10/1915
War Diary	Merris	06/10/1915	31/10/1915
Heading	21st Divl Sig: Coy: Vol. 3 121/7624 Nov 15		
War Diary	Merris	01/11/1915	11/11/1915
War Diary	Armentieres	12/11/1915	30/11/1915
War Diary	Armentieres	28/11/1915	28/11/1915
War Diary	Armentieres	24/11/1915	24/11/1915
Heading	21st Divl: Signals Coy Vol: 4 121/7935 Dec 15		
War Diary	Armentieres	01/12/1915	31/12/1915
War Diary	Armentieres	04/12/1915	28/12/1915
War Diary	Armentieres	20/12/1915	20/12/1915
Heading	21st Divisional Engineers 21st Divisional Signal Company R.E. January 1916.		
Heading	21st Divl: Signals Vol:5		
War Diary	Armentieres	01/01/1916	31/01/1916
War Diary	Armentieres	10/01/1916	23/01/1916
War Diary	Armentieres	01/01/1916	14/01/1916
War Diary	Armentieres	09/01/1916	30/01/1916
War Diary	Armentieres	19/01/1916	30/01/1916
War Diary	Armentieres	19/01/1916	31/01/1916
Heading	21st Divisional Engineers 21st Divisional Signal Company R.E. February 1916.		
War Diary	Armentieres	01/02/1916	29/02/1916
War Diary	Armentieres	17/02/1916	28/02/1916
War Diary	Armentieres	23/02/1919	28/02/1919
War Diary	Armentieres		
Heading	21st Divisional Engineers 21st Divisional Signal Company R.E. ::: March 1916.		
War Diary	Armentieres	01/03/1916	21/03/1916
War Diary	Armentieres	17/03/1916	29/03/1916
War Diary	Armentieres Merris	23/03/1916	30/03/1916
War Diary	Ribemont	31/03/1916	31/03/1916
War Diary	Ribemont	03/03/1916	03/03/1916

Heading	21st Divisional Engineers 21st Divisional Signal Company R.E. April 1916.		
War Diary	Ribemont	01/04/1916	30/04/1916
War Diary	Ribemont	05/04/1916	25/04/1916
War Diary	Ribemont	12/04/1916	12/04/1916
Heading	21st Divisional Engineers 21st Divisional Signal Company R.E. May 1916.		
Miscellaneous	Officer i/c AG's Office Base.	01/06/1916	01/06/1916
War Diary	Ribemont-Sur-Ancre	01/05/1916	31/05/1916
War Diary	Ribemont-Sur-Ancre	02/05/1916	13/05/1916
War Diary	Ribemont-Sur-Ancre	01/05/1916	01/05/1916
Heading	21st 7 Divisional Signal Company R E. 21st Divisional Signal Company R.E. ::: June 1916		
War Diary	Ribemont	01/06/1916	30/06/1916
War Diary	Meaulte	30/06/1916	30/06/1916
War Diary	Ribemont	01/06/1916	30/06/1916
Miscellaneous	88 G. The Following Additions Are Made To XV Corps 88 G. Dated 15/6/1916.	15/06/1916	15/06/1916
Miscellaneous	Telephone Communications.	04/06/1916	04/06/1916
Heading	21st Div Q		
Miscellaneous	2nd Indian Cavalry Division.		
Miscellaneous	Attached. Canadian Cavalry Brigade.		
Miscellaneous	5th. Division. Divisional Headquarters.		
Miscellaneous	95th Infantry Brigade.		
Heading	21st Divisional Engineers 21st Divisional Signal Company R.E. July 1916.		
War Diary	Ribemont	01/07/1916	04/07/1916
War Diary	Meaulte	01/07/1916	03/07/1916
War Diary	Ribemont	04/07/1916	04/07/1916
War Diary	Belloy Sur-Somme	04/07/1916	07/07/1916
War Diary	Cavillon	07/07/1916	10/07/1916
War Diary	Ribemont	10/07/1916	10/07/1916
War Diary	Ville	10/07/1916	10/07/1916
War Diary	Meaulte	11/07/1916	11/07/1916
War Diary	Meaulte	11/07/1916	19/07/1916
War Diary	Meaulte	16/07/1916	20/07/1916
War Diary	Cavillon	21/07/1916	23/07/1916
War Diary	Le Cauroy	23/07/1916	24/07/1916
War Diary	Fricourt	24/07/1916	24/07/1916
War Diary	Le Cauroy	27/07/1916	30/07/1916
War Diary	Duisans	30/07/1916	31/07/1916
War Diary	Belloy	05/07/1916	05/07/1916
War Diary	Le Cauroy	30/07/1916	30/07/1916
Miscellaneous	Signals.	02/07/1916	02/07/1916
Miscellaneous	Registered Addresses And Code Calls.	12/07/1916	12/07/1916
Miscellaneous	A		
Miscellaneous	21 Div. G. 46. 62 Inf. Bde.	12/07/1916	12/07/1916
Miscellaneous	21 Div. G. 68. 62 Inf. Bde. 64 Inf Bde.	13/07/1916	13/07/1916
Miscellaneous	List Of Registered Addresses & Code Calls 33rd. Division.	12/07/1916	12/07/1916
Miscellaneous	XIII Corps Code. 88. G.	12/07/1916	12/07/1916
Miscellaneous	88 G.	16/07/1916	16/07/1916
Miscellaneous	21 Div. G.138. 62 Inf. Bde. 64 Inf Bde.	16/07/1916	16/07/1916
Miscellaneous	21 Div. G.148. 62 Inf. Bde. 62 Inf. Bde.	17/07/1916	17/07/1916
Miscellaneous	88 G.	17/07/1916	17/07/1916
Miscellaneous	List Of Code Calls 33rd Division.	12/07/1916	12/07/1916

Miscellaneous	21 Div. G.155. 62 Inf. Bde.64 Inf. Bde.	18/07/1916	18/07/1916
Miscellaneous	List Of Registered Addresses & Code Calls 5th Division		
Miscellaneous	21 Div.G.307.		
Miscellaneous	XIII Corps Code. 88. G.	17/06/1916	17/06/1916
Miscellaneous	A Form. Messages And Signals.		
Operation(al) Order(s)	21 Div. O.O. No.61.	18/07/1916	18/07/1916
Miscellaneous			
Miscellaneous	21st Division.	08/07/1916	08/07/1916
Miscellaneous	Returns Required to Branch XIII Corps.		
Miscellaneous	Returns Required To Be Rendered To H.Q.II Corps.		
Miscellaneous	A Form. Messages And Signals.		
Miscellaneous	Instructions For Compilation Of Statements Of Surpluses And Deficiencies In Horse Transport.		
Miscellaneous	68th Div Battn. Leicestershire Regt.	09/07/1916	09/07/1916
Miscellaneous	Weekly Return Of Surpluses And Deficiencies In Horse Transport.		
Miscellaneous	State Of Trench Mortars, Trench Mortar Ammunition, Grenades And Smoke Candles At Noon, Sunday 1916		
Miscellaneous	Division Return Shewing In Detail Receipts And Expenditure Of Gun And Trench Mortar Ammunition During Week Ending Sunday 1916.		
Miscellaneous	Division-Return Shewing In Detail Remains Of Gun Ammunition At Noon, Sunday 1916.		
Miscellaneous	Formation Of Directorate. Return Of Labour, Unskilled And Semi-Skilled, Other Than That Provided By Fighting Troops Or Reinforcements, Employed On The 1st Of 1916.		
Miscellaneous	Return Of Reserves Of Supplies Maintained In Supporting Points On The Month Ending.		
Heading	21st Divisional Engineers 21st Divisional Signal Company R.E. August 1916.		
Heading	War Diary Of 21st Sig Coy. Period August. 1916.		
War Diary	Duisans	01/08/1916	26/08/1916
Heading	21st Divisional Engineers 21st Divisional Signal Company R.E. September 1916.		
War Diary	Duisans	01/09/1916	01/09/1916
War Diary	Le Cauroy	05/09/1916	12/09/1916
War Diary	Authie	13/09/1916	13/09/1916
War Diary	Buire	13/09/1916	21/09/1916
War Diary	Fricourt	22/09/1916	24/09/1916
War Diary	Montauban	25/09/1916	30/09/1916
Miscellaneous	21st Division Sick Wastage From Noon 2nd to 3rd Sept 1916.	03/09/1916	03/09/1916
Miscellaneous	21st Division Sick Wastage From Noon 1st to Noon 2nd Sept 1916	20/09/1916	20/09/1916
Heading	21st Divisional Engineers 21st Divisional Signal Company R.E. October 1916.		
War Diary	Montauban	01/10/1916	01/10/1916
War Diary	Fricourt	01/10/1916	01/10/1916
War Diary	Buire	02/10/1916	02/10/1916
War Diary	St Sauveur	03/10/1916	03/10/1916
War Diary	Ailly-Le-Haut-Clocher.	04/10/1916	08/10/1916
War Diary	Noeux-Les-Mines.	12/10/1916	12/10/1916
War Diary	Sailly La Bourse	12/10/1916	31/10/1916
War Diary	Sailly La Bourse	30/10/1916	30/10/1916

Heading	21st Divisional Engineers 21st Divisional Signal Company R.E. November 1916.		
War Diary	Sailly La Bourse	01/11/1916	29/11/1916
Heading	21st Divisional Engineers 21st Divisional Signal Company R.E. December 1916.		
War Diary	Sailly La Bourse	01/12/1916	29/12/1916
War Diary	Sailly La Bourse	00/12/1916	00/12/1916
War Diary	Ferfay		
War Diary	La Beuvriere	01/01/1917	28/01/1917
War Diary	Wormhoudt	12/02/1917	12/02/1917
War Diary	Wormhoudt	12/02/1917	14/02/1917
War Diary	Bethune	15/02/1917	17/02/1917
War Diary	Sailly La Bourse	18/02/1917	18/02/1917
War Diary	Sailly La Bourse	01/03/1917	11/03/1917
War Diary	Lucheux	12/03/1917	15/04/1917
War Diary	Yur	15/04/1917	30/04/1917
Diagram etc	Henin.		
Diagram etc	Circuit Diagram.		
War Diary	Hamelincourt	01/05/1917	12/05/1917
War Diary	Adinfer	13/05/1917	17/05/1917
War Diary	Adinfer Wood	20/05/1917	29/05/1917
War Diary	Adinfer	27/05/1917	30/05/1917
War Diary	Hamelinct	31/05/1917	31/05/1917
Diagram etc	Circuit Diagram. 21st Div. Signal Coy R.E.		
Diagram etc	Circuit Diagram. 21st Div. Signal Coy RE.		
Diagram etc	Circuit Diagram. 21st Div. Signal Coy R.E.		
Diagram etc	Royal Engineers 21st Division. Inter Company Sports Ransart.		
War Diary	Hamelincourt	01/06/1917	19/06/1917
War Diary	Adinfer Wood	20/06/1917	30/06/1917
War Diary	Adinfer Wood	05/06/1917	05/06/1917
War Diary	Adinfer Wood	25/06/1917	26/06/1917
Diagram etc	Diagram No.9. 30.6.17.		
War Diary	Adinfer Wood	01/07/1917	03/07/1917
War Diary	Moyenneville	04/07/1917	31/07/1917
Diagram etc	Sheet 51b S.W.		
Diagram etc	Visual Communication.		
Diagram etc	Route Diagram.		
Miscellaneous	Line Chances On Completion Of AG & MV Route. 19/7/17.	19/07/1917	19/07/1917
War Diary	Moyenneville	01/08/1917	26/08/1917
War Diary	Duisans	27/08/1917	31/08/1917
Diagram etc	All Lines "G.A"		
Miscellaneous	Diagram 13		
War Diary	Duisans	01/09/1917	01/09/1917
War Diary	Duisans	01/09/1917	07/09/1917
War Diary	Duisans.	07/09/1917	29/09/1917
War Diary	Duisans.	08/09/1917	16/09/1917
War Diary	Caestre	16/09/1917	18/09/1917
War Diary	Caestre	18/09/1917	22/09/1917
War Diary	Meteren	23/09/1917	30/09/1917
War Diary	Scottish Wood	30/09/1917	30/09/1917
Diagram etc	Diagram 14 29.9.17.		
War Diary	Scottish Wood	02/10/1917	05/10/1917
War Diary	Blaringhem	08/10/1917	11/10/1917
War Diary	Blaringhem	10/10/1917	10/10/1917

War Diary	Blaringhem	10/10/1917	19/10/1917
War Diary	Zevecoten	20/10/1917	22/10/1917
War Diary	Chau Segard	23/10/1917	31/10/1917
Diagram etc	Div No.1		
Diagram etc	Div No.2		
War Diary	Chau: Segard	01/11/1917	15/11/1917
War Diary	Vieux Berquin	16/11/1917	16/11/1917
War Diary	Barlin	18/11/1917	20/11/1917
War Diary	Victory Camp	22/11/1917	24/11/1917
War Diary	Villers Chatel	25/11/1917	30/11/1917
War Diary	Tincourt	01/12/1917	01/12/1917
War Diary	Villers Faucon	02/12/1917	07/12/1917
War Diary	Longavesaes	08/12/1917	13/12/1917
War Diary	Longavesaes	13/12/1917	31/12/1917
Diagram etc	Diagram Of Communications 21st Signal Coy. R.E		
Diagram etc	Diagram Of Communications.		
War Diary	Longavesnes	01/01/1918	30/01/1918
Miscellaneous	Orders Etc For Silent Day.		
Diagram etc	Visual And Wireless Communication.		
Heading	21 Signal Coy February 1918 Vol 30		
War Diary	Longavesnes	01/02/1918	01/02/1918
War Diary	Haut-Allaines	02/02/1918	28/02/1918
Heading	21st Div. War Diary 21st Divisional Signal Company, R.E. March 1918		
War Diary	Haut Allaines Longauesnes	01/03/1918	21/03/1918
War Diary	Templeux La Fosse	22/03/1918	22/03/1918
War Diary	Haut Allaines		
War Diary	Clery	23/03/1918	23/03/1918
War Diary	Maricourt	24/03/1918	24/03/1918
War Diary	Bray	25/03/1918	25/03/1918
War Diary	Sailly Laurette.	25/03/1918	25/03/1918
War Diary	Bresle	26/03/1918	26/03/1918
War Diary	Bayelincourt.	27/03/1918	28/03/1918
War Diary	Allonville	29/03/1918	31/03/1918
Heading	Appendices A, B & C.		
Diagram etc	Appendix A Lines.		
Diagram etc	Appendix "A" Visual		
Diagram etc	Appendix A Wireless		
Diagram etc	Appendix B Bury		
Diagram etc	Appendix C		
Heading	21st Divisional Engineers 21st Divisional Signal Company R.E. April 1918.		
War Diary	Allonville	01/04/1918	01/04/1918
War Diary	Caestre	02/04/1918	02/04/1918
War Diary	Dranoutre	03/04/1918	09/04/1918
War Diary	Chateau Segard	10/04/1918	12/04/1918
War Diary	Walker Camp	13/04/1918	15/04/1918
War Diary	Hoograaf	16/04/1918	18/04/1918
War Diary	G 15a 5.2. Sheet 28	19/04/1918	29/04/1918
War Diary	L 14a 2.0 Sheet 27	30/04/1918	30/04/1918
Diagram etc	Appendix. A.		
Diagram etc	Appendix. B.		
War Diary	L 14a 2.0	01/05/1918	01/05/1918
War Diary	Rubruck	02/05/1918	04/05/1918
War Diary	Romigny	06/05/1918	07/05/1918
War Diary	Romigny	07/05/1918	14/05/1918

Type	Location/Description	Start	End
War Diary	Chalons Le Vergeur	15/05/1918	27/05/1918
War Diary	Prouilly	27/05/1918	27/05/1918
War Diary	Rosnay	28/05/1918	28/05/1918
War Diary	Sarcy	28/05/1918	29/05/1918
War Diary	La Neuville	29/05/1918	29/05/1918
War Diary	Chaltrait Aux Bois	30/05/1918	31/05/1918
Diagram etc	Appendix A		
War Diary	Chaltrait	01/06/1918	06/06/1918
War Diary	La Noue	09/06/1918	14/06/1918
War Diary	Oisemont	15/06/1918	21/06/1918
War Diary	Gamaches	22/06/1918	30/06/1918
War Diary	Gamaches	23/06/1918	30/06/1918
War Diary	Gamaches	30/06/1918	30/06/1918
War Diary	Beauquesnes	01/07/1918	24/07/1918
War Diary	Raincheval	25/07/1918	26/07/1918
War Diary		25/07/1918	31/07/1918
Diagram etc	Visual Communications Map Reference Sheet 57d. Appendix I		
Diagram etc	Wireless & P.B. Communications.		
War Diary	Raincheval	01/08/1918	20/08/1918
War Diary	Acheux	21/08/1918	21/08/1918
War Diary	Mailly-Maillet	23/08/1918	24/08/1918
War Diary	Grandcourt	25/08/1918	27/08/1918
War Diary	Le Sars	30/08/1918	30/08/1918
Diagram etc	Grandcourt.		
Diagram etc	Le Sars.		
War Diary	Le Sars M 15a.9.8	01/09/1918	04/09/1918
War Diary	Les Boeufs T9a	05/09/1918	06/09/1918
War Diary	Le Mesnil	07/09/1918	27/09/1918
War Diary	P34 D 2.2 (Equancourt)	27/09/1918	30/09/1918
Diagram etc	(Sheet 57c) Appendix 1.		
Diagram etc	Appendix II		
Diagram etc	Appendix III		
Diagram etc	Appendix IV		
Diagram etc	Appendix V Communication.		
Diagram etc	21st Division. Communications. Appendix VI.		
Diagram etc	21st Divl Signals Coy, R.E. Appendix VII		
War Diary	Communications 14.9.18. Appendix VIII.		
Diagram etc	21st Division Communications At Zero+ 2 Hours Appendix IX		
Diagram etc	21st Division Communications Appendix X.		
Miscellaneous	21st Divisional Signal Orders For Divisional Communications. Appendix XI		
Diagram etc	Diagram I		
Diagram etc	Diagram II. Traffic.		
Heading	War Diary 21st Divl. Signal Coy., R.E. October 1st-31st 1918. Vol. 38		
War Diary	Equancourt	01/10/1918	04/10/1918
War Diary	Revelon W11a 5.8	05/10/1918	07/10/1918
War Diary	M 32 L 6.3.	08/10/1918	09/10/1918
War Diary	Walincourt	10/10/1918	20/10/1918
War Diary	Inchy	21/10/1918	21/10/1918
War Diary	Neuvilly	22/10/1918	24/10/1918
War Diary	Ovillers	25/10/1918	25/10/1918
War Diary	Neuvilly	26/10/1918	29/10/1918
War Diary	Ovillers	30/10/1918	30/10/1918

Type	Description	From	To
Diagram etc	Appendix I		
Diagram etc	Communications Appendix II		
Diagram etc	Divisional Communications. Appendix III		
Diagram etc	Line Communications Appendix IV		
Diagram etc	Communications. Appendix V		
Diagram etc	Line Communications. Appendix VI		
Heading	War Diary Of 21st Divl. Signal Company., R.E. From:- 1st November 1918. To 30th November 1918.		
War Diary	Ovillers	01/11/1918	01/11/1918
War Diary	Heuvilly	02/11/1918	02/11/1918
War Diary	Poix Du Nord	04/11/1918	04/11/1918
War Diary	S 24d 3.3	05/11/1918	06/11/1918
War Diary	Berlaimont	07/11/1918	11/11/1918
War Diary	Aulnoye	12/11/1918	30/11/1918
Diagram etc	21st Signal Coy, R.E. Communications On Novem. 1st 1918		
Diagram etc	21st Signal Coy, R.E. Lines At Zero, 5th Novem 1918.		
Diagram etc	21st Signal Coy, R.E.		
Heading	War Diary Of 21st Divl. Signal Company., R.E. From:- 1st December 1918. To:- 31st December 1918. Vol 40		
War Diary	Aulnoye	02/12/1918	13/12/1918
War Diary	Inchy	14/12/1918	18/12/1918
War Diary	Molliens Vidame.	19/12/1918	31/12/1918
Diagram etc	21st Div. Signal Coy, R.E. Communications In The Cavillon Area.		
Heading	War Diary Of 21st Divisional Signal Company., R.E. From:- 1st January 1919. To:- 31st January 1919. Vol 41		
War Diary	Molliens Vidame.	01/01/1919	30/01/1919
Diagram etc	21st Divl Signal Company, R.E. Communications January, 1919.		
War Diary	War Diary Of 21st Divl. Signal Coy, R.E. From:- 1st February 1919. To:- 28th February, 1919. Vol 42		
War Diary	Molliens-Vidame	01/02/1919	25/02/1919
Diagram etc	Appendix I.		
War Diary	Molliens Vidame	01/03/1919	30/03/1919
Diagram etc	Appendix I.		
Miscellaneous	O/C of 6 Sections 3rd Echelon	01/05/1919	01/05/1919
War Diary	Molliens Vidame.	01/04/1919	01/04/1919
War Diary	Conde Folie	05/04/1919	20/04/1919
Diagram etc	21st Division S1a. Communications-April-		
War Diary	Conde Folie	01/05/1919	19/05/1919
War Diary	L 'Etoile	19/05/1919	25/05/1919
Miscellaneous	21st. Division Group Packet No. A. 1276/1.	20/05/1919	20/05/1919
Miscellaneous	21st. Division Group Packet Details Camp-L 'Etoile. Regiment.		
War Diary	Conde Folie.	01/06/1919	22/06/1919

2145/1

Divisional Signal Company.

21ST DIVISION

21ST DIVL SIGNAL COY R.E.
SEP 1915 - JUN 1919

Army Form C. 2118

WAR DIARY or INTELLIGENCE SUMMARY

HdQrs & 22/Section 21st Divl Signal Co RE Vol 15

(Erase heading not required.)

Instructions regarding War Diaries and Intelligence Summaries are contained in F. S. Regs., Part II. and the Staff Manual respectively. Title Pages will be prepared in manuscript.

Place	Date	Hour	Summary of Events and Information	Remarks and references to Appendices
WITLEY CAMP	8.9.15	9am	Entrained at full strength at MILFORD Station to SOUTHAMPTON, & arrived at SOUTHAMPTON about noon. Embarked on transport CITY OF DUNQUERQUE during afternoon & sailed at 8pm. Strength Officers 3 O.R. 123 Horses 83. 12 Vehicles 1 30cwt. Daimler lorry 1 10HP Singer Car Major L.R.J.W. Taylor CSM Adams H. Lieut N. Porteous CQMS Hockaday F. 2nd Lieut A.I. Walker.	
HAVRE	9.9.15	7am	Disembarked & marched to rest camp, arriving there 2pm	
"	10.9.15	5am	Marched out from rest camp at 5am to GARE des MARCHANDISES & Entrained. Train started 10.15am arrived ST OMER at 6am on 11th, detrained & marched to WATTEN.	
WATTEN	11.9.15	11am	Arrived, established signal office at ECOLE COMMUNALE. Laid out lines to brigades at MOULE, NORDAUSQUES & BAYENGHEM. 2 French interpreters, Ptes HEIMANN, A. & BOUSQUIER attached to the Company	
"	12.9.15 to 20.9.15			

Army Form C. 2118

HdQrs & No 1 Section
21st Divl Signal Co RE

WAR DIARY
or
INTELLIGENCE SUMMARY
(Erase heading not required.)

Instructions regarding War Diaries and Intelligence Summaries are contained in F. S. Regs., Part II. and the Staff Manual respectively. Title Pages will be prepared in manuscript.

Place	Date	Hour	Summary of Events and Information	Remarks and references to Appendices
WATTEN	16.9.15		Lieut V Hook joined from 8th Divl Signal Co & took over No 2 Brigade Section from Lieut FASHAM.	
	20.9.15	8 pm	Marched out & proceeded with 2nd hdqrs via TILQUES, ARQUES to RACQUINGHEM	
RACQUINGHEM	21.9.15	2 am	Arrived, Signal Office at Chateau, company bivouacked in grounds	
"	"	7 pm	Marched out, via WITTES, AIRE to NORRENT-FONTES.	
NORRENT-FONTES	22.9.15	1 am	Arrived, bivouacked	
"	"	6 pm	Marched out, via LIERES, AMES to FERFAY.	
FERFAY	22.9.15	10 pm	Arrived, Signal Office at Chateau, company bivouacked.	
"	23.9.15		Laid cables to Brigades at BURBURE, CAUCHY-LA-TOUR & AMES.	
"	24.9.15		Reeled in cables by 3 pm. Marched out 7 pm via CAUCHY-LA-TOUR, AUCHEL, MARLES-LES-MINES to NOEUX-LES-MINES, arriving there at midnight.	
NOEUX-LES-MINES	25.9.15		Signal Office at Brewery, established communication with XI Corps.	

WAR DIARY
or
INTELLIGENCE SUMMARY

(Erase heading not required.)

Hd.Qrs & No1 Section Army Form C. 2118
21st Div. Signal Co.

3

Place	Date	Hour	Summary of Events and Information	Remarks and references to Appendices
NOEUX-LES-MINES	25/9/15		Received orders to march ~~about 12.30~~ during morning & marched off at 12 noon, via cross roads in NOEUX-LES-MINES. Delayed here an hour owing to traffic, arrived at MAZINGARBE about 2.30 p.m. & arranged for signal office in house selected as divl Hdqrs. Orders then received to move on to VERMELLES – PHILOSOPHE, & arrived there at 4 p.m. Established signal office & divl hdqrs in a row of houses N. of PHILOSOPHE Cross-roads. 11th Bde, whose advanced hdqrs were at SAILLY-LABOURSE, laid a line to this signal office at 6 p.m. One infantry brigade (62nd) was attached to another division. The 63rd & 64th moved forward & made night marches. Connection was kept up with them by runner, but was not satisfactory, chiefly owing to brigades not reporting their positions often enough, the country being strange & all roads congested with traffic.	
PHILOSOPHE	26/9/15		Three cable wagons commenced laying lines for Artillery at 6 a.m. Div Art Hdqrs was put at PHILOSOPHE & then at LA ROTOIRE. Cable laid & letter place, & point 69, S.W. of LOOS, & to artillery brigade headquarters. Connection to 63rd & 64th Inf Bdes maintained by runner, but was un-satisfactory, owing to difficulty in locating brigade headquarters. All three brigades commenced assembling on the PHILOSOPHE — SAILLY road	

WAR DIARY or INTELLIGENCE SUMMARY

Army Form C. 2118

HdQrs & No1 Section 21st Divl. Signal Co.

Place	Date	Hour	Summary of Events and Information	Remarks and references to Appendices
PHILOSOPHE	27/9/15		Cable wagons laid lines to new positions of 96th & 97th F.A. Bdes., at Fosse 9(?), & lines to other artillery brigades maintained. Altogether 20 miles of cable laid out for artillery on 26th & 27th, mostly under fire. Line laid also down the SAILLY LABOURSE road to ties taken off it to the three infantry brigades.	
"	28/9/15		Laid extra artillery lines & maintained then system. 2nd Lieut A.I. Walker, & Linesmen & 12 telegraphists detailed to remain with artillery. Remainder marched out from PHILOSOPHE at 9 pm towards BETHUNE.	
BETHUNE	29/9/15		Arrived 1 a.m., established signal office in Hotel de France. Men billeted in Ecole. Marched out at 2.10 pm, proceeded via CHOCQUES — LILLERS — ST. HILAIRE — RELY to LIETTRES.	
LIETTRES	30/9/15		Arrived 10 pm. Established signal office at Château; communicated to brigades in adjacent village by D.R.	
	Casualties		27.9.15 Lieut Lingard-Garred. Fractured. Lieut Hook.– gassed slightly. Returned to duty. Sapper C. Hall wounded (since died of wounds). M.C Corporal Dodd wounded & evacuated. M.C Corporal Turnbull. – gassed slightly. Remained at duty. Sergt Fletcher wounded 3.9.15 Evacuated 2 horses wounded 27.9.15 M.C Corporal Grund accidently hurt at LIETTRES on 30.9.15 Evacuated	

Wt. W593/826 1,000,000 4/15 J.B.C. & A. A.D.S.S./Forms/C. 2118. 1875

W. Wilkinson Major R.E.
O.C. 21 Divl Sig. Co. R.E.

121/7595

21st Kurrain

21st Afghil by Mr.
Vol 2

Oct 15

… Hdqrs v No 1 section
21st Div Signal Co. R.E.

WAR DIARY
INTELLIGENCE SUMMARY
(Erase heading not required.)

Army Form C. 2118.

Place	Date	Hour	Summary of Events and Information	Remarks and references to Appendices
LIETTRES	1st Oct	9 am	Left billet at CHATEAU by march route	
MORBECQUE	"	4 pm	Arrived, billeted at CHATEAU. Left by march route 9 am on 2nd Oct.	
HONDEGHEM	2nd Oct	6 pm	Arrived billeted in farm. Signal Office in ECOLE NATIONALE. Laid cable to brigades at CAESTRE, BORRE and STRAZEELE.	
"	3rd			
"	4th			
"	6th			
MERRIS	7th	9 am	Left by march route	
"	"	3 pm	Arrived, billeted in outbuilding of HOSPICE. Signal Office in HOSPICE. Laid cable connecting up HOSPICE. Frequent changes necessary owing to brigades leaving the area. Connected to artillery brigade at LA KREULE & vicinity. Ammunition cage laying improvised air line to replace D5 lines, on 28th. Materials used, 15 ft poles, 2" diam., obtained from the FORÊT DE NIEPPE, 100 lb. iron wire rings, loan issued, small porcelain insulators, commenced making brick house insulators on 30th.	
"	31st		Lieut. J W AITKEN R.E.(T.C.) joined as Supernumerary Officer	
			Strength on 31st Officers 4, Lieutenants 1, Other ranks 120, Attached (RSC) 3, Total 128, Horses 84	

2.ter Abtl. Sig. Cp:
Fol: 3

12/7924

Nov 15.

Army Form C. 2118.

Page 1

Instructions regarding War Diaries and Intelligence Summaries are contained in F.S. Regs., Part II. and the Staff Manual respectively. Title pages will be prepared in manuscript.

WAR DIARY or INTELLIGENCE SUMMARY.

HdQrs & No 1 Section 21st Div Signal Co. R.E.

(Erase heading not required.)

Place	Date	Hour	Summary of Events and Information	Remarks and references to Appendices
MERRIS	1.11.15		Carrying on with putting up improved airline to STRAZEELE BORRE CAESTRE and OUTTERSTEENE. Carrying on with horsestandings. Obtained brushwood & straw to making road to standing from MONT NOIR quarry through CE 2nd Corps.	
"	7.11.15 8.11.15	9am	4 Telegraphists & 2 linemen to Villa St Joseph, CASSEL, for course of instruction. 2 O.R. joined. 1 A.S.C. lorry driver evacuated.	
"	11.11.15	9am	Advance party, 2nd Lt Walker & 7 O.R. to ARMENTIERES.	
ARMENTIERES	12.11.15	11am	Company arrived by march route from MERRIS. Took over Signal Office at the ECOLE PROFESSIONELLE from 5th Signal Co. Office staff and despatch riders billeted at ECOLE, remainder with horses & wagons in bivouac at PONT DE NIEPPE. Accommodation at horse lines very poor, bivouacs consisting of tarpaulins stretched across poles. Brick standings for horses had been made, but no roads, nor paths, & the whole field was very muddy. Accommodation at Ecole good, with ample space.	
"	13.11.15 to 30.11.15		Party at ECOLE started sleeping in cellars, on account of shelling. A lot of work done in making lines safe, as a large number were cut by shellfire on night of 12th & subsequently. Some were laid in sewers & electric power mains (underground) were used for others. Safe lines were provided by these avenues to each F.A. Bde from Div. Art. hdqrs & 62nd, 64th Inf. Bdes. A road was made in the horselines up to the standings, stone being fetched by the G.S. wagon from a burnt-out factory in ARMENTIERES.	

2353 Wt. W3141/1454 1/790,000 5/15 D.D.& L. A.D.S.S./Form/C. 2118.

WAR DIARY

Hdqrs + No 1 Section
INTELLIGENCE SUMMARY. 21st Signal Co RE

Place	Date	Hour	Summary of Events and Information	Remarks and references to Appendices
ARMENTIERES	28.11.15		Three 20-men huts erected at Horse Lines.	
			Strength of Company on 30.11.15	
			Officers 4 Horses 84	
			Interpreter 1	
			Other ranks 120	
			Attached (ASC) 2 % of pigeons	
			" (G.H.Q. Sigs) 4	
			" (2nd Inf Bn Sigs) 10	
			" (Officer RE) 1	
			Total 142	
"	24.11.15		1 officer + 8 men of above, belonging to 2nd Corps Signal Co., joined as permanent party i/c communications of district.	

Murdoch Maj RE
O.C. 21st Sig Co RE

1/
2/ 2nd Divi Sjuala
vol: 4

D/
7935

Dec '15

WAR DIARY

Hdqrs & No. 1 Section 21st Divl Signal Co. R.E.

INTELLIGENCE SUMMARY

Army Form C. 2118.

Place	Date	Hour	Summary of Events and Information	Remarks and references to Appendices
ARMENTIERES.	1/12/15 to 31/12/15		Carried on with making important lines safe. In several cases, use was made of the town underground electric power cable system. These cables consist of three cores, which can be used as a metallic circuit + one earth return circuit. Replaced about 6 miles of poled D5 cable by airline. Picked up about 10 miles of damaged D5 lines. Altered the arrangement of office wiring between the Signal Office and the report centre, so that the change from one to the other could be made in the minimum of time. The Telephone Exchange transformers and sounder batteries were all put in the report centre, + duplicate leads to instruments installed to either office. Erected another 20 man hut at horse lines (B 28 b - 8.9 Sheet 36). Obtained from vacated camp of 2nd Mountain Battery, commenced putting up overhead shelter for horses over the brick standings, consisting of a roof of planks + felt supported on wooden frames.	
"	4/12/15		1 Driver evacuated to C.C.S BAILLEUL, — accidentally poisoned by	
"	16/12/15		1 Driver evacuated to No 8 CCS, BAILLEUL, —	
"	20/12/15		1 A.S.C. driver transferred to 21st Div. Ammn Sub park with Singer light car,	
"	26/12/15		1 Driver joined from R.E. Advanced Base	
"	27/12/15		1 O.S.C. driver rejoined from No 15 C.C.S	

WAR DIARY

INTELLIGENCE SUMMARY

Hdqrs & No 1 Section 21st Div. Signal Co. R.E.

Army Form C. 2118.

Place	Date	Hour	Summary of Events and Information	Remarks and references to Appendices
ARMENTIERES	20/12/15		1 Le Copt. A.S.C. transferred from 21st Div. Amm. Subpark with 12-16 H.P. Sunbeam car.	
			Strength of Company on 31.12.15.	
			Officers 4	
			Interpreter 1	
			Other ranks 121	
			Attached 3 (A.S.C.)	
			" 4 (G.H.Q. Signals, i/c of pigeons).	
			" 10 (2nd Corps. Signals)	
			Total 144	
			Horses 84.	

W.R. Shaughnessy Major R.E.
O.C. 21st Sig. Co. R.E.

21st Divisional Engineers

21st DIVISIONAL SIGNAL COMPANY R. E. :: JANUARY 1916.

2ⁿᵈ Set: Syrials
Vol: 5

Army Form C. 2118.

WAR DIARY

Hdqrs of 21st Division

INTELLIGENCE SUMMARY. 21st Div. Signal Co. R.E.

(Erase heading not required.)

Place	Date	Hour	Summary of Events and Information	Remarks and references to Appendices
ARMENTIERES	1.1.16 to 31.1.16		Carried on with ordinary maintenance & improving lines. Several D5 cable lines on river Lys that had been down 5 to 6 months became bad & had to be replaced. About 6 miles of airline was laid & a similar amount of D5 cable recovered. Bn. Hdqrs were shelled for short periods in evenings of 15th & 17th. On 28th orders were issued that front was to be held by 2 brigades instead of 3, & the necessary alterations in communications were carried out by 31st.	
"	10.1.16		Wireless (French pattern) set received with 3 operators & fixed up near Bgd. Hdqrs. Communication to front set at MIEPPE. British & French men taken by lty.	
"	12.1.16		"Ballot" 1 KW. Electric lighting set received & installed for lighting of Hdqrs Offices.	
"	23.1.16		From this date, 8 drivers & 8 pairs L.D. horses lent daily to Hdqrs 2nd Train, to assist in transport duties.	
"	1.1.16		1 a/Sergeant joined from RE Advanced base.	
"	6.1.16		1 driver evacuated to No. 8 C.C.S.	
"	14.1.16		1 driver rejoined from No. 8 C.C.S.	
"	9.1.16		2 drivers transferred to 2nd Corps Hdqrs Signal Co.	
"	14.1.16		3 drivers joined from RE Advanced base.	

Army Form C. 2118.

Hdqrs & No. 1 section
21st Divl Signal Co R.E.

WAR DIARY

INTELLIGENCE SUMMARY.

(Erase heading not required.)

Instructions regarding War Diaries and Intelligence Summaries are contained in F. S. Regs., Part II. and the Staff Manual respectively. Title pages will be prepared in manuscript.

Place	Date	Hour	Summary of Events and Information	Remarks and references to Appendices
ARMENTIERES	11.1.16		1 Sapper evacuated to No. 4 Stationary Hospt.	
"	30.1.16		1 Sapper joined from R.E. Advanced Base	
	19.1.16 to 30.1.16		2nd Lt G Conway Brown to Wireless G.H.Q. for course of instruction.	
	19.1.16 to 25.1.16		Lieut Grice R.E. attached for instruction.	
	25.1.16 to 31.1.16		Capt. Hennessy R.I. Fus. attached for instruction.	
			Strength of Company on 31.1.16	
			Officers.... 4	
			" .... 2 attached	
			Interprets... 1	
			Other ranks. 121	
			Attached 3 (A.S.C)	
			" 4 G.H.Q Signals (Lt pigeons)	
			" 12 (2nd Corps Signals)	
			" 3 Wireless operators	
			Total 150	Horses 84

R.A.W. Sunderson
Major R.E.
OC 21st Divl Signal Co R.E.

21st Divisional Engineers

21st DIVISIONAL SIGNAL COMPANY R. E. ::: FEBRUARY 1916.

Army Form C. 2118

WAR DIARY
INTELLIGENCE SUMMARY

HdQrs & No. 1 Section, 21st Divl. Signal Co. R.E.

(Erase heading not required.)

Instructions regarding War Diaries and Intelligence Summaries are contained in F.S. Regs., Part II. and the Staff Manual respectively. Title Pages will be prepared in manuscript.

Place	Date	Hour	Summary of Events and Information	Remarks and references to Appendices
ARMENTIERES.	1.2.16 to 29.2.16		General maintenance of lines. With the assistance of infantry working parties, provided shell protection to the Gris lenche Power station, which forms an important test point in the system of communications. A protected line was laid to a new H.Qrs. for the brigade in reserve.	
	17.2.16		A second wireless (trench pattern) set received & installed at Right Bde Adv.	
	17.2.16 to 29.2.16		Lieut. J.J. Heron to Wireless G.H.Q. for course of instruction.	
	23.2.16		1 Motor cyclist Corporal evacuated to No.1 Gen C.C.S. Accident to knee. Lieut. J.W. Aitken, Supernumerary Officer, left for 2nd Army Signals.	
	28.2.16		Lieut A.E. Collis joined as Supernumerary Officer. 2nd Lieuts. Hollings & G. Nickerson from Signal Depôt, Fenny Stratford, were each attached for one week's instruction.	
	26.2.16		Strength of Company on 29.2.16.	

WAR DIARY

Hqrs & W/ Section
21st Brit Signal Co RE

INTELLIGENCE SUMMARY

(Erase heading not required.)

Army Form C. 2118

Place	Dates	Hour	Summary of Events and Information	Remarks and references to Appendices
ARMENTIERES			Officers 4. 1 attached.	
			Interpreter 1	
			Other ranks 121	
			Attached 3 (A.S.C.)	
			" 4 (G.H.Q Signals, inc pigeons)	
			" 12 2nd Corps Signals	
			" 3 Wireless Operators	
			Total 149	

[signature]
W.H. Hamilton? R.E.
M/Sy R.E.
OC 21st Sigy Co RE

21st Divisional Engineers

21st DIVISIONAL SIGNAL COMPANY R. E. ::MARCH 1916.

Army Form C. 2118

WAR DIARY H.Qrs & No 1 Section
or 21st Div Signal Co RE
INTELLIGENCE SUMMARY

(Erase heading not required.)

Place	Date	Hour	Summary of Events and Information	Remarks and references to Appendices
ARMENTIERES	13/3/16		General maintenance of lines from 15th to 23rd inst. Infantry working parties were obtained for digging the trenches, in which 3 buried-sheathed 6pair cables were laid by night; two leading from the TISSAGE, HOUPLINES to the battalion hdqrs in PLANK Avenue, & one from the TISSAGE to the battalion hdqrs in SPAIN Avenue. Trench was 3 feet deep, with test boxes every 220 yards. Sergt W.I Russell did good work in organising details. Total length of trench dug 1600 yards.	
	21/3/16		Listening experiments were carried out, a receiver being connected to the German ends of power cables, whose cut in the front line opposite Trench 67.5 on the LILLE Road. The only signals picked up were some calls from the division on the right.	
	17/3/16		Lieut F.B Foster to Wireless G.H.Q for course of instruction. Capt J.W Pinsent R.E. attached till 23.3.16	
	17/3/16		Lieut Scurr posted to Co as Supernumerary Officer.	
	24/3/16		Lieut Scurr rejoined 2nd Corps Signal Co.	

WAR DIARY

INTELLIGENCE SUMMARY — HqFs & No 1 Section 21st Div. Signal Co R.E.

Army Form C. 2118

(Erase heading not required.)

Place	Date	Hour	Summary of Events and Information	Remarks and references to Appendices
ARMENTIERES	29.3.16		Handed over signal office to 17th Sig Co at 11 am. Marched out at 10 am. Arrived 1.30 pm. Established Signal Office in Hospice.	
MERRIS			No lines laid out; intended the brunie wirelines put up by the company in October. 19.15 pm Communicating with Brigades.	
	30.3.16		Marched out 6 pm. Entrained at GODEWAERSVELDE station at 8 pm. Sharing train with Cyclist Co & A.P. Cable Section. Train started 10.55 pm.	
RIBEMONT	31.3.16		Detrained at LONGUEAU station 10.15 am. Marched out to RIBEMONT, arriving 4 pm. Men billeted in barn &c. Horse accommodation fair, with overhead cover. Signal office established in same house as Div. H.Qrs.	
	3.3.16		1 Motor Cyclist Orderly joined from R.E. Signal Depot, Abbeville. Strength of Co on 31.3.16 — Officers 4, Interpreter 1, Other ranks 121, Attached 3 (A.S.C.) Total 129	

Lt. Col. Shanghan May R.E.
O.C. 21st Sig Co R.E.

21st Divisional Engineers

21st DIVISIONAL SIGNAL COMPANY R. E. :: APRIL 1916.

Army Form
Hdqrs & No 1 Section
21st Signal Co RE Vol 8

WAR DIARY or INTELLIGENCE SUMMARY

(Erase heading not required.)

Place	Date	Hour	Summary of Events and Information	Remarks and references to Appendices
RIBEMONT	1.4.16 to 30.4.16		Established communications with XIII Corps & with brigades at MEAULTE, VILLE and LA NEUVILLE. Utilised permanent telegraph lines on railway for most of these circuits. Commenced preparing a system of communications for an offensive, & worked out an estimate of 170 miles of cable required. Received 60 miles of cable. Carried on with digging cable trenches, preparing only towards this. Obtained working parties from infantry, averaging 100 testboxes &c by day & 200 by night. On 28.4.16, came under XV Corps, instead of XIII Corps. Lieut F.B. FINTER, No 3 Brigade Section, left for England. 2 Lieut G.H. RECKNELL, joined from XIII Corps as Supervising Officer. Lieut COLLIS, E.A. took over command of No 3 Brigade Section. 1 O.R. joined from base. Sergt J. Dinham left for England, with a view to getting a commission. B. Trevarten Lt	
	5.4.16			
	6.4.16			
	5.4.16			
	15.4.16			
	19.4.16 21.4.16			

Army Form C. 2118

WAR DIARY
or
INTELLIGENCE SUMMARY
(Erase heading not required.)

HQrs & No.1 Section
21st Div. Signal Co. RE

Place	Date	Hour	Summary of Events and Information	Remarks and references to Appendices
RIBEMONT	21.4.16		1 O.R. joined from base.	
"	25.4.16		1 O.R. joined from base.	
"	12.4.16		1 O.R. evacuated to Base hospital, Oxford	
			Strength on 30.4.16	
			3 Officers	Horses 81
			121 O.R.	
			2 Middlesex Regt ⎫	
			3 A.S.C. ⎬ attached	
			3 A.T. Cable Section ⎭	
			___	
			132	

W.R. Shanks (?)
Major R.E.
O.C. 21 Sig. Co. R.E.

21st Divisional Engineers

21st DIVISIONAL SIGNAL COMPANY R. E. ::: MAY 1916.

Officer i/c AG's office Base

Herewith war diary of Hdqrs &
No 1 sect of this company for months
Sept 1915 & May 1916.

B.E.F.
1/6/16

[signature]
Maj RE
O.C. 21 Sig Co RE

WAR DIARY or INTELLIGENCE SUMMARY

Army Form C. 2118

Hdqrs + No 1 Section 21st Divl Signal Co. R.E.

Place	Date	Hour	Summary of Events and Information	Remarks and references to Appendices
RIBEMONT-SUR-ANCRE	1.5.16 to 31.5.16		Maintained divisional communications & carried on with scheme of communications for an offensive. About forty miles of cable laid out, partly in cable trenches 3 foot deep (minimum) 5' deep (maximum), & partly slapped low down to sides of communication trenches. Unable to complete any section, as all dug-outs are still under construction & not yet ready for cables to be led in.	
	2.5.16		1 Sapper transferred to L Signal Co.	
	5.5.16		1 Sapper transferred from L Signal Co.	
	6.5.16		1 Sapper (harness maker) joined from base.	
	13.5.16		1 Pioneer joined from base.	
	1.5.16		Lt. B. Brereton, 30 O.R. with 30 horses joined from XV Corps, & attached to this Company as B.C. Cable Section.	
			Strength of Company on 31.5.16.	
			4 Officers (1 attached)	
			121 O.R.	
			2 Middlesex Regt. attached	
			3 A.S.C.	
			5 Wireless operators	
			30 B.C. Cable Section	
			165	
			111 horses	

L.W. Murphy R.E.
Capt
O.C. 21 Sig Co R.E.

21st 7 Divisional Signal Company R. E.

21st   DIVISIONAL SIGNAL COMPANY R. E. ::: JUNE   1916

WAR DIARY
INTELLIGENCE SUMMARY
(Erase heading not required.)

Hqrs No 1 Section Army Form C. 2118
21st Div Signal Co. R.E.
Vol 10

June

Place	Date	Hour	Summary of Events and Information	Remarks and references to Appendices
RIBEMONT	1.6.16 to 23.6.16		Maintenance work, with one brigade holding the FRICOURT sector of the front line, one brigade at VILLE & one at LA NEUVILLE. Carried on with preparations for the offensive, viz: digging cable trenches, laying cables & leading in to offices, trials & building emplacements for round signalling, making huts, shelters, terminal boards & buzzer switchboards for the whole division. The dug-out used as a forward exchange was not bombproof, & so the C.R.E. was made to help, the Signal Co added extra protection. Two lorry loads of girders were obtained from AMIENS, & a layer of girders placed across the roof, supported on longitudinal girders, one foot off the ground. About 3 feet of chalk & sandbags were put on top of this layer of girders.	
	23.6.16		One Officer, Lieut. A.I. Walker, & 13 O.R. proceeded to the forward exchange, Queen's Redoubt, BÉCOURT, & one Officer, Lieut. N. Porteous & #170R to the Divl. report centre, which was also C.R.A's advanced hdqrs, &	

Army Form C. 2118.

H.Qrs & No 1 Section 21st Divn Signal Co. R.E.

WAR DIARY
or
INTELLIGENCE SUMMARY.

(Erase heading not required.)

Place	Date	Hour	Summary of Events and Information	Remarks and references to Appendices
RIBEMONT	23.6.16 24.6.16 to 30.6.16		T.O.R. & travel stations & intermediate test points. Three parties ran the signal offices & maintained forward lines during the preliminary bombardment.	
NEAULTE	31.6.16		Major Taylor & H.O.R. proceeded to Report Centre, 3 O.R. to forward exchange & made up the full staff of these forward offices. 1 Cable detachment bivouacked near report centre. 6 linesmen of 17th Sig Co. were attached to give extra help. B.C. Cable Section ran the RIBEMONT office & maintained back lines. The RIBEMONT office was maintained as a back exchange.	
		5pm	Divn H.Q. closed at RIBEMONT & opened at the dug-outs (report centre) E.28.a.3.6. Sheet 62.D. Details of signal arrangements will accompany July report as an appendix.	

WAR DIARY
or
INTELLIGENCE SUMMARY

HQrs & No.1 Section, 21st Ind. Signal Co. R.E.

Army Form C. 2118.

Place	Date	Hour	Summary of Events and Information	Remarks and references to Appendices
RIBEMONT	1/6/16		4 pioneers joined from base, increase to establishment.	
"	11/6/16		Lieut. G. Gowing-Brown i/c No 2 section, evacuated to No 2 Stat. Hospt. Abbeville. A/Lieut G.H. Rockwell took over No 2 section.	
"	16/6/16		2/Lieut A.H. NIBLETT joined as Supernumerary Officer.	
"	17/6/16		Six wireless operators transferred to Co. as Sappers, increase to establishment.	
"	25/6/16		1 Sapper evacuated to C.C.S.	
"	29/6/16		3 sappers, including 1 of No 2 Section, killed in action at MEAULTE.	
"	30/6/16		4 O.R. joined from base.	
			Strength of Co. & attached on 30th	

WAR DIARY or INTELLIGENCE SUMMARY

HQrs & No 1 Sect. 21st Div¹ Signal Co RE

Place: RIBEMONT
Date: 30/6

Officers 4
O.R. 135

Officers 1 } BG Cable Section
O.R. 30 } attached

Interpreter 1

Attached {
O.R. 3   A.S.C. (lorry & car drivers)
O.R. 1   4th Middlesex R
O.R. 1   RFC wireless
O.R. 12 Cyclist orderlies
O.R. 6   Signallers, 14th Yorks¹ Fus.

Total 194

Horses 82
        30 B.G. section
       112

Major RE
O.C. 21 Sig Co RE

SECRET.   88 G.

The following additions are made to XV Corps 88 G. dated 15/6/1916 :-

	Registered Address.	Code Call.
17th Divisional Artillery H.Q.	Moth	MRM
"D" Coy. 12th (Labour) Battalion D.C.L.I.	Bugle	BD

H.Q., XV Corps,
23/6/1916.

[signed] E.V.J. Currie Capt.
For Brigadier General,
General Staff.

Copies to :-
7th Division   7
17th Division   7
21st Division   7
B.G.R.A.   7
C.E.   7
A.D.A.S.   3

No. 3 Squadron, R.F.C.   1
No. 3 Kite Balloon Sec. 1
"G"   4
"A" & "Q"   2
D.D.M.S.   1
A.D.O.S.   1
A.P.M.   1
Corps Commander   1

III Corps   1
XIII Corps   1 } for information.

TELEPHONE COMMUNICATIONS.

4/8/16.

VI CORPS SIGNALS.

A.D.A.S. VI Corps
A.D.O.S. VI Corps
A.P.M.   VI Corps
A.D.M.S. 11 Division
A.D.M.S. 21 Division

AMMUNITION PARKS:
VI Corps.
15 Reserve

AMMUNITION COLUMNS:
11 Division
21 Division

ANTI-AIRCRAFT:
No. 25 Section No 29 Sectn
No. 1 Gun
No. 2 Gun

ARMY SERVICE CORPS:
565 M.T. Coy. (No. 4
  Section) (Attached
  VI Corps H.Artillery)
NOTE: Other ASC units
  under Supply Cols. &c.

B.G.G.S., VI Corps

BRIGADES:
R.F.C. - 3rd
RFA - All Brigades in
  Corps.
Infantry - All Brigades
  in Corps.

CHIEF ENGINEER, VI Corps.

C.R.E. 11 Division
       21 Division

CAMP COMMANDANT: VI Corps

CASUALTY CLEARING STATION:
No. 37.

CORPS: VII
       XVII

D.A.& Q.M.G., VI Corps
A.Q.M.G., VI Corps.
  DDMS 6 Corps
DIVISIONS.
All Divisions in Corps

DIVISIONAL ARTILLERY.
All Divisional Artillery.

DIVISIONAL SCHOOLS.
5th Div. Details.
21 Division.

FIELD CASHIRE, VI Corps (ER)

FIELD AMBULANCES.
34   65
64

FRENCH MISSION VI Corps

GENERAL STAFF, VI Corps

HEAVY ARTILLERY, VI Corps
H.A.Ex for G.O.C. Gps.&c

INDIAN CAVALRY: Sialkot Bde

INTELLIGENCE, VI Corps.

I.O.M., VI Corps.
O.M.   O.Q.
KITE BALLOONS, No. 4 Squdn.
Nos.7 & 18 K.B. Sections

15 M.A.C.

MOUNTED TROOPS: Northants Yeo.

ORDNANCE: ADOS, VI Corps.
D.A.D.O.S. of Divisions.
O.M., (Avesnes). OQ
PIGEON LOFTS: GOUY & AGNEZ
6th P.O.War Coy.
"Q" Staff VI Corps.
15 Reserve Park.
ROYAL ARTILLERY.
B.G.R.A., VI Corps. All
RA Staffs, Bdes & Batts.
in Corps.
ROYAL ENGINEERS:
C.E. VI Corps: CRE of Divs.
235,144 A.T.Cos., NZ, 184,
256 T.Cos. 2/2 Glam. F. Co.
R.E. PARKS: Nos. 5,6, & 8,
and Laherliere.
ROYAL FLYING CORPS:
8,12,13,23 Squadrons
12,13 Wings.
3rd Brigade.
R.T.Os: Amiens, Aubigny,
Doullens, Mt.St.Eloi,
Saulty, Tincques.
SCHOOLS.
21 Div. (Hauteville)
SIALKOT BDE: 2 Ind.Cav.Div
SIGNAL SERVICE. A.D.A.S. &
Signal Master VI Corps.
All Div. Signal Officers.
STAFF.   All Staffs.
SUPPLY COLUMNS.
VI Corps.
11 Divisional
21 Divisional
TOWN MAJORS: Arras, Avesnes,
Gouy.
TRAINS: 11 Divisional
SURVEY POSTS. No. 7 Group.

AVESNES. Army Ex.
  Corps Ex.
  Town Major
  Field Cashier, &c.

ARRAS. Town Major
  Gendarmerie
  Sound Range Post

BARLY. 4 K.B. Squdn.
  11 Divisional Train
  34 Field Ambulance

BEAUFORT. 22 W.Yorks

BLAVINCOURT.

ETREE WAMIN.

FOSSEUX. 11th D.A.C.

GIVENCHY-LE-NOBLE.

GOUY. Town Major

GRAND RULLECOURT.
  5th Div. Details
  565 Co. ASC H.A. M.T.

HABARCQ. I.O.M. 6th
  Corps.
  Mounted Troops
  Wagon Lines H.A.Grp.

HAUTEVILLE. 21 Div.
  School.

LATTRE.

LE CAUROY.
  21 Div. R.A.

LIENCOURT. 65 F.A.

LIGNEREUIL. 64 F.A.

MANIN.

MONT ST. ELOI. R.T.O.

SAULTY. R.T.O.

SOMBRIN. 11 D.S.C.

SUS ST. LEGER.

TINCQUES. R.T.O.

WANQUETIN.
  R.F.A. Wagon Lines
  H.A.Group   do.

21st Div Q

SECRET

2ND INDIAN CAVALRY DIVISION.

G.O.C.	Major-General H.J.M. MACANDREW, D.S.O.
A.D.C.	2/Lieut. A.E. FORBES DENNIS, (Gen. List).
A.D.C.	2/Lieut. J.C.K.H. CHARTERS, (R. of O).
G.S.O. 1.	Lt. Col. R.G.H. HOWARD-VYSE, D.S.O.
G.S.O. 2.	Major A.F.C. WILLIAMS, D.S.O.
G.S.O. 3.	Captain F.B. NIXON.
A.A. & Q.M.G.	Lt. Col. H.H. COBBE, D.S.O.
D.A.A. & Q.M.G.	Bt.Major H.E. MEDLICOTT.
A.D.M.S.	Bt. Col. A.J. McNAB.
D.A.D.M.S.	Captain W.H.S. BURNEY.
A.D.V.S.	Major H.J. HOLNESS.
D.A.D.O.S.	Captain C.F. DOUGLAS-WHITE.
A.P.M.	Captain W. H. CLARK.

ROYAL ARTILLERY.

O.C. 2nd Ind. R.H.A. Bde.	Lt. Col. J.W.F. LAMONT, D.S.O.
Adjutant.	Lieut. K. T. GOOCH.
Orderly Officer.	2/Lieut. C.G.V. MIESEGAES.

SECUNDERABAD CAVALRY BRIGADE.

Commander.	Brig. General C.L. GREGORY.
A.D.C.	Captain G.P.R. JACQUES.
Brigade Major.	Major A.C. ROSS, D.S.O.
Staff Captain.	Captain M. C. RAYMOND.
7th Dragoon Guards.	Major J.E.F. DYER.
34th Poona Horse.	Lt. Col. W. G. COOPER.
20th Deccan Horse.	Lt. Col. E. TENNANT.
"N" Battery, R.H.A.	Major T.N. FRENCH.
M.G. Squadron.	Captain E. C. WATSON.

AMBALA CAVALRY BRIGADE.

Commander.	Brig. General C.H. RANKIN, C.M.G. D.S.O.
A.D.C.	Lieut. G.S. ROWLEY, (8th Hussars).
Brigade Major.	Major G. CRASTER.
Staff Captain.	Captain T.W. CORBETT.
8th Hussars.	Lt. Col. F.W. MUSSENDEN.
9th Hodson's Horse.	Lt. Col. G.A.H. BEATTY.
18th Lancers.	Lt. Col. V. E. MUSPRATT.
"X" Battery, R.H.A.	Major C. E. WALKER.
M.G. Squadron.	Captain A. H. BROOKE.

DIVISIONAL TROOPS.

2nd Ind. R.H.A. Bde. Ammunition Column.	Captain J.H.G. RILEY.
2nd Ind. Field Squadron.	Major R.C.R. HILL.
2nd Ind. Signal Squadron.	Captain W.R.P. HENRY.
2nd Ind. Cav. Divnl. A.S.C. Headquarters.	Lt. Col. M. SYNGE.
2nd Ind. Ammunition Park.	Captain P.S. WHITCOMBE.
2nd Ind. Supply Column.	Major C.A. CRAWLEY BOEVEY.
Sec'bad Cav. Field Ambulance	Lt. Col. A.N. FLEMING.
Mhow " " "	Major E.A.C. MATTHEWS, V.H.S.
2nd Ind. Cav. Sanitary Sec.	Captain R.H. LEE, I.M.S.
Sec'bad Mobile Vetny. Sec.	Captain HAYES.
Ambala " " "	Captain DEVINE.

- 2 -

Attached.

CANADIAN CAVALRY BRIGADE.

Commander.	Brig. General Rt.Hon. J.E.B. SEELY, C.B., D.S.O.
A.D.C.	2/Lieut. F. R. SEELY.
Brigade Major.	Bt. Major A.E. LAWSON.
Staff Captain.	Captain M. DOCHERTY.
Royal Canadian H.A.Brigade.	Lt. Col. H.A. PANET.
Royal Canadian Dragoons.	Lt. Col. C.M. NELLES, C.M.G.
Lord Strathcona's Horse (R.C).	Lt. Col. J.A. HESKETH, D.S.O.
Fort Garry Horse.	Lt. Col. R.W. PATERSON.
Can. Cav. Bde. Fld. Ambulance.	Major D.P. KAPPELE.
4th Can. Mob. Vetny. Section.	Captain J.H. HENNAN.

(NOTE - Canadian Ammunition Park and Supply Column are amalgamated with 2nd I.C. Ammunition Park and Supply Column respectively).

5th. DIVISION.

DIVISIONAL HEADQUARTERS.

SECRET

Commander.	Major-General R.B. Stephens, C.M.G.
A.D.C.	Captain F.G.B. Stephens.
A.D.C.	Lieut. G. Forsyth.
G.S.O.1.	Lt. Col. R.A.M. Currie, D.S.O.
G.S.O.2.	Major G.C.W. Gordon Hall, D.S.O.
G.S.O.3.	Major J.D.D. Brancker.
A.A. & Q.M.G.	Lt. Col. R.F.A. Hobbs, C.M.G., D.S.O.
D.A.A. & Q.M.G.	Captain J.H.S. Westley, D.S.O.
D.A.Q.M.G.	Captain H. Courtenay.
A.P.M.	Captain E. C. Coates.
D.A.D.O.S.	Captain C.J.T. Robertson.
A.D.V.S.	Major T. Bone.
A.D.M.S.	Colonel F.W. Hardy.
D.A.D.M.S.	Major J.G. Martin.

ROYAL ARTILLERY.

G.O.C., R.A.	Brig. General A.H. Hussey, C.B.
A.D.C.	2/Lieut. H.E.S. Paterson.
Brigade Major.	Major S. Gore Brown.
Staff Captain.	Captain A.E.L. Jones.
15th Brigade.	Lt. Col. C. St. L.G. Hawkes.
27th Brigade.	Lt. Col. J. Berkley.
28th Brigade.	Lt. Col. E. Harding Newman, D.S.O.
5th. Div. Amm. Col.	Lt. Col. G. Tyacke.
Divnl. T.M. Officer.	Lieut. N. C. Clery.
X.5. T.M. Battery.	Lieut. A. G. Harper.
Y.5. T.M. Battery.	2/Lieut. R. H. Slater.
Z.5. T.M. Battery.	2/Lieut. J. S. Seddon.

ROYAL ENGINEERS.

C.R.E.	Lt. Col. J. R. White, D.S.O.
Adjutant.	Lieut. H. J. Macnamara.
59th Field Coy.	Captain M. E. Morgan.
1/2nd Home Counties Fd.Co.	Major A. C. Ticehurst.
1/2nd Durham Fd. Co.	Captain A.P.W. Wedd.
5th Signal Co.	Captain H. Lee Wright.

13th INFANTRY BRIGADE.

G.O.C.	Brig. General L.O.W. Jones, D.S.O.
Brigade Major.	Captain W. T. Wyllie.
Staff Captain.	Captain G.A.H. Bower.
2nd K.O.S.B.	Lt. Col. D.R. Sladen, C.M.G., D.S.O.
1st R.W.Kents.	Lt. Col. H.D.B. Dunlop, D.S.O.
14th R.Warwicks.	Lt. Col. L. Murray.
15th R.Warwicks.	Lt. Col. C. Harding, C.M.G.
13th Bde. M.G. Coy.	Captain R.H. Cutting.
13th T.M. Battery.	Captain P. Clarke.

95th INFANTRY BRIGADE.

G.O.C.	Brig. General C.R. Ballard, C.B.
Brigade Major.	Captain D.K. McLeod.
Staff Captain.	Captain T. Balston.
1st Devons.	Lt. Col. D. H. Blunt.
1st E. Surreys.	Major E.M. Woulfe Flanagan.
1st D.C.L.I.	Major C. B. Norton, D.S.O. ∅
12th Gloucesters.	Lt. Col. M. Archer Shee, D.S.O.
95th Bde. M.G. Coy.	Captain E. A. Hodson.
95th T.M. Battery.	Captain J. S. Lorimer.

15th INFANTRY BRIGADE.

G.O.C.	Brig. General M.N. Turner, C.B.
Brigade Major.	Captain W.T. Brooks.
Staff Captain.	Major P.A. Wilson.
16th R. Warwicks.	Major R.M. Dudgeon.
1st Norfolks.	Lt. Col. P.V.P. Stone.
1st Bedfords.	Major W. Allason, D.S.O.
1st Cheshires.	Lt. Col. M. F. Clarke.
15th Bde. M.G. Coy.	Captain R.T. Neville.
15th T.M. Battery.	Captain H.W. Bubb.

DIVISIONAL TROOPS.

1/6th Argyll & Sutherland Highlanders (Pioneers).	Lt. Col. R. I. Rawson.
5th Divnl. Train.	Lt. Col. E. Wood.
13th Field Ambulance.	Lt. Col. P.J. Hanafin, D.S.O.
14th Field Ambulance.	Major D.O. Hyde.
15th Field Ambulance.	Major F.H. Bradley.
Divnl. Sanitary Section.	Lieut. A.H. Spicer.
Mob. Vet. Section.	Captain W. Halstead.

∅ Acting until arrival of Lt. Col. H. Fargus, D.S.O.

x 21st Divisional Engineers

21st DIVISIONAL SIGNAL COMPANY R. E. :: JULY 1916.

July

WAR DIARY Hdqrs & No.1 Section 21st Div Signal Co. RE Army Form C. 2118
Vol II

INTELLIGENCE SUMMARY
(Erase heading not required.)

Place	Date	Hour	Summary of Events and Information	Remarks and references to Appendices
ROZEMONT	1.7.16 to 4.7.16		Lt. NIBLETT remained in charge of men & horses not employed in the operations.	
MEAULTE	1.7.16 to 3.7.16		The 21st Div. attacked the portion of the German line, extending northwards from FRICOURT for about half a mile, & remained in action till the enemy of the 3rd when relieved by the 17th Div. During this period, the distribution of Hdqrs. & No. 1 Section was as follows:— At Div'l H.Q. (E 28 a 5.6 Sheet 62D). Major Taylor & 18 O.R. also 4 cyclist orderlies. XV Corps Mounted Troops. 2 Operators. B.9 cable Section. At Div'l Forward Exchange. (F 2 a 05.20) Lieut Portens Walker & 15 O.R. " 4 cyclist orderlies, IV Corps m.t.d. Troops. At BECORDEL relay post & wired receiving station S.A. (F 13 b 1.6). 5 O.R. also 4 cyclist orderlies. XV Corps m.t.d. Troops At each of the three inf. bde. Hdqrs, 2 O.R. At BELLEVUE farm wired receiving station. (F 11 b 3.9). 2 O.R.	

WAR DIARY
INTELLIGENCE SUMMARY

Hdqrs & No.1 Section 21st Bn.d Signal Co. R.E.

Army Form C. 2118

Place	Date	Hour	Summary of Events and Information	Remarks and references to Appendices
MEAULTE	1.7.16 to 3.7.16		During part of this period, 6 licencmen of 17th Sig Co were who attached. On the night 3rd/4th the 17th Bde relieved the 21st Bde, & the Command passed over at 9am on 4th.	
RIBEMONT	4.7.16		Detachments rejoined here during morning.	
		11.0am	Co marched off for BELLOY-SUR-SOMME, arriving there about 10pm. Lieut Walker remained behind at Fort Fournes Exchange, to look after the Communications of 21st Bde. Art., who remained in action.	
BELLOY-SUR-SOMME	5.7.16		Co billeted in Weaving factory. Bde HQ at CHATEAU de la ROCHEFOUCAULD. Communication established with II Corps, who were at VILLERS-BOCAGE.	
"	7.7.16	2pm	Co marched off to CAVILLON, arriving there about 5pm. Bde HQ in CHATEAU. Signal Office in stable. Co billeted in farm buildings near Church. Communication established with II Corps.	
CAVILLON	8.7.16		Laid D5-twis to RIENCOURT to 64 Inf Bde, established Communications with 62 Inf Bde at DISSY & 110 Inf Bde at HANGEST on existing air lines. 110 Inf Bde relieved 63 Inf Bde in the Division, but 263 Brigade section remained on.	

Army Form C. 2118

HdQrs & No 1 Section
21st Bird Signal Co R.E.

WAR DIARY
or
INTELLIGENCE SUMMARY

(Erase heading not required.)

Instructions regarding War Diaries and Intelligence Summaries are contained in F.S. Regs., Part II. and the Staff Manual respectively. Title Pages will be prepared in manuscript.

Place	Date	Hour	Summary of Events and Information	Remarks and references to Appendices
CAVILLON	9.7.16	2 pm	Coy marched off to QUERRIEU & bivouacked there for night.	
"	10.7.16	9.30 am	Div H.Q. closed down at CAVILLON & opened at RIBEMONT.	
RIBEMONT	"	9 am	Coy arrived from QUERRIEU.	
"	"	11 am	Coy marched off to VILLE & bivouacked at road junction VILLE – MEAULTE and MORLANCOURT roads.	
VILLE	"	6 pm	Detachments commenced taking over Signal Offices from 17th Sig. Co.	
MEAULTE	11.7.16	9.30 am	21 Div took over command from 17 Div & established HQ at F28a.5.6. From 11th — 19th the 21st Div was in action; its H.Q. remaining at F28a.5.6. As the Inf bdes. & artillery bdes. moved forward, the Brit Forward Exchange (F8a.05.20) was worked out of the system, & transferred to "DR" (F8a.7.3), & this in turn was worked out, & a forward exchange, both for Inf. & Art. bdes. established at FRICOURT CHATEAU.	
"	11.7.16 & 19.7.16		Owing to the great distance (6–7 miles) between Div. HQ & Inf Bdes, & to the fact that there were 8 Art. bdes fighting under 21 Div Art, the strain on personnel was heavy, & extra assistance was asked for.	

WAR DIARY

INTELLIGENCE SUMMARY   HQ & No.1 Section, 21st Div. Signal Co.R.E.

Army Form C. 2118

Place	Date	Hour	Summary of Events and Information	Remarks and references to Appendices
MEAULTE	16.7.16		Fourteen Linemen & Operators were sent by D.D.A.S, Fourth Army. 21 Div Art HQ transferred from E28a5.6 to FRICOURT Chateau. The staff at FRICOURT Chateau now consisted of 2 Officers (Lients. Porteous & Walker) 16 O.R. 4 Cyclists.	
"	"		2 Cable detachments were moved up to "DR" & bivouacked there.	
"	17.7.16		Co moved up from VILLE to MEAULTE, & bivouacked at E.17d.1.9. 11 of Fourth Army Linemen & Operators sent to 7th Div.	
"	18.7.16		3 remaining Fourth Army Linemen returned to Fourth Army.	
"	19.7.16		The 4 operators & the earth induction receiving & transmitting sets, that were sent by Signals, Cavalry Corps on 12th, were sent back to DAOURS.	
"	20.7.16		21 Div relieved by 33 Div. Closed down HQ at E28a5.6 at 9.30 a.m. 21 Div Art remained in action, with HQ at FRICOURT Chateau. Lieut Walker & 16 O.R. remained at FRICOURT Chateau, & the 2 cable detachments remained at "DR" under his orders, for Art. communications. Co. marched off for CAVILLON, arriving there 11.30 p.m.	

WAR DIARY or INTELLIGENCE SUMMARY

Army Form C. 2118

HdQrs & No. 1 Section 21st Div Signal Co. R.E.

(Erase heading not required.)

Instructions regarding War Diaries and Intelligence Summaries are contained in F.S. Regs., Part II. and the Staff Manual respectively. Title Pages will be prepared in manuscript.

Place	Date	Hour	Summary of Events and Information	Remarks and references to Appendices
CAVILLON	21.7.16		Established communication with Fourth Army, also with brigades by existing air-line. Signal office & billets same as on 7th.	
"	22.7.16	10.45pm	Co marched off to LONGUEAU station.	
	23.7.16		Entrained at LONGUEAU station 4-5am, left there 6.15am, detrained at PETIT HOUVIN 11am, marched to LE CAUROY, arriving there 2.30pm. Co billetted in farm buildings.	
LE CAUROY	"		Div. H.Q opened at Chateau 9.30am. Communication established with VI Corps at NOYELLE-VION & with 64 Inf Bde at HOUVIN-HOUVIGNEUL on existing airlines.	
"	24.7.16		Communication established with 110th Inf Bde at LIENCOURT on existing airline.	
FRICOURT	"	4pm	Lieut. Walker, 46 OR & two cable wagons left FRICOURT with 21 Div Art- & marched to CORBIE for night 24th/25th. Marched to BETHENCOURT for night 25th/26th. Marched to near DOULLENS for night 26th/27th. Rejoined at LE CAUROY at 2.30pm 27th.	
LE CAUROY	27th 28th		Advanced parties to DUISANS, who commenced taking over 11th Sig Co's Signal Office.	

Army Form C. 2118

WAR DIARY
or
INTELLIGENCE SUMMARY
(Erase heading not required.)

Hdqrs & No.1 Section 21st Divl Signal Co. R.E.

Remarks and references to Appendices 6

Place	Date	Hour	Summary of Events and Information
LE CAUROY	30.7.16	8 am	Marched out to DUISANS, arriving there 12 noon.
DUISANS	30.7.16	10 am	Took over Signal Office from 11th Divl Sig Co, which moved to WARLUS. Brigade took over J & K sectors, north of ARRAS, from 14th Div. Gt. billeted in barns, horses & wagons picketed out.
"	30 to 31.7.16		Communications with VI Corps at NOYELLE-VION, 64th Inf. Bde, PLACE ST. CROIX, ARRAS, 62nd & 110th Inf Bdes (together), PLACE ST. CROIX, ARRAS; 60th Div at ETRUN, 11th Div at WARLUS. Strength on 31.7.16. 4 Officers 131 O.R. 3 A.S.C (attached) 1 Interpreter 3 VI Corps Signals (attached) 7 Orderlies to —— 149 Horses 83

1875 Wt. W593/826 1,000,000 4/15 J.B.C. & A. A.D.S.S./Forms/C. 2118.

Army Form C. 2118

WAR DIARY

HdQrs & No. 1 Section 21st Div. Signal Co. R.E.

INTELLIGENCE SUMMARY

(Erase heading not required.)

7

Place	Date	Hour	Summary of Events and Information	Remarks and references to Appendices
BELLOY	5.7.16		1 Sapper (Shoeing Smith) evacuated to 2nd Western General Hospt, Manchester.	
LE CAUROY	30.7.16		1 Motorcyclist Corpl (Cpl. Rogers RS) to England, to join Cadet School. Copy of letter received from 21 Div. HQ attached.	A

L.W.Shuyler Major R.E.
O.C. 21 Sig Co. R.E.

Signals.

The General Officer Commanding has directed me to convey to you, and to the 21st Div: Signal Co; his appreciation of the very good work done by the Company during the recent operations.

The success of any operations is so dependant on the Signal Service, that it is only right that your Officers, N.C.Os, and men, should know how pleased the General is and what a large part the Company has played in the re-establishment of the reputation of the 21st Division.

The 21st Division has played a very big part and is now recognised to be one of the best Divisions in France.

Please let all ranks in your Company know how pleased the G.O.C. is.

(sd) A. Paley. Lt: Col:
G.S.

8.7.16.

21 Div.
G.43.

REGISTERED ADDRESSES AND CODE CALLS.

21st Division No. G.5 dated 11th July 1916 is cancelled
Registered addresses and Code Calls will continue to be
used in accordance with this office Nos. G.307 and G.128
dated 16th June and 8th July 1916, respectively.

A. Sparks
Major,
G.S. 21 Div.

12/7/16.

Distribution.

62 Inf. Bde.	2	"A"	1
64 : :	2	A.D.C.	1
110 : :	2	C.Comdt.	1
Div. Art.	2	A.D.M.S.	1
Div. Eng.	3	A.D.V.S.	1
Signals	3	A.P.M.	1
Pioneers	1	D.A.D.O.S.	1
Train	1	Supply Coln.	1
F.Ambs.	3	Salvage Co.	1
San. Sec.	1		

SECRET.

21 Div.
G. 46.

62 Inf. Bde.
64 "   "
110 "   "
Div. Art.
"Q"
Signals.

Herewith "List of Code Calls for 33rd Division" for your information.

(signature)
Major.

12.7.16.

General Staff.
21st Division.

SECRET.

21 Div.
G. 68.

62 Inf. Bde.
64 "   "
110 "   "
Div. Art.
Signals.
"Q"

Herewith "List of Registered Addresses and Code Calls for the XIIIth Corps, and 33rd Division, for your information.

(signature)
Major.

13.7.16.

General Staff.
21st Division.

SECRET.

88.G.

List of Registered Addresses & Code Calls

33rd. DIVISION.

Unit.	Registered Address.	Code Call.
Divisional Headquarters	JEWEL	JF
C. R. A.	.....	JG
156th Brigade, R.F.A.	LINNET	JJ
162nd " R.F.A.	STORK	JK
168th " R.F.A.	WREN	JL
167th " R.F.A.	ROBIN	JM
33rd D. A. C.	MARTIN	JP
X/33 T.M. Battery	BEAR	JR
Y/33 " "	BIFF	JS
Z/33 " "	BING	JT
C. R. E.	....	JU
11th Field Coy. R.E.	BOIL	JV
212th " " R.E.	BLUFF	JW
222nd " " R.E.	BAIN	JAQ
19th Infantry Bde. H.Q.	JAY	J
20th Royal Fusiliers	JACKAL	JA
2nd Royal Welsh Fusiliers	JACKDAW	JB
1st Scottish Rifles	JAM	JC
5/6th Scottish Rifles (T)	JAR	JD
19th Bde. M.G. Company	JOIST	JE
19th Bde. T.M. Battery	SPARROW	JAN
98th Infantry Brigade H.Q.	QUAIL	Q
4th Liverpool Regt.	QUINCE	QB
1/4th Suffolk Regt.	QUIET	QC
1st Middlesex Regt.	QUILL	QE
2nd Argyle & Sutherland Hlrs.	QUAD	QF
98th Bde. M.G. Company	QUART	QG
98th Bde. T.M. Battery	BLOT	JAB
100th Infantry Bde. H.Q.	POPPY	U
1st R. West Surrey Regt.	PEAR	UA
2nd Worcester Regt.	PEACH	UB
13th K.R.R. Corps	PEPPER	UC
1/9th Highland L.I. (T)	PEN	UD
100th Bde. M.G. Company	PLUM	UE
100th Bde. T.M. Battery	DASH	JAR
Pioneer Battalion) 18th Middlesex Regt.)	PINE	UAB
19th Field Ambulance	BATH	JAS
99th " "	BOUGH	JAT
101st " "	BASIN	JAU
Sanitary Section	BUSH	JAV

Contd........ (2) 88. G.

Unit.	Registered Address.	Code Call.
Reserve Park	BAY	JAC
Supply Column	BUCK	JAD
O.C. Train	BEAN	JAE
S.S.O.	BEAT	JAF
170th Company, A.S.C.	BEND	JAG
171st " "	BIGHT	JAK
172nd " "	BANK	JAL
173rd " "	BEAST	JAM
Mobile Veterinary Section.	BIRCH	JAP

H.Q. XV Corps,
12-7-1916.

for Brigadier-General,
General Staff.

Copies to :-

```
    7th Division   - 7.      Corps Mtd. Troops -      3.
   17th Division   - 7.      No. 3 Sqdn. R.F.C.-      1.
   21st Division   - 7.      No. 3 Kite Balloon Sec. - 1.
   33rd Division   - 7.      No. 4 Kite Balloon Sec. - 1.
   B.G. R.A.       - 10.     "G"                    - 4.
   C.E.            - 7.

   III Corps.      - 5.)
   XIII Corps.     - 5.) for information.
   Fourth Army.    - 1.)
```

SECRET. 88. G.

XIII Corps Code.

Unit.	Registered Address.	Code Call.
XIII Corps H.Q.	NERVE	-
" " Heavy Artillery	FLASH	F W
No. 12 Kite Balloon	HAWK	A K
3rd Division H.Q.	BUGLE	-
8th Infantry Brigade	PEPPER	P P R
9th Infantry Brigade	SALT	S L T
76th Infantry Brigade	MUSTARD	M T D
3rd Divisional Artillery	SAUCE	S C E
9th Division H.Q.	CENTRE	-
26th Infantry Brigade	ROME	Q A
27th Infantry Brigade	NAPLES	Q D
South African Brigade	VENICE	V C
9th Divisional Artillery	NORWAY	W P
18th Division H.Q.	HEART	-
53rd Infantry Brigade	FRUIT	F R
54th Infantry Brigade	STAR	S S
55th Infantry Brigade	OAK	K W
18th Divisional Artillery	FUZE	F E
30th Division H.Q.	TREE	-
21st Infantry Brigade	TRUNK	T R
89th Infantry Brigade	ROOT	R J
90th Infantry Brigade	BRANCH	R C
30th Divisional Artillery	FISH	F S

III Corps Code.

Unit.	Code Name and Signal Call.
III Corps H.Q.	C V
" " Heavy Artillery	C V
" " Kite Balloon	K W
1st Division H.Q.	
1st Infantry Brigade	Q U
2nd Infantry Brigade	F D
3rd Infantry Brigade	L B
19th Division H.Q.	
56th Infantry Brigade	A R
57th Infantry Brigade	C A V
58th Infantry Brigade	M V
23rd Division H.Q.	
24th Infantry Brigade	K I
68th Infantry Brigade	L E
69th Infantry Brigade	A I
34th Division H.Q.	
101st Infantry Brigade	D L
102nd Infantry Brigade	C E
103rd Infantry Brigade	D G

H.Q., XV Corps,
12-7-1916.

Brigadier-General,
General Staff.

Copies to :-   7th Div. - 7   33rd Div. - 7
           17th Div. - 7   B.G.R.A. - 7/12
           21st Div. - 7   **A.D.A.S.** - 4

SECRET

88 G.

With reference to XV Corps No.88 G dated 12th July, 1916, the following are to be added to the list of XIII Corps Registered addresses and code calls:-

	Registered address	Code Call
XIII Corps	FORTUNE	-
35th Division		
104th Infantry Brigade	EMBLEM	EMB
105th Infantry Brigade	SUNSHINE	SSH
106th Infantry Brigade	BEAUTY	BEA

Capt.
For Brigadier-General,
General Staff.

H.Q. XV Corps

16/7/16.
Copies to - 7th Div. 7   B.G., R.A. 12
           21st Div. 7   A.D.A.S.   3
           33rd Div. 7

SECRET.

21 Div.
G. 138.

62 Inf. Bde.
64 " "
110 " "
Div. Art.
"Q"
Signals.

Herewith "List of Registered Address and Code Calls for 35th Division (XIII Corps)" for your information.

[signature]
Major.

General Staff.
21st Division.

16.7.16.

SECRET.

21 Div.
G. 148.

62 Inf. Bde.
64 "   "
110 "   "
Div. Art.
Signals.
"Q"

      The attached alteration is to be made to the Code Calls for the III Corps issued under this office No. G.68 dated 13th July, 1916.

                                      Major.

17.7.16.   General Staff.
                                      21st Division.

SECRET

88 G.

The following alteration is to be made to Code Calls issued under XV Corps No.88 G. dated 12/7/16:-

<u>III CORPS.</u>
Delete "24th Infantry Brigade   K I"
Add   "70th Infantry Brigade   K I"

Brigadier-General,
General Staff.

H.Q. XV Corps
17/7/16.

Copies to 7th Div. - 7   A.D.A.S. 3
~~17th Div. - 7~~
21st Div. - 7 ✓
33rd Div. - 7
B.G.R.A. -12

SECRET.

LIST OF CODE CALLS
33rd DIVISION.

88 G.

Unit.	Code Call.
Divisional Headquarters	JF
156th Brigade, R.F.A.	JJ
162nd " "	JK
166th " "	JL
167th " "	JM
33rd D.A.C.	JP
X/33 T.M. Battery	JR
Y/33 " "	JS
Z/33 " "	JT
11th Field Coy., R.E.	JV
212th " " "	JW
222nd " " "	JAQ
19th Infantry Bde., H.Q.	J
20th Royal Fusiliers	JA
2nd Royal Welsh Fus.	JB
1st Scottish Rifles	JC
5/6th Scottish Rifles (T)	JD
19th Bde., M.G. Company	JE
19th Bde. T.M. Battery	JAN
98th Infantry Bde., H.Q.	Q
4th Liverpool Regt.	QB
1/4th Suffolk Regt.	QC
1st Middlesex Regt.	QE
2nd Argyle & Sutherland Hlrs.	QF
98th Bde., M.G. Company	QG
98th Bde., T.M. Battery	JAB
100th Infantry Bde., H.Q.	U
1st R. West Surrey Regt.	UA
2nd Worcester Regt.	UB
16th K.R.R. Corps	UC
1/9th Highland L.I. (T)	UD
100th Bde., M.G. Company	UE
100th Bde., T.M. Battery	JAR
Pioneer Battalion) 18th Middlesex Regt.)	UAB

H.Q., XV Corps,
12/7/1916.

J.R.Wethered Maj.
for Brigadier-General,
General Staff.

Copies to :-
7th Division	7	Corps Mtd. Troops	3	
17th Division	7	No. 3 Squadron, R.F.C.	1	
21st Division	7	No. 3 Kite Balloon Sec.	1	
33rd Division	7	No. 4 Kite Balloon Sec.	1	
B.G.R.A.	10	"G"	4	
C.E.	7			
III Corps	5)			
XIII Corps	5) for information.			
Fourth Army	1)			

SECRET.

21 Div.
G. 155.

62 Inf. Bde.
64 "   "
110 "   "
Div. Art.
Signals.
"Q"

The attached "List of Registered Addresses and Code Calls for the 5th Division" is forwarded for your information.

[signature]

Major.
General Staff.
21st. Division.

18.7.16.

SECRET.

88 G.

List of Registered Addresses & Code Calls
5th DIVISION

UNIT.	REGISTERED ADDRESS.	CODE CALL
Divisional Headquarters	SALMON	QM
13th Infantry Brigade H.Q.	EEL	QI
14th Royal Warwick Regt.	ROACH	QIA
15th Royal Warwick Regt.	TROUT	QIB
2nd K.O. Scottish Borderers	SNOEK	QIC
1st R. West Kent Regt.	BREAM	QID
13th Bde. M.G. Coy.	CHUB	QIE
13th T.M. Battery	CRAB	QIF
15th Infantry Brigade H.Q.	PRAWN	QK
16th Royal Warwick Regt.	WHELK	QKA
1st Norfolk Regt.	MUSSEL	QKB
1st Bedford Regt.	COCKEL	QKC
1st Cheshire Regt.	WINKLE	QKD
15th Bde. M.G. Coy.	TURBOT	QKE
15th T.M. Battery.	COD	QKF
95th Infantry Brigade H.Q.	SPRAT	QL
1st Devon Regt.	SPAWN	QLA
12th Gloucester Regt.	SKATE	QLB
1st E. Surrey Regt.	SHARK	QLC
1st D. of Cornwall's L.I.	SHRIMP	QLD
95th Bde. M.G. Coy.	SARDINE	QLE
95th T.M. Battery.	SOLE	QLF
15th Brigade, R.F.A.	PAPER	QP
52nd Battery, "	PULP	QPA
80th Battery, "	PRINT	QPB
"D" Battery, "	PUFF	QPC
27th Brigade, R.F.A.	PIOUS	QR
119th Battery, "	PSALM	QRA
120th Battery, "	PURGE	QRB
121st Battery, "	PURPLE	QRC
37th Battery, "	PROWL	QRD
28th Brigade, R.F.A.	PRUNE	QS
122nd Battery, "	PUSSY	QSA
123rd Battery, "	PEEP	QSB
124th Battery, "	PENAL	QSC
65th Battery, "	PROXY	QSD

5th Division, Contd......   2.   S E C R E T.

                                                            88. G.

UNIT.	REGISTERED ADDRESS.	CODE CALL.
X5 T. M. Battery, R.A.	POLAR	QT
Y5 T. M. Battery, "	POUT	QTA
Z5 T. M. Battery, "	PRATE	QTB
5th Divisional Amm. Column	JURY	QTC
59th Field Coy. R.E.	JUDGE	QTD
1/2nd Home Counties Fld. Coy. R.E.(T).	JOLLY	QTE
1/2nd Durham Fld. Coy. R.E. (T).	JOIN	QTF
5th Divisional Signal Company	JELLY	YE
Pioneer Bn. 1/6th Arg. & Suth'd. Highrs.	JACK	QTI
5th Divisional Train (Nos. 4,6,33 & 37 Coys. A.S.C.)	JILT	QTK
13th Field Ambulance	JERK	QTL
14th Field Ambulance	JUST	QTM
15th Field Ambulance	JUICE	QTP
No. 6 Sanitary Section	JOY	QTQ
5th Mobile Vet. Section.	JOT	QTR

H.Q. XV Corps,
    17-7-1916.

J R Wethered Major
for
Brigadier-General,
General Staff.

Copies to :-

5th Division	- 7.	A.D.A.S.	-	3.
7th Division	- 7.	Corps Mtd. Troops	-	3.
17th Division	- 7.	No. 3 Sqdn. R.F.C.	-	1.
21st Division	- 7.	No. 3 Kite Balloon Sec.		1.
33rd Division	- 7.	No. 4 Kite Balloon Sec.		1.
B.G.R.A.	- 10.	"G".	-	4.
C.E.	- 7.			

III Corps   - 5.)
XIII Corps.   - 5.) for information.
Fourth Army   - 1.)

Yx Div. DAB
17x LACE
50 Inf Bde LACK

SECRET.

21 Div.
G.307.

From 12 midnight 18th June, 1916, all previous Registered Addresses and code calls will be destroyed and the following list substituted :-

---

21ST DIVISION.	Registered Address.	Code Call.
Divisional Headquarters.	SOME	S
Divisional Artillery H.Q.	SUCH	SU
94th F.A. Brigade.	SHAG	UK
95th F.A. Brigade.	SHED	UL
96th F.A. Brigade.	SHIN	UM
97th F.A. Brigade.	SHOP	UG
Divisional Ammunition Column.	SHUT	UF
V/21 T.M.Battery. (Heavy)	STUN	UP
W/21 T.M.Battery. (Heavy)	SNUG	UT
X/21 T.M.Battery. (Medium)	SNAG	UQ
Y/21 T.M.Battery. (Medium)	SNIP	UR
Z/21 T.M.Battery. (Medium)	SNOW	US
Divisional Engineers H.Q.	SAP	SP
97th Field Coy. R.E.	SIP	SPA
98th Field Coy. R.E.	SOP	SPB
126th Field Coy. R.E.	SUP	SPC
Divisional Signal Company.	STACK	SW
62nd Infantry Brigade H.Q.	SCAN	T
12th North'd Fus.	SKEW	TA
13th North'd Fus.	SKIN	TB
1st Lincoln Regt.	SCOT	TC
10th Yorks Regt.	SCUD	TD
Brigade M.G.Coy.	SKY	TL
62nd T.M.Battery.	SAT	TM
110th 63rd Infantry Brigade H.Q.	SLAY	V
~~8th Lincoln Regt.~~ 6 Leicester	SLED	VA
~~8th Som. L.I.~~ 7 "	SLIM	VB
~~4th Middlesex Regt.~~ 8 "	SLOT	VC
~~10th Yorks & Lancs Regt.~~ 9 "	SLUG	VD
Brigade M.G.Coy.	SLY	VL
63rd T.M.Battery.	SET	VM

S E C R E T   XIII Corps Code.   88. G.

                                         Registered address.   Code Call.

XIII Corps H.Q.   NERVE   -
 "   "   Heavy Artillery.   FLASH   F W

    No. 12 Kite Balloon.   HAWK   A K

    18th. Division H.Q.   HEART   -
        53rd. Infantry Brigade.   FRUIT   F R
        54th. Infantry Brigade.   STAR   S S
        55th. Infantry Brigade.   OAK   K W
    18th. Divisional Artillery.   FUZE   F E

    30th. Division H.Q.   TREE   -
        21st. Infantry Brigade.   TRUNK   T R
        89th. Infantry Brigade.   ROOT   R J
        90th. Infantry Brigade.   BRANCH   R C
    30th. Divisional Artillery.   FISH   F S

    9th. Division H.Q.   CENTRE   -
        26th. Infantry Brigade.   ROME   Q A
        27th. Infantry Brigade.   NAPLES   Q D
        South African Brigade.   VENICE   V C
    9th. Divisional Artillery.   NORWAY   W P

                        III Corps Code.
                                          Code Name and Signal Call.

III Corps H.Q.

 "   "   Heavy Artillery.   O V

 "   "   Kite Balloon.   K W

    8th. Division H.Q.
        23rd. Infantry Brigade.   K I
        25th. Infantry Brigade.   L E
        70th. Infantry Brigade.   A I

    19th. Division H.Q.
        56th. Infantry Brigade.   A R
        57th. Infantry Brigade.   C A
        58th. Infantry Brigade.   M V

    34th. Division H.Q.
        101st. Infantry Brigade.   D L
        102nd. Infantry Brigade.   O E
        103rd. Infantry Brigade.   D G

                                                    Brigadier-General,
H.Q. XV Corps,   General Staff.
   17-6-1916.

    Copies to :- 7th. Div.- 7.   "Q"   - 1
                17th. Div.- 7   D.D.M.S.   - 1
                21st. Div.- 7   A.D.O.S.   - 1
                B.G.R.A.   - 7   A.D.A.S.   - 3
                C. E.   - 1   A.P.M.   - 1

"A" Form.
Army Form C. 2121.

MESSAGES AND SIGNALS.

TO	SCAN	SAP	"Q"	C.Comdt.
	SLAY	STEP	A.D.M.S.	D.A.D.O.S.
	SPAR	STACK	A.P.M.	

Sender's Number.	Day of Month.	In reply to Number.		AAA
G. 159.	18			

Reference	21	Div.	O.O.	61
of	to-day	the	operations	referred
to	therein	are	postponed	till
further	orders	AAA		

From: SOME
Place:
Time: 3.45 p.m.

Copy No. 24

21 Div. O.O. No. 61.

18th July 1916.

Ref:- MARTINPUICH Map, 1/20,000

1. (a) The 4th Army will continue the attack on 19th July in conjunction with the Reserve Army and French 6th Army at an hour Zero.

   (b) The XV Corps is to attack HIGH WOOD and the German SWITCH Line between HIGH WOOD and the RAILWAY Line at S 2 a 0.2.

2. The position, when gained, is at once to be consolidated. A Support Line will be dug behind SWITCH TRENCH at the earliest opportunity.

3. The 21st Division will be in Corps Reserve and will be ready to move at 2 hours notice from Zero on 19th July.

4. Today, and on any following days during which the Division is in Reserve, every effort will be made to re-organise Lewis Gun Detachments by training fresh Officers and men.

   Grenadier Squads will be reorganised as far as possible, and the number of bombs carried by each Battalion should be made up. Demands for bombs and buckets should be made to 21st Division "Q" as soon as possible.

5. Brigades, R.E. Companies and Pioneers will forward to Div. H.Q. tomorrow morning table showing strength in Officers and O.R. per unit fit to return to action.

   This table will only show numbers of Officers and O.R. who would move forward in an attack and will not include 1st Line

P.T.O.

21 Div. O.O. No. 61.   Copy No. 25

                                        18th July 1916.

Ref:- MARTINPUICH Map, 1/20,000

1. (a)   The 4th Army will continue the attack on 19th
         July in conjunction with the Reserve Army and French
         6th Army at an hour Zero.

   (b)   The XV Corps is to attack HIGH WOOD and the German
         SWITCH Line between HIGH WOOD and the RAILWAY Line at
         S 2 a 0.2.

2.   The position, when gained, is at once to be consolidated.
         A Support Line will be dug behind SWITCH TRENCH at the
         earliest opportunity.

3.   The 21st Division will be in Corps Reserve and will be
         ready to move at 2 hours notice from Zero on 19th July.

4.   Today, and on any following days during which the
         Division is in Reserve, every effort will be made to re-
         organise Lewis Gun Detachments by training fresh Officers
         and men.
         Grenadier Squads will be reorganised as far as possible,
         and the number of bombs carried by each Battalion should be
         made up.   Demands for bombs and buckets should be made to
         21st Division "Q" as soon as possible.

5.   Brigades, R.E. Companies and Pioneers will forward to
         Div. H.Q. tomorrow morning table showing strength in Officers
         and O.R. per unit fit to return to action.
         This table will only show numbers of Officers and O.R. who
         would move forward in an attack and will not include 1st Line

                                                         P.T.O.

21 Div. O.O. No. 61.

Copy No. 26

18th July 1916.

Ref:- MARTINPUICH Map, 1/20,000

1. (a) The 4th Army will continue the attack on 19th July in conjunction with the Reserve Army and French 6th Army at an hour Zero.

   (b) The XV Corps is to attack HIGH WOOD and the German SWITCH Line between HIGH WOOD and the RAILWAY Line at S 2 a 0.2.

2. The position, when gained, is at once to be consolidated. A Support Line will be dug behind SWITCH TRENCH at the earliest opportunity.

3. The 21st Division will be in Corps Reserve and will be ready to move at 2 hours notice from Zero on 19th July.

4. Today, and on any following days during which the Division is in Reserve, every effort will be made to re-organise Lewis Gun Detachments by training fresh Officers and men.

    Grenadier Squads will be reorganised as far as possible, and the number of bombs carried by each Battalion should be made up. Demands for bombs and buckets should be made to 21st Division "Q" as soon as possible.

5. Brigades, R.E.Companies and Pioneers will forward to Div. H.Q. tomorrow morning table showing strength in Officers and O.R. per unit fit to return to action.

    This table will only show numbers of Officers and O.R. who would move forward in an attack and will not include 1st Line

P.T.O.

- 2 -

Transport and others who would normally be left behind.

6. Div. H.Q. will remain in their present position.

[signature]
Lieut-Colonel,
General Staff,
21st Division.

Issued at 10.0 a.m. to

	Copy No.
War Diary & File	1 - 2
62nd Inf. Bde.	3 - 7
64th " "	8 - 12
110th " "	13 - 17
Div. Eng.	18 - 21
Pioneers	22
Signals	23
"Q"	24 - 26
A.D.M.S.	27
A.P.M.	28
C.Comdt.	29
D.A.D.O.S.	30

- 2 -

Transport and others who would normally be left behind.

6. Div. H.Q. will remain in their present position.

[signature]
Lieut-Colonel,
General Staff,
21st Division.

Issued at 10.0 a.m. to

	Copy No.
War Diary & File	1 - 2
62nd Inf. Bde.	3 - 7
64th " "	8 - 12
110th " "	13 - 17
Div Eng.	18 - 21
Pioneers	22
Signals	23
RGA	24 - 26
A.D.M.S.	27
A.P.M.	28
Comdt.	29
D.A.D.O.S.	30

Transport and others who would normally be left behind.

6.   Div. H.Q. will remain in their present position.

[signature] Lieut-Colonel,
General Staff,
21st Division.

Issued at 10.0 a.m. to

	Copy No.
War Diary & File	1 - 2
62nd Inf. Bde.	3 - 7
64th : :	8 - 12
110th : :	13 - 17
Div. Eng.	18 - 21
Pioneers	22
Signals	23
M.G.	24 - 26
A.D.M.S.	27
A.P.M.	28
C.Comdt.	29
D.A.D.O.S.	30

21st Division.
~~1st Cavalry Division.~~
~~3rd Cavalry Division.~~

    The attached list of "Q" Returns, with pro-formas, required to be rendered to II Corps Headquarters, are forwarded for information and guidance.

    The return of Surpluses and Deficiencies in Horse Transport should reach this office by 6 p.m. 9th instant.

H.Q. II Corps.
8th July 1916.

J. P. Villiers-Stuart Major
for Lieut-Colonel,
A.Q.M.G. II Corps.

RETURNS REQUIRED ... BRANCH XIII CORPS.

Name of Return.	Whom from.	Date due here.	Due Corps.
Daily.			
Ammunition and Trench Mortar Expenditure.	Div: Art: & Bde: in Line.	Soon after noon as possible.	By.2.30p.m.(wire)
Weekly. **Saturday.**			
Feeding Strength.	Div: Train.	Sat: Morn:	2.0.p.m.
Transport, (surplus & Deficient.)	All Units.	Fri. "	9.0 a.m. Saturday.
Sunday.			
Report on Supply Services.	Div: Train.	Sat: "	Noon Sunday.
Refilling Points.	Div: Train.	" "	" "
A.F. F.773.	" "	" "	" "
Ammunition, rounds in possession.	Div: Art:	Soon after noon as possible.	Soon after noon as possible.
Grenades on hand.	3 Bdes:Div:Art: S.I.H. 14th N.F. Cyclists.	" "	" "
Trench Mortars, guns & ammunition.	Div:Art: & Bdes: in line.	" "	" "
Monthly.			
Return of Labour	CRE	2 Sept q to 1st day	2 Day of new
No. of rounds fired with various propell- -ants.	Div: Art:	Last day of each month.	4th of each month.
Machine Guns in possession.	"	alternate Sundays from May 21	11th & 27th of each month.
Gendarmes & Interpreters.		last day of month	1st of each month.
Return of Claims.	Doulens	" "	6th " " "
Supplies in Support- -ing points.		" "	27th " " "
Motor Cars & Bicycles.		" "	Last day " "
S.A.A. on charge.		" "	29th of " "
Saturdays			10 pm Saturday
Ammunition & Trench mortar guns			
Trench stores in possession	3 Bdes. R.E. R.A. Cyclists S.I.H.	13th & 29th of each month.	1st & 15th of each month.
P.B. Men Nows			1st of each month

RETURNS REQUIRED TO BE RENDERED TO H.Q. II Corps.

DAILY.

Expenditure of Gun Ammunition	By wire as soon as possible after noon

WEEKLY

Surplus & Deficient Horse Transport	To reach II Corps H.Q. by 6 p.m. Sundays.
Gun Ammunition, Trench Mortars and Ammunition, Grenades and Smoke Candles on hand noon Sunday.	To reach II Corps H.Q. by 6 p.m. Sundays.

MONTHLY

Returns of Labour	To reach II Corps H.Q. by 6 p.m. 1st of each month.
Supplies in Supporting Points and Defended Localities	To reach II Corps H.Q. by 6 p.m. on 24th of each month.

****

"A" Form.
Army Form C.-2121.

MESSAGES AND SIGNALS.

No. of Message _____

Prefix _____ Code _____ m.	Words	Charge	This message is on a/c of:	Recd. at _____ m.
Office of Origin and Service Instructions.	Sent		_____ Service.	Date _____
	At _____ m.			From _____
	To _____			
	By _____		(Signature of "Franking Officer.")	By _____

TO { 2nd Corps Q.

Sender's Number.	Day of Month	In reply to Number	
* —	—		A A A

Ammunition expended 24 hours ended noon today AAA A three two four AX Six B Nil BX forty nine AAA Guns A Forty eight B Twelve.

From: Divison.
Place:
Time:

The above may be forwarded as now corrected.   (Z)

Censor. Signature of Addressor or person authorised to telegraph in his name.

* This line should be erased if not required.

Instructions for compilation of statement of
Surpluses and Deficiencies in Horse Transport.

****

1. This return will be rendered to D.D.S. & T., Fourth Army, by Monday of each week.

2. Return should include all 1st line and Train Transport vehicles, but not technical vehicles and will show the nett surplus and deficiency in the Corps after adjustments have been made between Divisions.

3. The return will show :-

    (a) Whether transport is complete turnsout or vehicles only.
    (b) Whether serviceable or unserviceable.
    (c) Whether deficiencies have been demanded from A.O.D.

4. No steps will be taken to return surplus transport pending instructions from D.D.S & T.

8th Serv Batt. Leicestershire Regt.

Ref. N.R.O. 564 — Saddle blankets
of July 5/16

The second saddle blanket allowed per horse was returned to Ordnance 3)th Division before we marched here.

J Simpson Lt Col
Comg 8th Leicestershire Regt.

July 7/16
The Field

WEEKLY RETURN OF SURPLUSES AND DEFICIENCIES IN HORSE TRANSPORT.

WEEK ENDING..................1916.

FORMATION	SURPLUSES										DEFICIENCIES									Remarks.
	Carts Forage	Carts S.A.A.	Carts Tool.	Carts Water	Carts.	Travelling Kitchens.	Wagons Ambulance	Wagons Civilian	Wagons G.S.	Wagons G.S. Limbered.	Carts, Forage	Carts, S.A.A.	Carts, Tool	Carts, Water.	Carts.	Travelling Kitchens.	Wagons Ambulance.	Wagons Civilian.	Wagons G.S.	Wagons G.S. Limbered.	

All deficiencies have been indented for and are complete turnsout except where otherwise stated. Certified that there is no horse transport held by this formation surplus to authorised establishment, other than that shewn above.

(Signed)

State of Trench Mortars, Trench Mortar Ammunition, Grenades and Smoke Candles at Noon, Sunday .... 1916.

.... ARMY, CORPS OR TRENCH MORTAR SCHOOL.

I. Trench Mortars and Trench Mortar Ammunition.

DESCRIPTION.	No. of Mortars.	ROUNDS.				Rounds per Mortar.	REMARKS*
		With Troops.	In Parks.	Corps or other Reserve.	Total.		
1.57 in.							
2 in.							
4 in.							
3.7 in.							
3 in. } Stokes							
4 in. }							
240 m/m.							

II. Grenades and Smoke Candles.

DESCRIPTION.	GRENADES.				REMARKS.
	With Troops.	In Parks.	Corps or other Reserve.	Total.	
Rifle Grenades:—					
No. 3					
No. 20					
Percussion Grenades:—					
No. 1					
No. 2					
No. 19					
Time Grenades:—					
No. 5					
Smoke Candles:—					

* To show mortars received, lost, captured, destroyed by enemy fire or other cause.

_____ DIVISION.

Return shewing in detail receipts and expenditure of Gun and Trench Mortar Ammunition during week ending Sunday _____ 1916.

	18-pdr			4.5" How.		TRENCH MORTARS.	
	A	AX	B	BX		2"	3" STOKES.
Expended /16.							
" :/ /16.							
" :/ /16.							
" :/ /16.							
" :/ /16.							
" :/ /16.							
" :/ /16.							
Retd to A.S.P.							
TOTAL.							
Receipts /16.							
" :/ /16.							
" :/ /16.							
" :/ /16.							
" :/ /16.							
" :/ /16.							
" :/ /16.							
TOTAL.							
On hand // 18.							
GROSS TOTAL EXPENDED							
REMAINS / /16.							

_____ DIVISION.

Return shewing in detail remains of Gun Ammunition at noon,

Sunday, _____ 1916.

UNITS.	Guns 18 pdr.			Guns 4.5" Howr			Guns	Guns	Guns	Guns
	A Shp	A.X Lyd	B Shp	B Lyd	BX Lyd					
Bde R.F.A.										
Bde R.F.A.										
Bde R.F.A.										
Bde R.F.A.										
Div. Ammn. Col.										

Total on hand
Noon _____ 1916.

Q. 1493.

Formation or Directorate.

....

Return of Labour, unskilled and semi-skilled, other than that provided by fighting Troops or Reinforcements, employed on the

1st of ...., 1916.

	ROADS.		QUARRIES.		DEFENCES.		RAILWAYS.		FORESTS.		WORKSHOPS & STORES.		DOCKS.		MISCELLANEOUS.		TOTAL.
	Unit.	Strength.	Unit.	Strength.	Unit.	Strength.	Unit.	Strength.	Unit.	Strength.	Unit.	Strength.	Unit.	Strength.	Unit.	Strength.	
Military:—																	
British ...																	
French ...																	
Belgian ...																	
Civilian:—																	
French ...																	
Belgian ...																	
Other labour...																	
*TOTAL ...																	
Total preceding month ...																	

1st Printing Co., R.E. 4th Army Section. 278

Return of Reserves of Supplies maintained in Supporting
Points on the month ending

Division.	Quantities maintained		Remarks.
	Commodity	No. of Rations.	

Only complete Iron Rations are authorised for this purpose
consisting of a two days reserve.

21st Divisional Engineers

21st DIVISIONAL SIGNAL COMPANY R. E.

AUGUST 1916.

Cover for Documents.

Nature of Enclosures.

War Diary

of

21st Sig. Coy.

Tenoid August 1915

Notes, or Letters written.

21st Divisional Engineers

21st DIVISIONAL SIGNAL COMPANY R. E. :: SEPTEMBER 1916.

WAR DIARY
INTELLIGENCE SUMMARY

of 21st SIGNAL COMPANY R.E.
SEPTEMBER 1916

Army Form C. 2118

Place	Date	Hour	Summary of Events and Information	Remarks and references to Appendices
DUISANS	1/9/16		Sec 5th. Preparations for coming operations. Scheme been hindered by difficulty in obtaining cord for making telephone lines and test apparatus.	
LE CAUROY	5/9/16		Moved to training area. Disposed at LE CAUROY. Brigade returns to consist of divisional equipment and personnel. No 4 section did not come in on Brigade decides to do combined training. Other Brigade section	Vide letter A.
	7/9/16		Officers were told training of battalion signals. Mr Parsons leave to England. Horse transport of company marches to AUTHIE.	
LE CAUROY	12/9/16			
AUTHIE	13/9/16		2/Lieutenant NF. with one section and Air Service camp. 2/Walker must no later at BELLEVUE then ALBERT/r RA	
BUIRE	13/9/16		Company left section to BUIRE	
BUIRE	14/9/16		Company less W/Parsons to camp at PICOURT F well, section/r RA 10-15 up. Lt Walker remained at BELLEVUE then with RA	

WAR DIARY of 21st SIGNAL COMPANY R.E.

INTELLIGENCE SUMMARY for SEPTEMBER 1916

Army Form C. 2118

Place	Date	Hour	Summary of Events and Information	Remarks and references to Appendices
BUIRE	14/9/16		64th Brigade signals did not carry out instructions as to having connection to Corps exchange at POMMIERS redoubt. This caused considerable trouble and has eventually been put right by Capt. Yule from at night and mng ? of cable.	
	15/9/16 — 18/9/16		64th Brigade attacked FLERS DIVION. Sn HQ moved to TRICOURT.	
	19/9/16		Capt. Yule visited Brigade. De Montgomery suffering from effects of gas shell. Lt A.H. Millett took Capt. Yule round lines MORVILLE wood and various pts. Lt. Montgomery show ? him some Lt. Millett and Montgomery knocked out by shell. Shock ? Lt. Millett partens thigh & flesh wound. capt. wd ? body on extremities, 2nd 36 ccs	
	20/9/16		Work on lining for adv DiV H/Q at MONTAUBAN. Lt Lasso arrives to replace Lt Millett. Septembe Lts (a.c.s.n.) Livingpool & Attached Div Signal Company.	V. app. 13
	21/9/16		Lt. A.H. Millett died in No 26 c.c.s. Leg amputated previous to death.	

WAR DIARY of 21st Signal Company, R.E.
INTELLIGENCE SUMMARY
SEPTEMBER 1916

Army Form C. 2118

(Erase heading not required.)

Place	Date	Hour	Summary of Events and Information	Remarks and references to Appendices
TRICOURT	22/9/16		Work of preparation continued. 2 pairs twisted DZ laid in exps cable trench for ½ mile during day and ¾ mile during night. Cable trench to be only dug as far as S17a.5.9. (LONGUEVAL sheet).	
	23/9/16		Lines extended from MONTAUBAN to YORK TRENCH right Brigade. Polis not available owing to stores not been forth coming. Heavy shelling delved day from Brigade Hd Qrs to comp cable trench.	
	24/9/16		Line completed but not put through. Se leased to MONTAUBAN two hours to rffn. 110th Brigade moved out at 10 pm.	
MONTAUBAN	25/9/16		Division Advd. to MONTAUBAN. One hour before Op 22 Pv. Communication in telephon, through G.H.Q to Brigade Speaking for dispatches up to Brigade. Sapper Peck wounded.	
	26/9/16		Cavalry in GUEUDECOURT. Lyt Allen with troop S.I.H. all wires he rerouts but it was found that they but lave. Wires wounded on return journey N.G.D ELVILLE WOOD	

Army Form C. 2118

21st SIGNAL CO RE

WAR DIARY
INTELLIGENCE SUMMARY SEPTEMBER 1916

(Erase heading not required.)

Instructions regarding War Diaries and Intelligence Summaries are contained in F.S. Regs., Part II. and the Staff Manual respectively. Title Pages will be prepared in manuscript.

Place	Date	Hour	Summary of Events and Information	Remarks and references to Appendices
MONTAUBAN	27/9/16		Capt. Yule visited Brigades. 2 Brigades in and small day out. I make nothing difficult. Noticeable lack of cooperation between the two Brigades and officers of 110th and 64th Brigades. 62nd Brigade reports complaints of bad handwriting. Matters were improved after this. 62n took over night of 26th/27th. Wire to battn claim satisfactory. Capt. Collin slightly wounded. At Montauban Brigade and to point in 8th Section and establish 64 Brigade head qrs. a battle HQ.	
	28/9/16		Relief of 164th Brigade by 123rd Brigade which then came under 21 DHQ Division. Line cleared to 123rd Brigade at 9.45 a.m. Line arranged through to N11DA at 8 p.m. though not required till new next day.	
	29/9/16		Capt. Yule visited Brigades. Found 123rd Signals had not been enabled by 110th Brigade although the Brigade was only 53 yards away. 123rd Brigade had first system of battalion lines. Walked through battalion lines of 120th Brigade. Noticeable lines of Westmoreland police. Reports EADASAS possible between Bn.	
	30/9/16		from PIERS to LES BOUFS still started. 1st LINCOLNS the whole GUEDECOURT was Advance had proceeded. Chances had proceeded. Small durin advance - only 3 killed and three casualties small durin advance - only 3 killed and three by stray shell in his area.	

21st Division

Sick wastage from noon 2nd to noon 3rd Sept 1916.

	Admitted	Evacuated	Remaining
62nd Inf Brigade	—	2	30
64th " "	—	1	35
110th " "	—	1	27
Div. Artillery	—	3	26
" Troops	2	1	36
Totals	2	8	154

H.Q. 21. Div.
3. 9. 1916.

C. C. Thomson
Major
Colonel
A.D.M.S.

21st Division

Sick wastage from noon 1st to noon 2nd Sept. 1916.

	Admitted	Evacuated	Remaining
62nd Inf. Brigade	10	2	51
64th " "	5	3	41
110th " "	5	-	35
Div. Artillery	7	2	47
" Troops	8	2	50
Totals	35	9	224

H.Q. 21. Div.
2. 9. 1916.

Colonel
A.D.M.S.

21st Divisional Engineers

21st DIVISIONAL SIGNAL COMPANY R. E. OCTOBER 1916.

Army Form C. 2118

WAR DIARY of 21st Signal Company R.E.
INTELLIGENCE SUMMARY
(Erase heading not required.)

OCTOBER 1916

Vol 1

Instructions regarding War Diaries and Intelligence Summaries are contained in F.S. Regs., Part II. and the Staff Manual respectively. Title Pages will be prepared in manuscript.

Place	Date	Hour	Summary of Events and Information	Remarks and references to Appendices
MONTAUBAN	1/10/16		D.H.Q. decided to move back to TRICOURT arriving to have offices behind. Signal Officers in charge were early arranged and a close hold full during flight apart from Signal Office.	
TRICOURT				
"	2/10/16.		Change to TRICOURT at 11 a.m.. L/Platoon supervises changes at TRICOURT.	
IN USE			Six Knives. Company by road. One lantern left behind with Pt. under Lt Walker.	
ESTANVEUR	3/10/16		Company ESTANVEUR. Billets poor.	
MILLY-LE-HAUT-CLOCHER	4/10/16		Company to MILLY - LE - HAUT - CLOCHER. Billets fair. Miners clean french	
"	5/10/16		Routine.	
"	6/10/16		Routine. Capt. Wm. 6[?] 1st ARMY 62 mm taking over.	
"	7/10/16	5.30	Coy. marched to LONGPRÉ Station (7 mils.) Entrained for FOUCQUEREUIL arrived there 7.30 a.m. Brigade Section with Brigade H.Q. to rest areas near BETHUNE.	
	8/10/16	12 noon	DIV. H.Q. opened at NOEUX les MINES. Lines ready to 1st Corps & Corps exchange. All Brigades on 'phone'.	

O.C. 21st Signal Co. R.E.

WAR DIARY or INTELLIGENCE SUMMARY

Army Form C. 2118

H.Q. & No 1 Sect. 21st SIGNAL COY.

OCTOBER 1916

Place	Date	Hour	Summary of Events and Information	Remarks and references to Appendices
NOEUX-LES-MINES	11/10/16	9.30 am	Captain J.S. YULE R.E. left for Canadian Corps Signal Company. Linesmen & instruments sent to 5th. Div. Signal Offices to take over estab. Lt. Pickawa O/c company now taking over arrangements. 62 & 110 Inf Bde Sigs	
	12/10	2.30 pm	Coy. moved to old 5th. Div. Sig. H.Q. at SAILLY - LA BOURSE. Took over at 6 pm. Taking over was carried out with Lt. Walker and one section still with 21 Div. Att. East Yorks. took over	
Sailly La Bourse	12/10		Captain A.G. SHAW 4th. Bn. East Yorks. took over command of 21st. Signal Coy. 40th. Div. on right. 32nd. Div. on left.	
	14/10	2 pm	6th. Inf Bde Sig. (C/c Lt. JACKSON, 13R. N.F.) took over from 97R. Inf Bde Sig. 32nd Div. Taking over was without hitch.	
	15/10 to		Maintenance of routes & signal arrangements. Preparation for move of 6 Bth R. Inf. Bde. to new HQ at ANNEQUIN. 1st Corps Instld 9-way route NOEULLES to ANNEQUIN on 16th Oct	

A.W. Stewart Capt
O.C. 21st Signal Co. R.E.

WAR DIARY

Army Form C. 2118

HQ – No, I Section

INTELLIGENCE SUMMARY 21st Div Signal Coy R.E.

(Erase heading not required.) October 1916

Instructions regarding War Diaries and Intelligence Summaries are contained in F. S. Regs., Part II. and the Staff Manual respectively. Title Pages will be prepared in manuscript.

Place	Date	Hour	Summary of Events and Information	Remarks and references to Appendices
Sailly La Bourse	18/10/16	2pm	64th Inf. Brigade move to new HQ at Annequin. Move carried out without a hitch. Communication working satisfactorily.	
	19/10/16		Lt Walker and cable section rejoined Company from the Somme battle.	
	20/10/16	noon	21st Div artillery relieve 8th D** artillery. Communication in working satisfactory.	
		2.30pm	Party under Lt Faram left for six weeks class at Divisional School at Terfay. Object of school to train battalion + artillery signallers.	
	22/10/16		2/Lt C. Hedderwich joined Company as supernumery officer from 14th Army Corps Signal Coy.	
	23.10.16 & 31.10.16		No matter of interest. Usual routine and work of improvement of Divisional communication necessary in trench warfare.	
30.10.16			24th Div Division relieve 110th Division and are now in our Right Flank.	

O.C. 21st Signal Co. R.E.

21st Divisional Engineers

21st DIVISIONAL SIGNAL COMPANY R. E. :: NOVEMBER   1916.

WAR DIARY 2/2 Divisional Signal Company Rfs.
or
INTELLIGENCE SUMMARY

Army Form C. 2118

Place	Date	Hour	Summary of Events and Information	Remarks and references to Appendices
Sailly La Bourse	1/11/16 to 2/11/16		General routine work. — Improvement of D Corps buried Cable system and laying lines into new Divisional dugouts 500 yards south of Div HQ.	
	3/11/16			
	4/11/16		Sappers W.H. Cook + T. Fletcher of No 3 Section of the Company awarded military medals for conspicuous bravery and good work on the Somme operations. —	
	5/11/16	11 am	G.O.C. 1st Army Corps distributed medal ribbons to the Division. 2 Officers 30 Other Ranks of the Company proceeded attached	
	6/11/16 to 14/11/16		Nothing of any mention. General routine maintenance work and instruction at Divisional Signal School. —	
	15/11/16 to 23/11/16		Nothing of importance. General maintenance of lines. —	
	29/11/16		64th Bde relieved by 18th Brigade. 6th Division all lines handed over correct. A. Phanarum	

21st Divisional Engineers

21st DIVISIONAL SIGNAL COMPANY R. E. :: DECEMBER 1916.

Original.

DEC 1916.
21st Divisional Signal Coy. R.E.

WAR DIARY or INTELLIGENCE SUMMARY

Army Form C. 2118

(Erase heading not required.) Headquarters - N°. 1. Section

Place	Date	Hour	Summary of Events and Information	Remarks and references to Appendices
SAILLY LABOURSE	1/12/16		Div. H.Q. Sig Office at SAILLY LABOURSE (nr BETHUNE). 64th Div Sig in nr BETHUNE. 26 Squads on George. 110th. H.Q. at VERMELLES Groeing HOHENZOLLERN Redoubt & 2nd at VERMELLES Groeing QUARRIES sector. 94th + 95th Bdes R.F.A. at NOYELLES Groeing 62nd and 110th. Inf Bdes supporting 64th in Cambrin sector opposite 15th Inf Bde Gr. Div. 64th Div on Right. Position cables relieved by 1st Army taken into use.	SS 16
	11/12/16 Noon		Lt A.B JACKSON, 13th N.F. transferred to Signal Service & posted to 21st Sig Coy.	
	9th		Divisional Signals Dugout Shelter in Bn. defence line near Sully Labourse to circle E of Chateau now completed wired up & connected to all Brigades.	
	12th.		Inf. 14th 9 + 1st Corps. Trial moves to any out exercise 11.30 pm with Signal Staff to familiarise personnel with routine of change. Worked well; all unite got in to connecto from time of getting order "move to dugouts". Telephone wires & for Corps Commanders interrupted at all.	
15th	3 pm		64th Div Sigs. relieved 110th Div Sigs who took over Res place in Bethune	
	19th		110th Sigs to AUCHEL for training with Brigade	

2.

DEC. 1916   21st. SIG. COY. R.E.

WAR DIARY
or
INTELLIGENCE SUMMARY — H.Q. & No.1 SECTION.
(Erase heading not required.)

Army Form C. 2118

Place	Date	Hour	Summary of Events and Information	Remarks and references to Appendices
	22/12/16		Lt. E.J. LASSEN posted to 1st. Corps. Signal Coy.	
	25/12/16		CAPT. A.C. SHAW to 65th. F.A. (Sick) then to DIV. rest Stn., then 33 C.C.S., No. 20 Gen. Hosp. & to England 2.1.17.	
			A/CAPT. N. PORTEOUS in command of company.	
	26/12/16		62nd Inf. Bde. relieved by Bde. of 6th. DIV. and went to rest at FERFAY ALLOUAGNE.	
	28/12/16		64th Inf. Bde. relieved by Bde. of 6th. DIV. and went to rest at FOUQUIÈRES.	
	29/12/16	10 a.m.	21st DIV. Relieved by 6th. DIV.: Closed Office at LABEUVRIÈRE 10 a.m. Telephone power & single line to Corps- Buses on Corps & Army lines. 21 Div. Art. at SALLY. 96th. Bde. H.Q. at NOEUX-LES-MINES. 95th. Bde. H.Q. at NOEUX-LES-MINES. Batteries in Hohenzollern Sector. Sth. H.Q. NOYELLES Batteries in evening @ V ARRAS SECTOR.	

H.Q. & No.1 Section. Now in Labeuvrière & Lapugnoy. Horse lines Lapugnoy. Billets in houses fair. Hope Lines Lapugnoy. Billets in houses fair in the area for troops. Billets in houses fair, huts ditto. Country flat, very wet.

DEC. 1916.
21st SIGNAL COY Army Form C. 2118
HQ. + NO. 1 SECTION

WAR DIARY
or
INTELLIGENCE SUMMARY
(Erase heading not required.)

Place	Date	Hour	Summary of Events and Information	Remarks and references to Appendices
SAILLY LABOURSE	Dec. 1916		Work of HQ + No. 1. Section during December 1916:- Maintaining + improving lines taken over from 8th Div. Join signals. Every route to ANNEQUIN from NOYELLES put up by A Co on our request. Every route (rest) running E↔W - south of FOSSE 9 to clear up that area + give alternative route to ANNEQUIN. Every route built CRA to Dunkirk. Every Gnr 9 to Cenelin. Dib. DuS outs relaid + wired up to Corps, Brigades of Inf. Harry, and to dug outs of Staff + C.R.A. Temporarily built Dis. Dugout for 7? Lamp Station built into S. slope of Gnr 9 for work to Vermelles Brigades. Terror line now extends much further in forward trenches thoroughly ov'erhauled & made up a great deal of cable relaid & up & sent to base. Assistance given to ACO for clearing up + rewiring Fevin Prin. Avenue routes. Vermelles routes to Front H. line cleared up since H. + 3 Front line Linguets routes put into area as area stores by ACO at our request. Six weeks sources of Sigt. DIV. SCHOOL Signal Class 75 men dealt with. Lt Laver brought by Lt Jackson 835 first class signallers in charge. ||	
FERFAY				

WAR DIARY

JANUARY

INTELLIGENCE SUMMARY

H.Q. & No. 1. SECTION
21 SIGNAL COY.

Vol 17

Army Form C. 2118

Place	Date	Hour	Summary of Events and Information	Remarks and references to Appendices
LABEUV-RIERE	1/1/17		Div. H.Q. Signal Office at LABEUVRIÈRE, near BETHUNE. Brigades at ALLOUAGNE (62m) AUCHEL (110r.) FOUQUIÈRES (64th.). Communication to Brigades & Artillery through 1st Corps & 1st Army exchanges. Local airline run out to Chocheau & local offices.	
	5/1/17		N.C.O. & 2 sappers with Lt. WALKER for 21 Div. Art. at SAILLY LABOURSE. 21 Div. Art. S/g. Coy. near N.C.O. to Labeuvrière. 21 Div. Pet. to AMETTES. WORK:— Training in cable work & reorganizing of detachments owing to recent promotions & reinforcements. Overhaul of all equipment & technical stores. Rising and training drill, foot drill, infantry drill, communication drill for N.C.O's. Construction of Cane shelters for at LAPUGNOY. Lectures on Signal work and organization, I.T. work, and contact aeroplane signalling Recreation, routemarches & physical training, football. Divisional School – Signals carried on under Lt. JACKSON.	
	13/1/17		CAPTAIN A.E. GOULD "L" ARMY SIGNAL COY. took over command of 21 S. Coy. Div. H.Q. Signal Office closed at Labeuvrière at 7:30 a.m. & opened at WORMHOUDT (6 miles N. of CASSEL) at 10 a.m. Transport moved by MERVILLE. Signal Staff under Capt. PORTEOUS moved by lorries by HAZEBROUCK 27/1. H.Q. at	
	28/1/17		Chateau. 3 pairs run 3 Coy. also Local lines. Brigades on Corps lines (8th Cple) (8th Cyc) 62m at Camp X (Peperinghe) 110r. HOODERQUEQUES – 64th. at WORMHOUDT.	

1875 Wt. W593/826 1,000,000 4/15 J.B.C. & A. A.D.S.S./Forms/C. 2118.

WAR DIARY or INTELLIGENCE SUMMARY

Army Form C. 2118

FEBRUARY 1917

21st Signal Co. R.E.
HQ. No. 1 Section
Vol 16

Place	Date	Hour	Summary of Events and Information	Remarks and references to Appendices
WORMHOUDT	12/2/17		Bde. Signal Office was close to 2nd Army Sub-exchange; HQ. in Chateau. Bdes:- 62nd at "X" CAMP (POPERINGHE); 110th at HAUTKERQUE; 64th at WORMHOUDT. Local lines to Chateau; Div. Arty. and 64th Bde. Communication to 62nd Bde. on Army route to 8th Corps, to 62nd Bde. through Corps and to 2nd Army to 94th Bde RFA through WATOU Sx. and 95th Bde RFA through 110th Bde. Signal Coy. transport marched Div. Arty. closed and moved to HAZEBROUCK to BETHUNE.	AW
	13/2/17	9am	64th Bde. closed moved by train to old HAZEBROUCK. Signal office moved to Chateau utilising existing lines to old office for communication to 2nd Army; 8th Corps; and WORMHOUDT Exchange; 110th Bde. through WATOU Sx. Artillery Bdes. disconnected. Signals Coy. took an officer tone office relief to advanced "G" + "Q". opened at 2.50 pm. Local lines were run at WORMHOUDT and to BETHUNE CIVIL EX. Div. HQ. also at BETHUNE executing line to 5th Div. Arty. Div. Ant. opened in BETHUNE utilising executing line to 5x. for communication.	AW
	14/2/17		BETHUNE. 2nd office relief and stores from WORMHOUDT to BETHUNE by lorry. 64th Bde. closed at BETHUNE and relieved 6th Bde. 6th Div. in CAMBRIN SECTION. 110th Bde. closed at HAUTKERQUE and opened in BETHUNE	AW

O.C. 21st Signal Co. R.E.

Army Form C. 2118

FEBRUARY 1917

WAR DIARY or INTELLIGENCE SUMMARY

21st Signal Co RE
H.Q. No 1 Section

Place	Date	Hour	Summary of Events and Information	Remarks and references to Appendices
BETHUNE	15/2/17	1.30pm	110th Bde closed at BETHUNE and relieved Centre Bde 6th DIV in HOHENZOLLERN Section	VM
		noon	Bri 110 closed at WORMHOUDT and opened in BETHUNE.	
		4 pm	62nd Bde opened in BETHUNE.	A.D.W.
	17/2/17	10 am	Bri Arty closed and relieved 6th Div Arty at SAILLY LABOURSE	
		10 am	62nd Bde closed at BETHUNE and relieved right Bde 6th Div in QUARRIES Section	A.D.W.
SAILLY LABOURSE	18/2/17	10 am	Bri HQ opened at SAILLY LABOURSE relieving 6th Div. Communication to Corps (1st) by telephone and sounder; telephone to HQ by telephone sounder; telephone to BETHUNE CIVIL Ex and Rear DIV. SIG. telephone and buzzer to test station and exchange at NOYELLES; local circuits to G.Q, Bri Arty Ex, BASD, CRE, ADMS, Tunnelling Coy, Pigeon Loft. Local circuits from NOYELLES Ex to Field Corps RE; Pioneers and Corps Wireless Station. Telephone lines from NOYELLES to Right Centre Bde Bri Arty Ex; - Telephone lines to 94th, 95th Bdes RFA, and to 38th Army F.A Bde, to Bri Ex; 1st Corps Heavy Arty Ex; No 30 Kite Balloon Section and DAC, Buzzer lines to 94th and 95th Bde RFA, and to 38th Army F.A. Bde	A.D.W. A. Harold Parrott Capt RE

Army Form C. 2118

21 Signal Company R.E.

MARCH 1917 WAR DIARY or INTELLIGENCE SUMMARY

FEBRUARY

(Erase heading not required.)

Place	Date	Hour	Summary of Events and Information	Remarks and references to Appendices
SAILLY-LABOURSE	MARCH 1		Communications as at end of February 1917.	
		11:30am	62nd Inf. Bde. relieved in the QUARRIES SECTION by 71st Inf. Bde. (6th Dvn.) moved to BETHUNE. Telephone communication to 62nd Inf. Bde. through BETHUNE Exchange.	
		4pm	62nd Inf. Bde. closed at BETHUNE and opened at La MIQUELLERIE 2 miles N.b.E. of LILLERS. Telephone communication established through 1st Army Exchange.	
	2		NIL	
	3	1pm	62nd Inf. Bde. closed at BETHUNE and opened at La MIQUELLERIE 2 miles N.b.E. of LILLERS. Telephone communication established through 1st Army Exchange.	
	4	1:30pm	71st Inf. Bde. moved their HQ from VERMELLES to La PHILOSOPHE where they had formerly been a Brigade HQ.	
		3pm	G.O.C. 6th Division took over command of front covered by 71st Inf. Bde. + 110th Inf. Bde. (HOHENZOLLERN SECTION) + 94th Bde. R.F.A. gone + 37th Div. Arty. was taken over by 95th Bde. R.F.A. (HOHENZOLLERN) 6th Div. took over all lines at (NOEUX-LES-MINES) Signals at 21st Div. H.Q. except one pair to 95th Bde. (on which Noeux Schno informed) one pair to 110th Inf. Bde. one pair to 95th Bde. R.F.A. one pair to 94th Bde. R.F.A. (which remained in their H.Q.) Lines to	

WAR DIARY or INTELLIGENCE SUMMARY

Army Form C. 2118

21 Signal Company R.E.

MARCH 1917

Place	Date March	Hour	Summary of Events and Information	Remarks and references to Appendices
SAILLY-LABOURSE	4 (cont.)		BETHUNE Exchange; 6th Divn. 1st Corps Heavy Arty; 64th Infy Bde (who remained under command of G.O.C. 21st Bde) and local circuits. 6th Divn. H.Q. were at NOEUX-LES-MINES; circuits were put through on the Bethune road at 21 Divn H.Q. as up 2 by 6th Divn. Sig.	
	5.	3 pm	64th Infy Bde relieved in CAMBRIN SECTION by 15th Infy Bde (5th Divn—) 64th Bde moved to BETHUNE. Exchange established. Telephone communication through 5th Divn Exchange. Direct line to 6th Divn Sigs to then Bde taken over by 6th Divn Sigs to then	
	6.	9.30 a.m.	own use.	
		10 a.m.	Command of 95th Bde. R.F.A passed to G.O.C R.A 6th Divn Arty. Command of CAMBRIN GROUP R.F.A passed to G.O.C R.A 5th Divn Arty.	
		1 pm	64th Infy Bde closed at BETHUNE opened at ROBECQ; telephone communication through 1st Army Exchange. (ROBECQ 2 miles S.W. of ST. VENANT)	
	7.		NIL.	
	8.		NIL.	

Army Form C. 2118

21st Signal Company / R.E.

WAR DIARY
or
INTELLIGENCE SUMMARY
(Erase heading not required.)

MARCH

Instructions regarding War Diaries and Intelligence Summaries are contained in F. S. Regs., Part II. and the Staff Manual respectively. Title Pages will be prepared in manuscript.

Place	Date March	Hour	Summary of Events and Information	Remarks and references to Appendices
SAILY-LABOURSE	9		62nd Inf. Bde. closed at LA MIQUELLERIE + opened at RELY, 5 miles N. of Lillers.	
		4 pm.	Telephone communication was established thro' 1st Army Exchange.	
		6.30 pm.	Communication broken between 1st Army Exchange + 62nd Bde. 1st Army disposed of message.	
		2 pm.	64th Inf. Bde. opened telephone communication from NORRENT FONTES (N. by N. of LILLERS)	
			62nd Inf. Bde. opened at ANTIGNEUL CHATEAU (on St. Pol - BRUAY road)	
	10	12 noon	21st Sig. Co.	
	11	3 pm.	Advanced party arrived by lorry at LUCHEUX (4 miles N.E. of DOULLENS). Local lines to join to LE SOUICH were found led into an old Sig. office at the Chateau; also a pair to VII Corps. The latter was tested + found to be clear; + a sounder was superimposed, though by the line gave much trouble intermittent faults being caused by workmen + parties some miles away on the line. A lineman was sent on bicycle to LE SOUICH + the total clear of this office was picked up outside the office to 18th Corps + found in good order.	

WAR DIARY or INTELLIGENCE SUMMARY

Army Form C. 2118.

21st Signal Company RE

MARCH (Cont'd)

Place	Date	Hour	Summary of Events and Information	Remarks and references to Appendices
SAILLY-LABOURSE	11 (cont)		Linesman sent to HALLOY to test pair from that point to 18th Corps	
LUCHEUX	12.	9 a.m.	Office closed at SAILLY-LABOURSE and opened at LUCHEUX. 62nd Bde at HALLOY on telephone through 18th Corp	
		12 noon	Div. HQ opened at LUCHEUX Chau.	
	13.		64th Bde opened at Le SOUICH; working round superimposed. Second line to VII Corps hy through SAULTY Exchange. Div. Art. at LUCHEUX. 110th Bde. still at VERMELLES.	
	16.		In view of 21st Div. going to ARRAS, 8 linesmen with a dept sent to SIGS. 14th Divn to assist in work and lean lines at 14th Divn Exchange. ARRAS and the CAVES at RONVILLE.	
	17.		Divl. School closed at FERFAY + 1 officer + 3 O.R. rejoined this unit. Farrier officer proceeded to 14th Divn Signals.	
	23.		64th Bde. moved to POMMERA Chau. Communication this Army buttered at MONDICOURT.	
	25		62nd Bde. opened at BERLES-AU-BOIS in 58th Divn area in 58th Divn area. Officer from ARRAS proceeded to BAVINCOURT 58th Divn HQ., in view of 21st Divn now going into line to relieve 58th Divn.	

Army Form C. 2118.

21st Signal Co RE

WAR DIARY
or
INTELLIGENCE SUMMARY.
(Erase heading not required.)

MARCH (cont'd)

Place	Date	Hour	Summary of Events and Information	Remarks and references to Appendices
LUCHEUX	27	8am	2 Officers and mounted portion of the company left LUCHEUX for ADINFER – Map SHEET 51c SE (1/20000) – x 21 D., to build new lines in rear of Div. HQ. moving to ADINFER WOOD. 58th Bgde. had one Inf. Bde. and 2 Arty. Groups in the line; the 62nd relieved Bde of 58th Div. at BOIRY. ST-RICTRUDE	
	28	11am	on this day. 2 pairs of airline received from BERLES-AU-BOIS to ADINFER. picking up old German route from there to BOIRY. 64th Inf. Bde. opened at BERLES-AU-BOIS. 21st Div. relieving 58th Div. Office stood at BAVINCOURT.	
		10am	Party at ADINFER putting new 8-way airline near ADINFER WOOD to BOIRY ST. RICTRUDE. Reconnecting route left partly standing by the Germans. Poles were collected from derelict routes to build new airline, and one route with little labour was made good from ADINFER to MOYENVILLE – SHEET 51B SW – S.28.c.	
	30		Party from BAVINCOURT to ADINFER WOOD to prepare to forward Sx. All lines led into test board in this forward by working thro' on morning of 30th. 2 pairs of Cable laid forward from BOIRY by M/fork route to 62nd Bde. advanced HQ at S11 d 9.0.	

O.C. 21ST SIGNAL Co R.E.

2/1st Div Signal Coy
April 1917.
H.Q. & No 1 Sector

Army Form C. 2118.

WAR DIARY
or
INTELLIGENCE SUMMARY.
(Erase heading not required.)

Vol 20

Place	Date	Hour	Summary of Events and Information	Remarks and references to Appendices
	1st	10am	Div HQ closed BAVINCOURT and opened ADINFER WOOD X 26 a 4.3 Sheet 57 D.	
		10am	64th Inf Bde left BERLES AU BOIS	
		2pm	64th " " opened at BOIRY ST RICTRUDE Sheet 51 B.	
			62 " " at S17a 9.9	GWP
			110th " " at POMMIER	GWP
	2nd	5.15a	Attack by 62nd Inf Bde commenced.	
		5.30p	All lines disconnected, owing to snowstorm. All cable cut out and Communications reestablished 11.30pm	GWP
	3rd	night	Lieut WALKER and Wires detachment laid its cable from MAISON ROUGE cross roads to ST LEGER for 110th Bde HQ. Lieut JACKSON and party put through circuit on French Rly pole and Boche hop pole to MAISON ROUGE. Heavy snowstorms and cold winds.	GWP
	4th	night	64th Inf Bde took over left of 62nd Inf Bde front 110th Inf Bde took over Right front of 62nd Inf Bde and spoken of 7th Inf Bde	GWP
	5th		62nd at BERLES AU BOIS, 64th at S17d 9.9, 110th at HAMELINCOURT	GWP

Army Form C. 2118.

WAR DIARY April 1917. (2)
or
INTELLIGENCE SUMMARY. H.Q. Y No.1 Section
21 Sig. Coy.

(Erase heading not required.)

Instructions regarding War Diaries and Intelligence Summaries are contained in F. S. Regs., Part II. and the Staff Manual respectively. Title pages will be prepared in manuscript.

Place	Date	Hour	Summary of Events and Information	Remarks and references to Appendices
	6th		Lieut JACKSON with party completed airline on existing poles to HAMELINCOURT. Another party made up cable laid to ST LEGER for 110th Inf Bde.	
	6th	4pm	Visual station established at S21.b.3.3 in old Boch trench or M.G. emplacement. Trench was kept with forward Brigade and a wire laid to BOIRY to wire to Division HQ. During the working of this station it was attacked by hostile aeroplane which descended to about 500 feet and opened machine gun fire. No damage was done. Advanced exchange opened at BOIRY ST RICTRUDE. 62nd Bde at BOIRY, but at S.M. a 9.9, 110th at HAMELINCOURT.	
	7th	12 noon	Captain N. PORTEOUS returned to duty.	
	8th		Lieut JACKSON and Sarti moved from Beaty to cellars in YW.	
	9th	4.15pm	Attack by 64th Inf Bde began.	
	10th	11.25a & 10.15p	VIII Corps complain of their own operator at 2" Bn. man probably changed. Their request Lines to 110th Inf Bde give trouble — intermittent faults on old airline. 62nd Inf Bde and 64th Inf Bde changed places.	

2353 Wt. W2514/1454 700,000 5/15 D. D. & L. A.D.S.S. Forms/C. 2118.

Army Form C. 2118.

WAR DIARY
or
INTELLIGENCE SUMMARY.

(Erase heading not required.)

April 1917. H.Q. & No 1 Section 21st Div. Sig. Coy.

Place	Date	Hour	Summary of Events and Information	Remarks and references to Appendices
	11th	2pm	Town lines across BAPAUME - BOISLEAUX Railway broken by traffic. Cable South and part of lines tried these lines under Railway finishing midnight	C&M W.P.
	12th	6pm	62nd Inf Bde move to shelters on roadside at S.79.c.6.1 moving Batten lines to old position	
		4pm	Cable wagon and transport left ADINFER. Owing to three long trains delays BOIRY ST MARTIN not reached till 8.0pm	
		8pm	Advanced office opened at S.17.b.9.9 relaying exchange at BOIRY as test point	
		9pm	Capt PORTEOUS with cable detail under Sgt TIPPER laid D.3 pair to 62nd Bde HQ. Owing to traffic delays and obstructions (@ Crater at Cross roads, 6 ammunition carts left in Rly cutting S.17.b.9.9) lines were not begun till 3.0am and were through at 6.0am	W.P.
			Cpl JOHNSON and 2/Cpl NEWTH with two Barrow parties laid D5 single to 62nd Inf Bde HQ. Through at 6.0am	W.P.
	13th	6.30am	This party also laid D3 pair 62nd Bde to 75th Bde on L. pt at T.3.a.7.7	
		8.0am	OC Signal arrived YUR	
		9.30am	General Staff arrived YUR. Staff phones not on their lines till 10.15am	W.P.

Army Form C. 2118.

WAR DIARY
or
INTELLIGENCE SUMMARY.

(Erase heading not required.)

April 1917 H.Q. 4 No 1 Section
21 Sqn Coy

Place	Date	Hour	Summary of Events and Information	Remarks and references to Appendices
	13th		Owing to Staff not deciding on which dugouts they were to occupy	
		9.30am	21st Div Arty moved S.17d 9.9	
		9.55am	Attack by 62nd Inf Bde commenced. Lines laid well as any	MR
	14th	6.20am	VII Corps linesmen crossed lines YUR-VII Corps and YUR-YU. Corpl JOHNSON (21st Div Sig) sent out to rectify mistake.	
		5.20pm	21st Div linesmen discover length of line 1652=Bde cut out near 37th TMAC BOYELLES.	
		5.45pm	Linesman reports 4 poles and 250 yds of D.5 plain cut out of line by RFC at Sucrerie.	
		6pm	G. Staff and 21st Div Arty Repl S.17 F 9.9	
		8pm	Signal Coy transport left BOIRY ST MARTIN and returned ADINFER CAMP	
			62nd Inf Bde relieved by 19th Inf Bde (33 DIVN)	MR
		night	YUR closed down and front taken over by 33 DIVN until HQ Signal	
	15th	11am	Office at HAMELINCOURT. 21st DIVN opened at old office in ADINFER WOOD. 62nd Inf Bde at BELLACOURT CHATEAU, 64th Bde BLAIREVILLE QUARRY. 110th Inf Bde at BASSEUX. Brigade connected up to ADINFER exchange during afternoon.	MR

Army Form C. 2118.

WAR DIARY
or
INTELLIGENCE SUMMARY

April '17 (3) HQ 7 No 1 Sect
21 Div Sig Coy

(Erase heading not required.)

Place	Date	Hour	Summary of Events and Information	Remarks and references to Appendices
YUR	15th	11am	Lieut A.T. WALKER appointed O/Captain whilst 1/c Signals 2 Div Art (Arty) (S/m) during his 15 days leave, know and snow made maintenance of Corps airlines very difficult. Vapour lines and shafts of varying lengths of cable by personnel thereof, also added to difficulty of maintenance. Three horses died from weather conditions and exposure, and shortage of forage over a long period. Forage supply began to improve and Signal Cy horses were turned onto paddocks improved by C.S.M. Smith. Want of exercise and maintenance of circuits on a continuous and trying round to weather, traffic and other conditions. The following N.C.O's did particularly good work C.S.M. SMITH, Corpl JOHNSON, 2/Cpl NEWITH (Lines), 2/Cpl COOPER (Superintendent). Maintenance of airline, department of circuits to came Rue Neuve by 38 miles of D5 cable taken up and used up and replaced by and broken by airline party organized under L/Cpl JOHNSON and given H.Q. labour from Corps lines to Corps Brigades required constant maintenance by	
	16th/20th		'21st' Signal Cy Emanuce	
	21st		Constructed line No No 8 R.F.C. at 9.25 and R.S.G. at report of F.T. by	

Army Form C. 2118.

WAR DIARY
or
INTELLIGENCE SUMMARY.
(Erase heading not required.)

Army Form C. 2118.

April 1917   HQ + No 1 Section
21/50/6

Place	Date	Hour	Summary of Events and Information	Remarks and references to Appendices
	23rd	3pm	6th Inf Bde left Blaireville and moved to NERGATEL.	
			Capt PORTEOUS went to TELEGRAPH HILL to investigate condition of 50th Div. Signal system	MP
	24th	7.30am	110th Inf Bde at BOIRY	
		4pm	6th " " "	
		6.20	" " at BOIRY (Sq a 9.4)	
		5.20am	Leave BLAIREVILLE for MERCATEL — arrived and reported	
			on GCO line at D.10 km	
	25th	11am	Capt PORTEOUS and Lieut JACKSON ran Signal through from MERCATEL to HAMELINCOURT	MP
		9am	After consultation with Signals 33rd Div. Capt PORTEOUS and Lieut JACKSON	
			to construct 2 direct pairs by cable as bte at T9 E 6.1	
		7.30pm	6th Inf Bde leave BOIRY and open at T3a 3.3	
		9.50pm	110th " " " "	
			BASSEUX and open near JUDAS FARM	
	26th	10am	31st Signal returns	
			33rd Signals at HAMELINCOURT	MP
		11am	6th Inf Bde arrives Sig 9.9 (from 50th Div area)	
			6th " " at T3a 3.3, 110th Bde at JUDAS FARM T27a 6.7	
			21st Div Art and 37th Div Art at HAMELINCOURT, 95th Bde RFA at HAMELINCOURT, 9th Bde RFA at SigF 9.9.	MP

Army Form C. 2118.

WAR DIARY April 1917 (1)
or
INTELLIGENCE SUMMARY.
(Erase heading not required.)

HQ 2nd/1st Sig
21 S.S. Coy

Place	Date	Hour	Summary of Events and Information	Remarks and references to Appendices
	26th	7.45pm	Signal office at T9.6.8.1 taken over as YUR took new pairs in use and one extended to 6th on existing lateral. Sounder to arc Bt SgP	9/6.
			worked correctly during evening.	
			All lines comp'td and tested either airline or cable either diagram	
	28/4/17		attached. The diagram now got out on the assumption that	9/6.
			the DIVISION would advance towards the Right Brigade.	
	29	6.30pm	62nd Inf Bde close at S.9.6.9.9 and open at T.21.d.7.8 as Right Brigade	
			YUR office moved to T9.C.7.7 as it seemed likely that T.9.5.8.1 would	
			be heavily shelled within next few days.	
	10am		Vionne station was taken over from 33rd DIV at T4.b.2.7 but a new	
			D's pair amo laid to it. this station was never actually used	
			32 unbranced reinforcements joined Coy. They are being used	
			to reinvest generally, cable allocated to filling Bde Stations.	9/6.
	30th		All lines shewn on diagram are working satisfactorily and	
			with good results. Visual at YUR and on HINDENBURG LINE	
			at T.4.b.	9/6.

2353 Wt. W2544/1454 700,000 5/15 D.D.& L. A.D.S.S. Forms/C. 2118.

WAR DIARY
INTELLIGENCE SUMMARY
(Erase heading not required.)

Army Form C. 2118.

April 1917 HQ, No 1 Sec, 2/9 Sig Co

Place	Date	Hour	Summary of Events and Information	Remarks and references to Appendices
	30th		The lines system having been completed as per line diagram dated 28th and on key satisfactorily, instructions were issued to prepare for two Brigades taking up HQ on HINDENBURG LINE T5-T9.8 in dugouts No 17, 18, 19 and 20. Arrangements were also made to recast the whole system. Working and weather conditions were every bad during first half of April. The Company continued to work well and work began to show an improvement technically. Circuit diagrams area 28/4/17 and 1/5/17 with each copy.	[signatures]

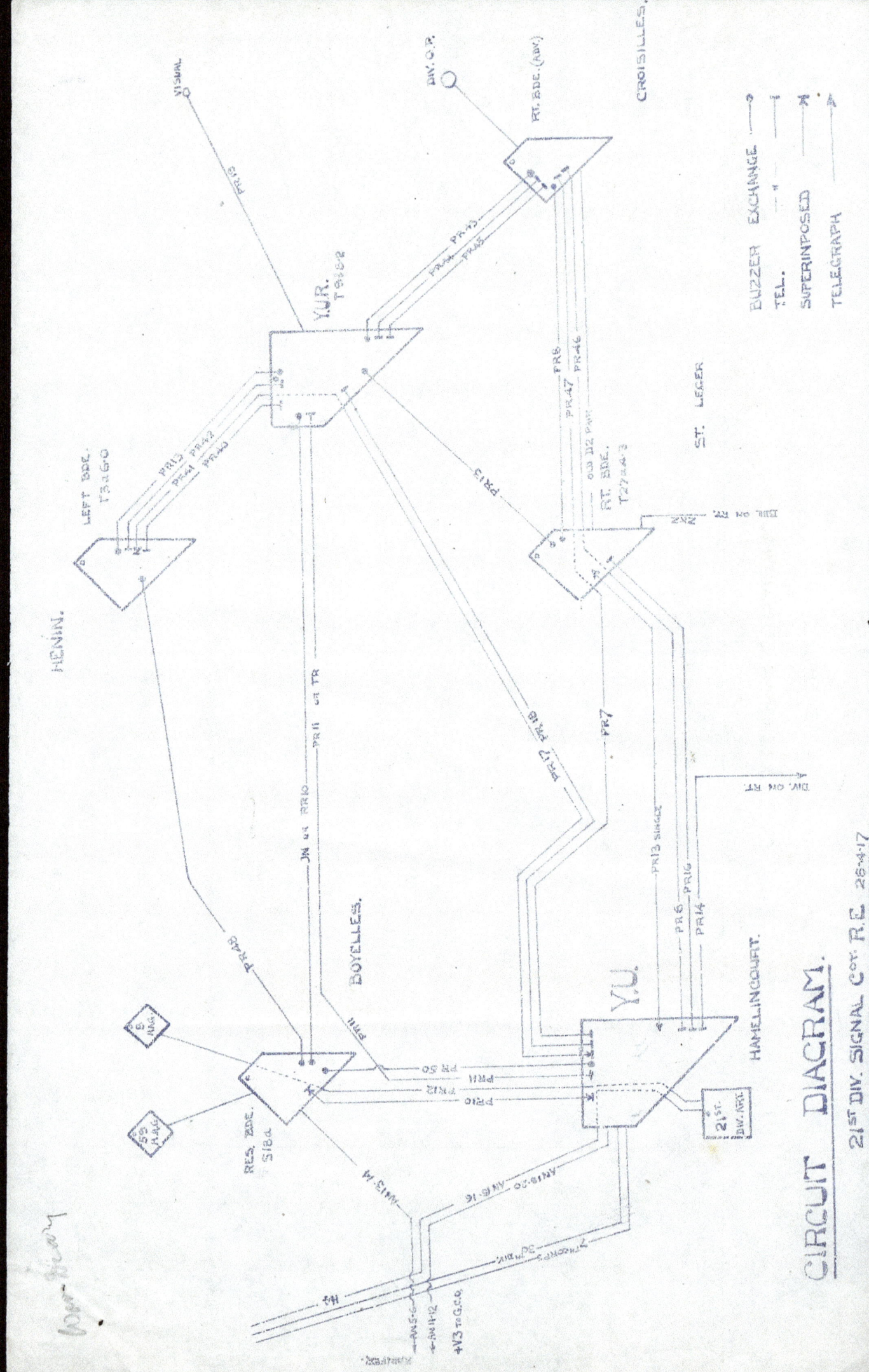

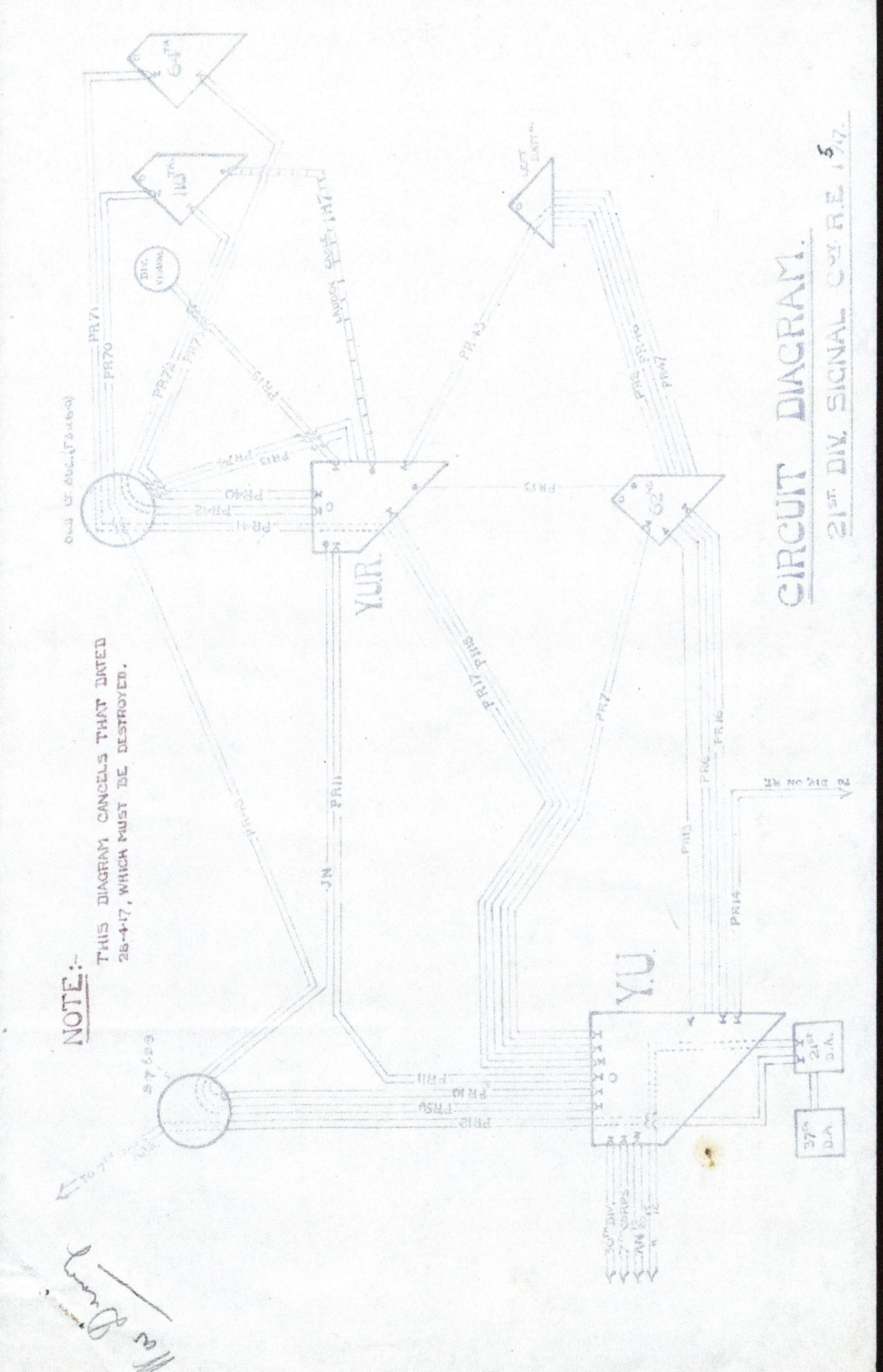

WAR DIARY or INTELLIGENCE SUMMARY

Army Form C. 2118.

21st Brit Signal Coy
May 1917
1/Q No 7 Section
2nd Spine Co RE
Vol 21

Place	Date	Hour	Summary of Events and Information	Remarks and references to Appendices
HAMELINCOURT	1/5/17	4 am	Note - All Map references are Sheet 51 B SW. Work began on charge of line system, i.e. division of communication trenches from Right area to Left area. CM's party commenced work at 4.0am by collecting poles from MOYENVILLE area. These poles were taken to Bn HQ on HENIN-CROISELLES road at T3a.8.1 and erected by Sgt TIPPER'S party to Hindenburg Line at N.35.c. Sgt SKINNER laid 2 pair of D5 twisted cable on these to the Hindenburg Line. Parties under CSM SMITH and Cpl JOHNSON laid two armoured cables between same points. This work was under the general supervision of Capt PORTEOUS and Lieut JACKSON. Arrived at the Hindenburg Line the former officer reorganized the parties. Parties under the CSM., Cpl JOHNSON, Sgt TIPPER and Sgt WILKES continued the lines which extend the tunnel under the Hindenburg support line to dugout 19 at T3a.15.70. CSM and Cpl JOHNSON finished their lines by 8.0pm. The others had about two hours work to complete but ran out of cable owing to Cpl BOND'S party at Negro sending up 8 drums of cable instead of 10 as ordered. The whole party got back to HQ about midnight. From Ervsieurs were left with Brigade under 2/Cpl TERRY.	

Army Form C. 2118.

WAR DIARY May 1917
INTELLIGENCE SUMMARY.
(Erase heading not required.)

HQ / No 7 Section
2nd Signal Co R.E.

Place	Date	Hour	Summary of Events and Information	Remarks and references to Appendices
	2nd		62nd Brigade on right at T.21.d.5.8, 110th at T.5.a.15.90 and 64th at T.5.a.2.70	
	3rd		On morning of attack by 110th and 64th Bdes the whole line system as per diagram dated 15/4 was completed, all lines were paired except the armoured cable and the laddered cable. During the attack communications to Brigade held. At one time all forward lines except one were broken by shell fire but were repaired by H/Cpl TERRY, Sappers BROWN, COUTTS and JOHNSON in very short time. DRLS work was performed by 15 mounted men of Northumberland Hussars under Sgt SCOTT. Wireless telegraphy exchanged test messages but was not used for operations. Power Buzzer was also tested but neither of these were needed as were not used for messages.	
	3rd	9.0 am	Capt PORTEOUS moves to YUR and El JACKSON to Test Point in Hindenburg Tunnel T.5.a.5.9	
	4th	8.0 pm	62nd Bde relieved 110th Bde and line changes were carried out by Lt JACKSON.	
	5th		110th Bde took over right position. Line changes carried out were altered according to new dispositions.	
4/6/17			Work was continued by the Coy of strengthening and improving lines, laying cable and erecting airline in lieu, in relays up at B.11.70 and in instructing	

WAR DIARY or INTELLIGENCE SUMMARY

Army Form C. 2118.

May, 1917 HQ No 1 Section
2nd Div Signal Co RE

Place	Date	Hour	Summary of Events and Information	Remarks and references to Appendices
	7th		Drivers and reinforcements in line work. The Company was reorganised on following lines:— All operators (Telegraph) to H.Q. Section. Artist party, 2 Inst repairers, 4 Telephonists, 4 F.S. men together with Cyclists completed the H.Q. Section. No 1 Section consisted of 4 detachments each with 2 N.C.O.s and 9 working members. 2 N.C.O.s & men mounted for detachment. The arrangement forces to work very well in practice as the cable detachments have always has enough men to work them and the old practice of having operators in No 1 Section which have never had the slightest practical value since 1914 was done away with.	
	8th		6th Bde moved into reserve at BOYELLES. During this period the weather remained fine and the health of the men and horses improved. Supplies of all kinds came forward well.	
	10th & 11th		21st Divn was relieved by 18th and 33rd Divns — the latter taking over. Div H.Q. at HAMELINCOURT. The arrangement for relief worked well and 21 Sig Co. Personnel stayed on whilst 33 Div worked the system for several hours.	

Army Form C. 2118.

(4) May 15.17
HQ No.1 Section
2nd Army Sig. Coy AG

WAR DIARY
or
INTELLIGENCE SUMMARY.
(Erase heading not required.)

Place	Date	Hour	Summary of Events and Information	Remarks and references to Appendices
	11th		The company suffered no casualties	
	12th	10am	Bde HQ closed at HAMELINCOURT and opened at ADINFER WOOD. Signal Office established near well at X29C 8.7 (sheet 51C) 62nd Bde at BLAIREVILLE QUARRY, 10th at POMMIERS, 64th at BASSEUX. Connection by VII Corps lines which were very unsatisfactory and required constant work and maintenance by Brig[Sig] Coy	
ADINFER	13th		Standing orders for HQ at ADINFER and Signal Camp issued. Installation of lines began. Spur cable reeled up between BOIRY + Railway (2 miles)	
	14th		2/Lieuts COLLIS E.A. and MONTGOMERIE F.J.D. promoted Lieutenant from 6th Jany 1917. Sergt ROBERTS evacuated to No 20 C.C.S. Major A.E. GOULD leave to U.K.	
	15th		Party working all day on Corps lines to POMMIER to improve them. Redirect on BS cable near ADINFER and layout line to DADOS, and 54th Sig Co. Capt WALKER, Lieut COLLIS, Cpl NEWTH and Sapper SHEPHERD mentioned in despatches	
	17th		Capt PARRISH to I Corps School as instructor to	

Army Form C. 2118.

WAR DIARY (5) May 1917
or
INTELLIGENCE SUMMARY.
(Erase heading not required.)

No.1 No.1 Section
21st Signal Coy. RE

Place	Date	Hour	Summary of Events and Information	Remarks and references to Appendices
ADINFER WOOD	20th		21 Signal Coy ran Inter-Company sports at RIVINSART organized by CRE Lt Col ADDISON D.S.O. Match Signal Coy 39, 126th Field (7) 6, 97th Field (7) 20, 128th Field (7) 6. There sports were extremely successful, knower a good turn out and keen competition. GOC and Staff paid a visit during afternoon. The weather was fine and the arrangements good. A copy of the certificate is attached — there were no prizes.	
	21st 22nd 23rd 24th		Weather broken interfering with training. Working parts again on the VII Corps lines.	
	25th		2/Capt COCKBILL reports from I Corps School as rejoins No 3 Section. 2/Lieut F. H. GREATREX joins the Coy from 3 Army Signals and posted to No.1 Section. 2e Capt OWEN A.V. rejoins from 21st Bn. School Ist mot and training of horses & reinforcements The weather improved since 23rd and training of horses & reinforcements was proceeded with. Health of Company good. Office work easy to Cope but continued to improve throughout the week and 3 wagon horses were cast. Trazmin of Communications attached.	
	26th 27th		Training in line work and riding continued. Weather good.	

Army Form C. 2118.

WAR DIARY (6) May 1917
or
INTELLIGENCE SUMMARY. HQ & No 1 Section
(Erase heading not required.) 21 Signal Coy RE

Instructions regarding War Diaries and Intelligence Summaries are contained in F.S. Regs., Part II. and the Staff Manual respectively. Title pages will be prepared in manuscript.

Place	Date	Hour	Summary of Events and Information	Remarks and references to Appendices
ADINFER	28th	6pm	Major GOULD returned from leave to UK.	
RONSSOY	29th	11a	2 Lieut C. HEDDERWICK left to report 25th Signal Coy RE	
			Reinforcements arrived from Signal Depot for RA HQ Signal sections and were sent to HAMELINCOURT for Capt WALKER	
	30th	6pm	Lieut and me H [in] relief went forward to HAMELINCOURT kept acquainted with lines and offices before taking over	
			2 Lieut R.W.P. YATES attached from 3 Army Sig Coy in place of 2/Lt. F.H. GREATREX who was withdrawn and returned to 3 Army Signal Coy	
HAMELINC	31st	10a	Relief of 33 Div Signals by this Coy at HAMELINCOURT. Through to all Brigades and other units.	
			No 1 Section Camp remained at X.29 C.8.7 Central as the water supply at the front was extremely good and grazing available	
			Effective strength found: 6 Officers, 277 O.R., 64 Riding, 77 & D. Horses	

[signature]
Major RE
O.C. 21ST SIGNAL COY R.E.

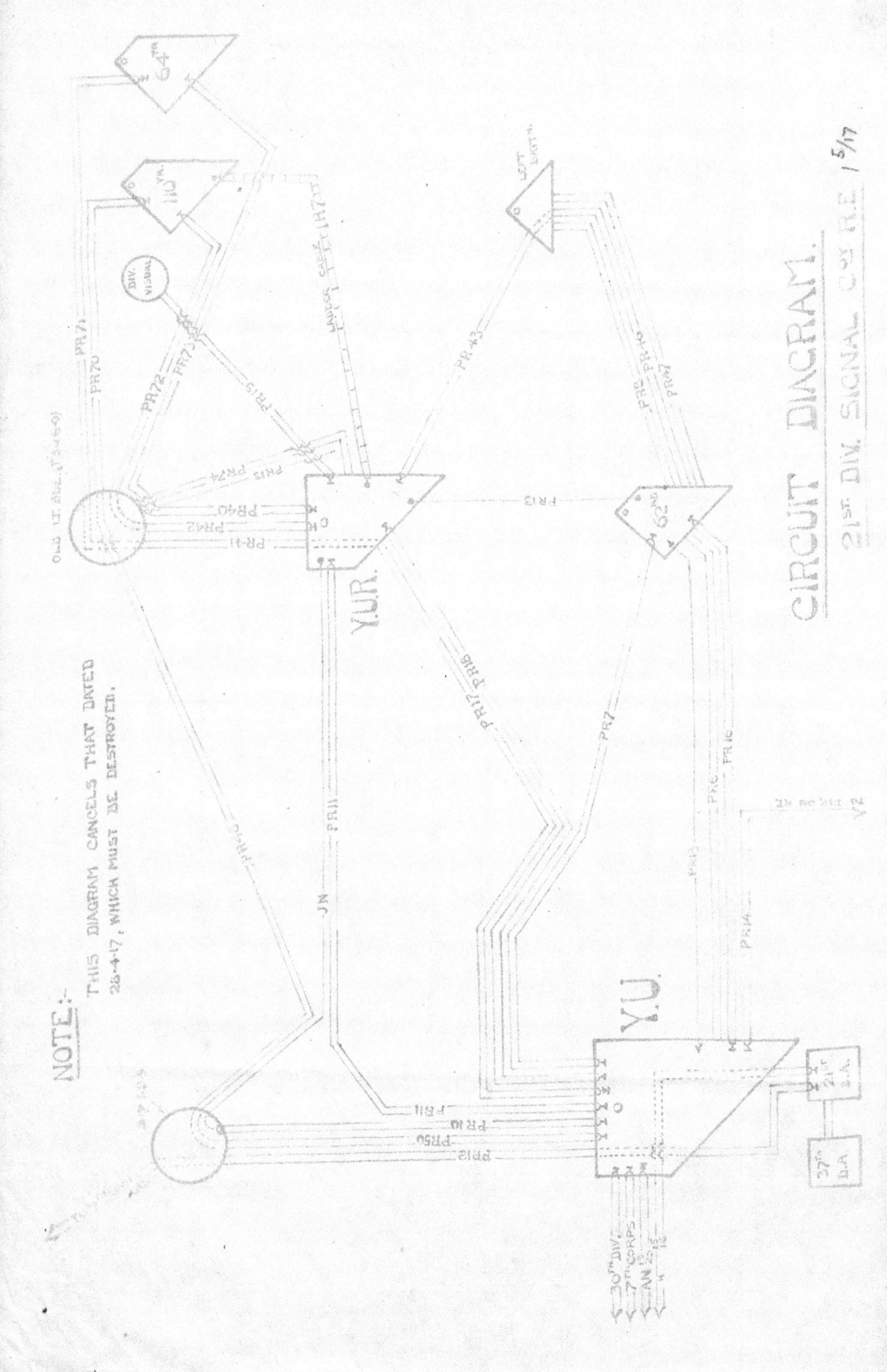

NOTE:—

THIS DIAGRAM CANCELS THAT OF 15/1/17, WHICH MUST BE DESTROYED

CIRCUIT DIAGRAM

21st DIV. SIGNAL CO. R.E. 5/17

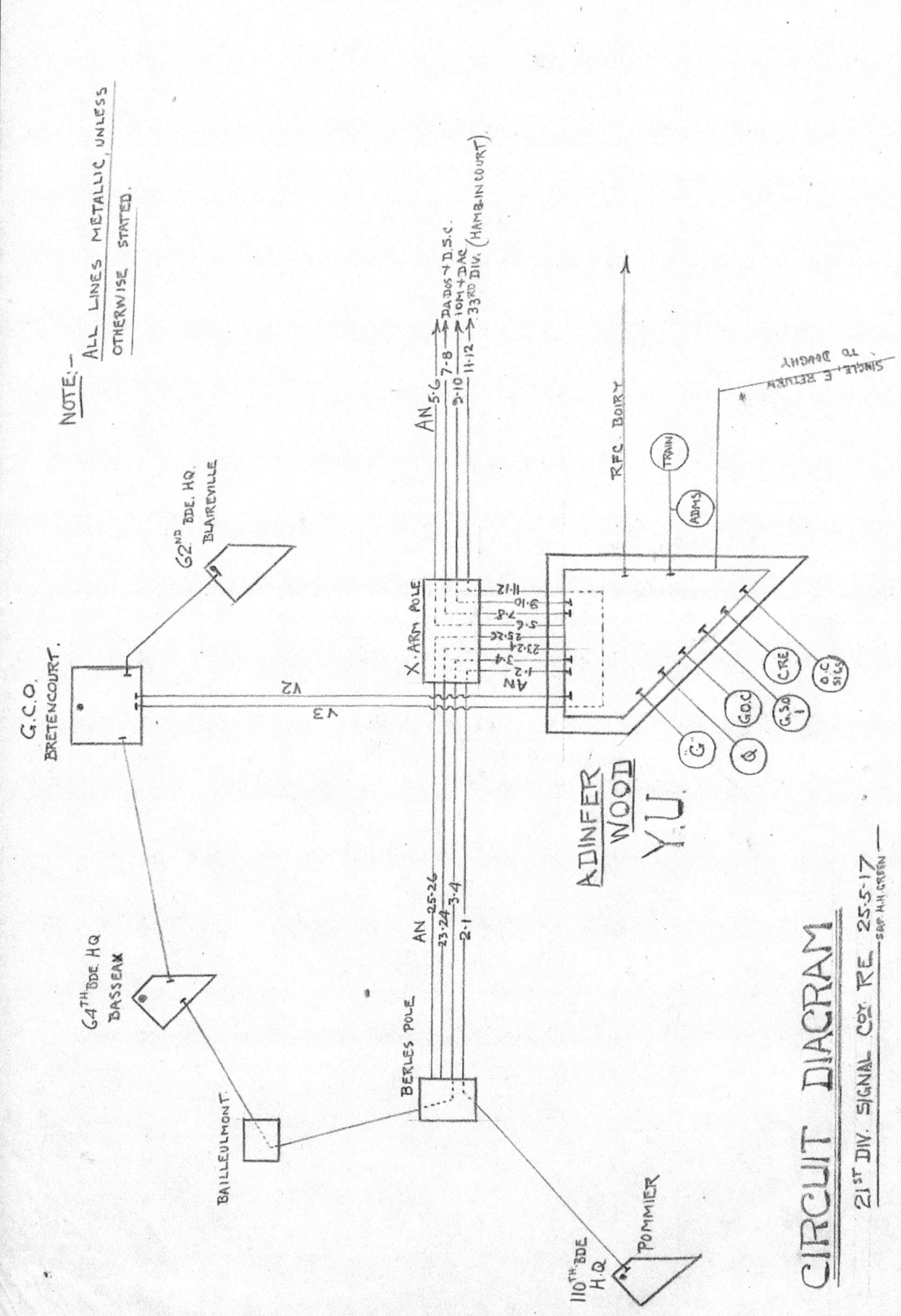

CIRCUIT DIAGRAM.
21st DIV. SIGNAL Coy R.E.

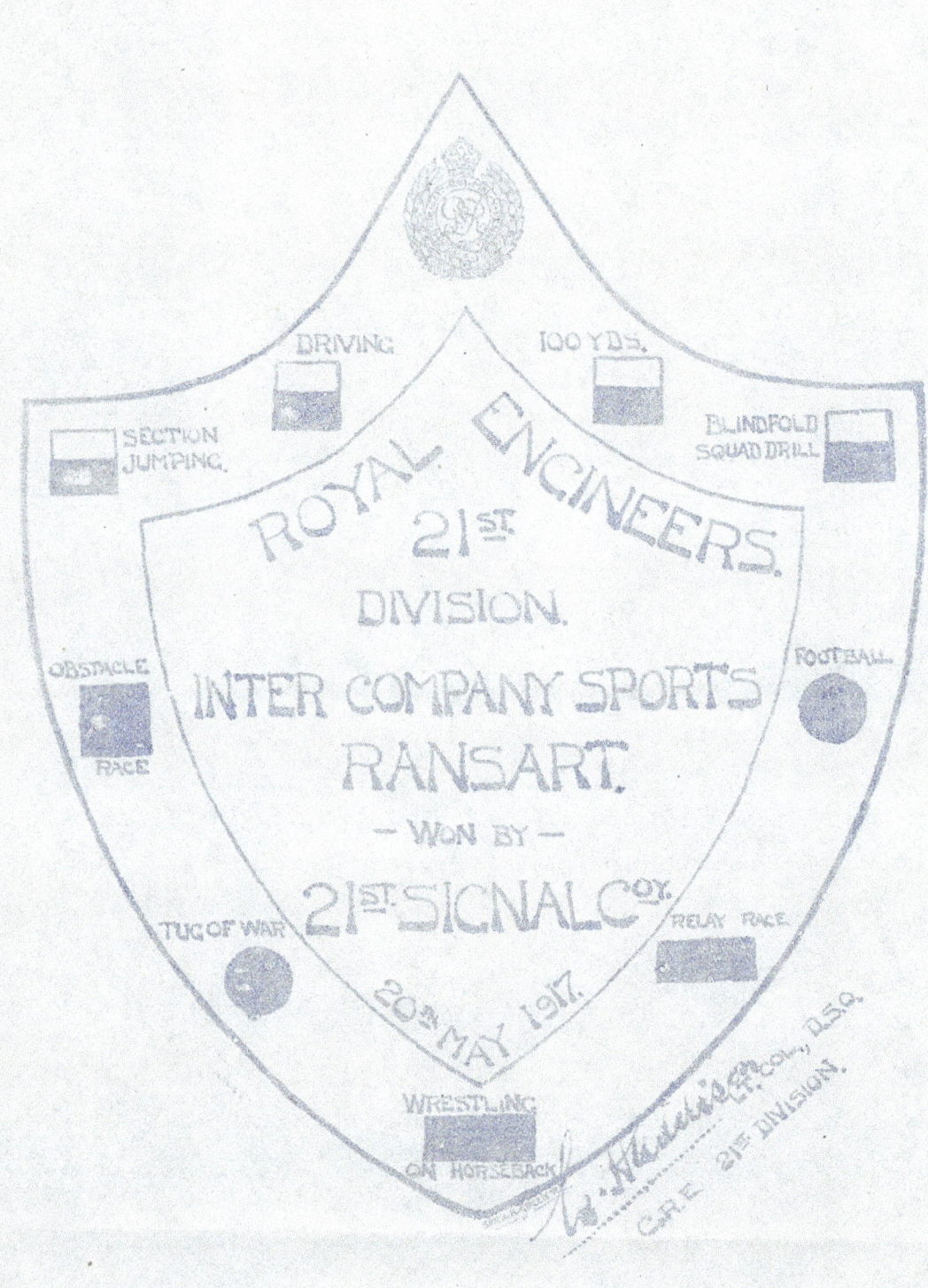

Army Form C. 2118.

WAR DIARY
or
INTELLIGENCE SUMMARY.
(Erase heading not required.)

June 1917
HQ No 1 Section
2¹ Signal Co RE

Place	Date	Hour	Summary of Events and Information	Remarks and references to Appendices
HAMELIN-COURT	1/6/17		"D" detachment moved from Camp at X.29.C.8.7 to 110 HAMELINCOURT and also 3 mile cable. Maintenance parties on airline routes 110th Bde moved to MOYENNEVILLE, in reserve; communication by telephone from north moved circuit superimposed.	
"	2/6/17		Commenced construction of signal dugout, as HQ occasionally shelled. Maintenance parties continued on airline route. Cable detached enemy cable in back areas	
	3/6/17		Enemy airline route commenced between left & right Bdes, 2 poles wired only, thus giving alternate route to either Bde. From 1.45pm to 3.0pm HAMELINCOURT shelled in vicinity of horse lines with H.E. Camp moved to NW of village. No damage to personnel, horses or signal office. Construction of two OP exchanges for Artillery commences at T.11.a.5.2 & T.6.c.9.5. Connecting trench for Forward cable between these points partly dug. En personnel from Trench Mortar Batteries, not completed. Survey of Buried Cable system by 2 Lieut YATES & Sergt WILKES between left & right Bdes Brigade Headquarters complete.	
	4/6/17			

Army Form C. 2118.

WAR DIARY
or
INTELLIGENCE SUMMARY

(Erase heading not required.)

HQ + No 1 Section (2)
21 Signal Co RE

Place	Date	Hour	Summary of Events and Information	Remarks and references to Appendices
HAMELIN- COURT.	5/6/17		Labelled and overhauled all lines to Brigade. Lieut J.J. HERON RE. SR. No 4 Section assumed Military duties.	
	6/6/17		Staff check on new position for Bde HQ. to relieve further to new position X 29 b. Route reconnoitred. "A" detachment from Coups at X 29 c 8.7 to relieve 'C' detachment. 8 way airline route construction for 62nd Bde forward to replace pole's cable commencing Left Bde 11B and finishing T 90 7.7 about 25 to 5 hr. Maintenance on other airline routes, always an accomplice	
	7/6/17		62nd Bde relieved by 110th Bde. exchange of positions only, communications as before New 11B, airline running of Signal office and local telephone system commenced.	
	10/6/17		Construction of three new routes from HAMELINCOURT to new HQ constitution of present system commenced.	
			110th Bde Signalling school opened with 60 signals from battalions this Bde very short of signallers owing to casualties in action May 3rd. 62nd + 64th Bde possess normal number of signallers with battalions.	
	11/6/17		Final of three new D line airline routes from 11B complete.	

WAR DIARY or INTELLIGENCE SUMMARY

Army Form C. 2118.

June 1917 (3)

HQ r No 1 Section
2 S/[?]nl C RE

Place	Date	Hour	Summary of Events and Information	Remarks and references to Appendices
HAMELIN-COURT	12/7		Signals dugout at HAMELINCOURT completed except inside boarding. No 192355 Cpl SMITH with party of eight laid armoured wire (pair) from right Bde HQrs to advanced Battalion HQrs in front line U13b 4.5 (sheet 51B 5w) and orchards trenches to avoid 110th Inf Bde for coming action. Power Buzzers also installed. Line working back by relay of power buzzers at T18d 9.7 to Arr Bde HQrs. Line very difficult to keep through owing to hostile shelling.	No 192355 Cpl SMITH
	13/7 14/7		Inside wiring and local telephone system at new camp completed. Complete system of visual - Companies to Battns - Battns to Brigade - to Brigade HQrs to Division establishes for 110th Bde.	
	15/7		½ mile of armoured cable sent to advanced Battalion for use when moving forward after attack. Weather very fine. Clan Smith and party of eight repairing and relaying lines from 110th Bde to front line. Work under heavy shell fire & lines completed all lines to 110th Bde from own carefully maintained. Weather very fine.	
	16/7/17	3.30am	Attack on TUNNEL TRENCH by 110th Bde. All forward lines cut by heavy barrage at 12.15 am. Enemy counterattack on own on right Power Buzzer works satisfactorily	

Army Form C. 2118.

WAR DIARY June 1917
or
INTELLIGENCE SUMMARY.
(Erase heading not required.)

H.Q. & No 1 Section
2" Signal Co. N.E.

Instructions regarding War Diaries and Intelligence Summaries are contained in F. S. Regs., Part II. and the Staff Manual respectively. Title pages will be prepared in manuscript.

Place	Date	Hour	Summary of Events and Information	Remarks and references to Appendices
HAMELIN-COURT	16/6/17	12.30a	New line from Bde forward to left Bn Hqrs on front line laid by Cpl A T WALKER with Artillery personnel.	
		9.0a	All lines again through forward after being relaid. Triple signals runners throughout, also good wire under heavy shell fire. No wires. Sgt HUFTON	
	18/7	3.0a	No trouble on the lines from Bn to Brigade, good speaking throughout acknowledged.	
			Very heavy thunderstorm which damaged air insulators on switchboard, also twelve fuses blown on kolboard	
		5a	Everything working again satisfactorily	
		9.30a	62nd Bde move from MOYENNEVILLE to BASSEUX. Communication through	
			33rd Division at ADINFER WOOD	
	19/6/17	6.20p	New direct telephone from HAMELINCOURT H.Q. to ADINFER WOOD H.Q. pri through to simplify relief	
ADINFER WOOD	20/6/17	9am	Bn H.Q. closed at HAMELINCOURT and opened ADINFER WOOD same time	
		9.30a	Phone and sounder cct No 62nd Infy Bde at BASSEUX established	
		12.25p	Phone and sounder cct. to 64th Infy Bde at POMMIER established	
		2.35p	110th Infy Bde open at BLAIREVILLE. Phone circuit through 111 Corps	

Army Form C. 2118.

WAR DIARY June 1917 (5)
or
INTELLIGENCE SUMMARY.

HQ. "No.1 Section"
21 Signal Coy R.E.

(Erase heading not required.)

Instructions regarding War Diaries and Intelligence Summaries are contained in F. S. Regs., Part II. and the Staff Manual respectively. Title pages will be prepared in manuscript.

Place	Date	Hour	Summary of Events and Information	Remarks and references to Appendices
ADINFER WOOD	21/6/17	9a	Buss return for reinforcements opened - subject, relay drill, line work etc. Large number of reinforcements to complete forward divisional establishment arrived without training for their work and were residents in this branch. Good type of men. Training continued.	
	22/6/17 to 24/6/17		Training continued	
	25-30/6/17		Took over Bde HQ at MOYENNEVILLE Command Office test panels & switchboards being fitted in anticipation of relief of 33rd DIVN on 1st July.	
	28/6/17	5a	Violent thunderstorm, several fuses blown, no interference with lines. Training continued.	
	29/6/17	2pm	6th Bde close at POMMIER reopen same hour MOYENNEVILLE. Circuit through 33rd Division HAMELINCOURT	
	30/6/17		6th Bde to right sector Circuit as above. 62nd Bde to left sector " "	
			Office complete for opening	
	5/6/17		No.44626 Sergt. RUDDICK J. awarded the D.C.M.	
	25/6/17		No.44415 Sergt. HUFTON. J., No.18207 Sapp. BURTON. T., No.533351 Pte BURNS. J. awarded Military Medal	
	26/6/17		No.152355 A/C/S C.S.M. SMITH. E. H. awarded Military Medal	

O.C. 21ST SIGNAL Co R.E.

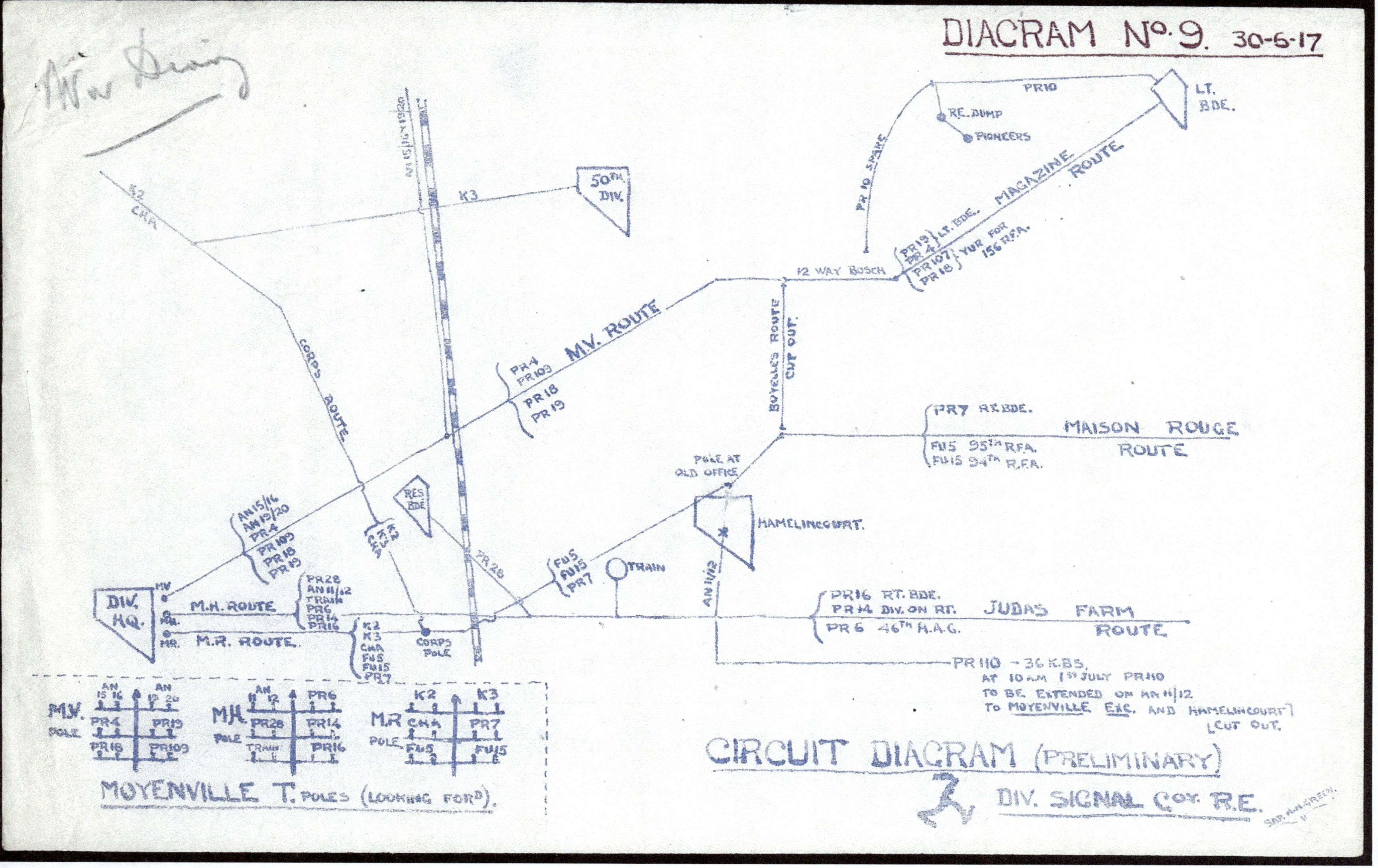

DIAGRAM No. 9. 30-6-17
LT. BDE.
PR10
RE. DUMP
PIONEERS
PR 10 SPARE
50TH DIV.
K2
CHA
K3
AN 15/16 Y 19/20
MAGAZINE ROUTE
PR19 PR4 LT. BDE.
PR107 PR18 YUR FOR 156 R.F.A.
12 WAY BOSCH
M.V. ROUTE
PR4 PR109
PR18 PR19
BOYELLES ROUTE CUT OUT.
CORPS ROUTE
PR7 RT. BDE.
MAISON ROUGE ROUTE
FU5 95TH R.F.A.
FU15 94TH R.F.A.
POLE AT OLD OFFICE
RES BDE
HAMELINCOURT.
AN 15/16 AN 19/20 PR4
PR109 PR18 PR19
K2 K3 CHA
PR28
FU5 FU15 PR7
TRAIN
AN 11/12
MV
DIV. HQ.
MH.
MR.
M.H. ROUTE
M.R. ROUTE.
PR28 AN 11/12 TRAIN PR6 PR14 PR16
K2 K3 CHA FU5 FU15 PR7
CORPS POLE
PR16 RT. BDE.
PR14 DIV. ON RT.
PR6 46TH H.A.G.
JUDAS FARM ROUTE
PR110 → 36 K.B5.
AT 10 A.M. 1ST JULY PR110
TO BE EXTENDED ON AN 11/12
TO MOYENVILLE EXC. AND HAMELINCOURT
CUT OUT.
M.V. POLE
AN 15 16
AN 19 20
PR4
PR19
PR18
PR109
M.H. POLE
AN 11 12
PR6
PR28
PR14
TRAIN
PR16
M.R. POLE
K2
K3
CHA
PR7
FU5
FU15
MOYENVILLE T. POLES (LOOKING FORD).
CIRCUIT DIAGRAM (PRELIMINARY)
DIV. SIGNAL COY. R.E.
SAP. H.A. GREEN.

Army Form C. 2118.

July 1917
21st Div: Signal Co RE HQ + No 1 Section

WAR DIARY
or
INTELLIGENCE SUMMARY
(Erase heading not required.)

Place	Date	Hour	Summary of Events and Information	Remarks and references to Appendices
ADINFER WOOD	1/7/17	10.0 am	Office closed ADINFER WOOD + reopened at MOYENNEVILLE relieving 33rd Division at HAMELINCOURT. This type of relief is difficult: Moyenneville is in rear of Hamelincourt + line changes had to be made at the hour of relief. Spare circuits were established to Right + Left Brigades + to Right Artillery Brigade for change then commenced.	
		N.0	110th Brigade Office closed at BLAIRVILLE.	
	2/7/17		All line changes completed giving two circuits to Right + Left Brigade. Right Centre + Left Artillery Brigades 2 circuits to Corps. One circuit to Reserve Brigade + one to HA Group.	
			110th Brigade Office opened at MOYENNEVILLE.	
			Buried cable route commenced - diagram attached, appendix A. Two companies of pioneers were allotted for digging cable trench 8' deep from O to H. 20 pair route - between each led box + the n.s. 440 yards.	
	3/7/17		AG airline route commenced as third forward route - diagram attached, appendix B. Buried cable route commenced from O to E - 30 pair route by artillery personnel (appendix A).	

Army Form C. 2118.

WAR DIARY
or
INTELLIGENCE SUMMARY.
(Erase heading not required.)

July 1917

Place	Date	Hour	Summary of Events and Information	Remarks and references to Appendices
MOYENNEVILLE	4/7/17		A & B Detachments worked on Buried cable & the AG airline route.	
	5/7/17		Do	
	6/7/17		Do 2 pairs wire added to ML route for use of Artillery.	
	7/7/17		The AG route was completed. A & B Detachments worked on the Buried cable route.	
	8/7/17 from 4.20		A & B Detachments worked on Buried cable route & on camp improvement. 110th Bde relieved 64th Brigade in Right Sector. 64th Bde to MOYENNEVILLE.	
	9/7/17		A & B detachments - Buried cable route & maintenance of airline routes to Brigades. 2/Lt G.E. ROBERTS joined the Company from 3rd Army Signal Co.	
	10/7/17		A & B detachments. Buried cable route. Dismantling & detaching lines not in use.	
	11/7/17		Do Airline party completing MV route.	
	13/7/17		Do News faun laid to DAC to replace faulty pair.	
	14/7/17		Do Airline party MV route. Divisional & Artillery	
	15/7/17		lines to Right Bde MV route on account of shelling	
	16/7/17 from 5.0		Weather wet. Day devoted to sheathing stones equipment etc. & overhauling cable wagons. 64th Brigade relieved 62nd Bde in Left Bde position. Latter to Reserve positions	

Army Form C. 2118.

July 1917 (3)

WAR DIARY
or
INTELLIGENCE SUMMARY.
(Erase heading not required.)

Instructions regarding War Diaries and Intelligence Summaries are contained in F. S. Regs., Part II. and the Staff Manual respectively. Title pages will be prepared in manuscript.

Place	Date	Hour	Summary of Events and Information	Remarks and references to Appendices
MOYENNEVILLE	17/7/17		A & B detachments. Buried cable route. Airline party MV route. Weather over, little rain	
	18/7/17		A.B.& C. do do do dull	
	19/7/17		do do do MV route completed. " fine shot	
	20/7/17		No 50250 Spr Cook. W.H was killed by shell-fire. Lieut E.A. COLLIS, R.E. & No 41445 Sgt HUFTON, J.T. were wounded by shell-fire. These casualties occurred at Quarry bed found K. Buried cable continued. Maintenance of airlines on MB route. Weather dull.	
	21/7/17		B.& C. Detachments, buried cable. New route. (MM) was laid from Judas Farm giving an airline route in place of a number of bad cables.	
	22/7/17		B.& C. Detachments, buried cable. Number of disused lines reeled up.	
	23/7/17		do do 6 pairs of cable were laid on MK route from end of MJ route (Judas Farm). Weather fine shot.	
	24/7/17 5.0 pm		B & C detachments on buried cable. 62nd Brigade relieved 64th Bde in left Bde position: latter to Reserve Bde position.	
	25/7/17		Airline party renewed lateral between 94th & 51st Brigades RFA. - Route MP.	
	26/7/17 6.0 am		" " on MP route. B & C detachments buried cable. Heavy Thunderstorm.	

WAR DIARY or INTELLIGENCE SUMMARY

Army Form C. 2118.

July 1917 (4)

Place	Date	Hour	Summary of Events and Information	Remarks and references to Appendices
MOYENNEVILLE	27/7/17		A detachment continued work on buried cable. Airline party completed M.P. route. Military Medal awarded to No 44693 Spr WRIGHT. R. & No 9994 Spr ABLETT. J.	
	28/7/17		Airline party put two additional pairs on MS route. A & B detachments worked on buried cable & D detachment on maintenance.	
	29/7/17		Airline party completed MS route. D detachment picked up disused cable. Heavy thunderstorm - 6 lines Down	
	30/7/17		Airline party repaired damage to MH & ML routes caused by storm on 29th. All detachments spent the day straightening up lines & reeling up disused cable.	
	31/7/17		Airline party carried out minor line changes. B & C detachments rected up spare lines in left Brigade area & 10th detachment laid two pairs from the MK route to the new Artillery H.Qrs., also bringing 3 lines from there for Divisional Kite Balloon Station & one spare.	

C.W.B. [?]
Major R.E.
O.C. 21st SIGNAL Co R.E.

SHEET 51ᴮ S.W.

BURIED ROUTE.

3 DIV. SIGNAL COY. RE. 5·8·17

SCALE 1:20,000

SHEET 51B

VISUAL COMMUNICATION

2 DIV. SIGNAL COY. RE. 5·8·17
MA.6

SCALE 1:40,000

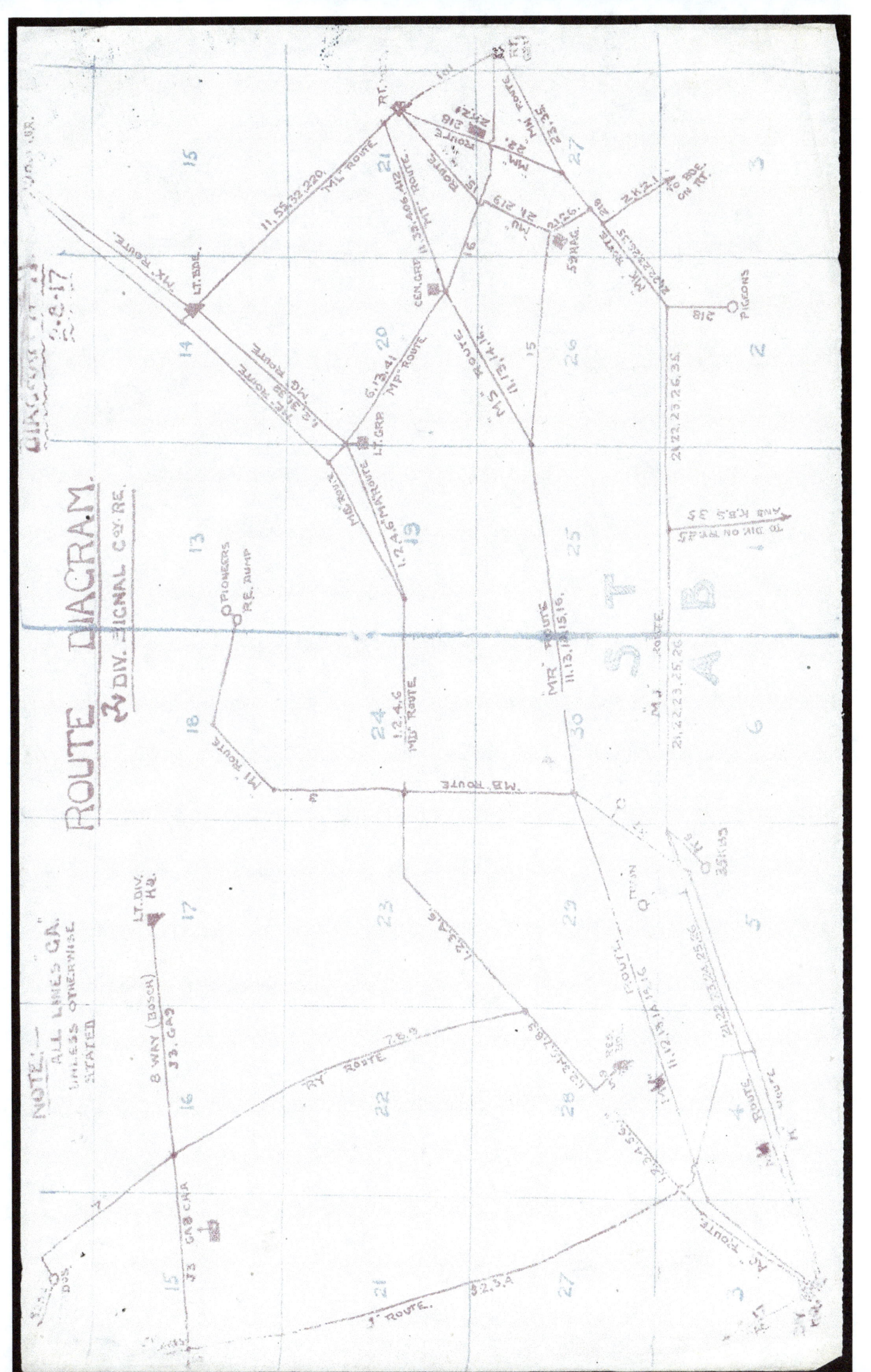

LINE CHANGES ON COMPLETION OF AC & MV ROUTES. 19/7/17 a.m.

MAIN ROUTE	SECOND ROUTE	THIRD ROUTE	OFFICE	NOTES
AC 1	MD 91	MC 21	LT. GROUP	OLD PR 107
AC 2	PR in AN 1/16		U.A.D.O.S.	TEMPORARY UNTIL MONTH HQ COMPLETE
AC 3	MB 123		CORPS H.A.	THIS CHANGE MAY BE LEFT OVER HEAVIER
AC 4	MD 94, MA 24	MC 34	LT. BDE.	OLD PR 19
AC 5			RES. BDE.	OLD PR 14. FROM LIGHT TO LT BDE EXTEND TO RT BDE
AC 6	MD 96	MA 26	LT. GROUP	OLD P.R.C.
MV 7	MR 57	EXISTING	CENTRE GRP	PR 15
MV 8	MR 58		RT. GROUP.	PR 5.
MV 9	MR 59	MS 99	RT. BDE.	OLD PR 7
MV 10	MR 60	MS 100	CENTRE GRP	PR 20. TEMPORARY UNTIL HQ COMPLETE
MV 11	MB 105, MD 95	MG 25, MG 25	LT. BTE.	PR 17. SOMEWHERE CUT.
MV 12	MR 62		RT. BDE.	
MR 13	(R&S) 103		35 MTS	
MR 14	MJ 64	NK 114, MM 214	RT. BM.	OLD PR 12
MR 15			HAMEL T.P.	
MR 16			TRAIN	
MR 17	MJ 67		DIV ON RT.	OLD PR 14
MR 18	MJ 68		1 K. 135.	
K 2	J 2		7TH CORPS.	
K 3	J 3		DIVON RT.	
K 4	J 4		7TH CORPS	
K 5	MB 104, 124		CORPS SOMEWHERE OUT	JONELLES
K 6	MB 106, 126.		LT DV D.A.	OLD PR 11 ALONG OUT FARM
K 7	MA	MJ 65	SIGNAL	

August 1917
21 Army C. R.E.
(I.O. No 1 Section)

Army Form C. 2118.

WAR DIARY
or
INTELLIGENCE SUMMARY.
(Erase heading not required.)

Vol 24

Place	Date	Hour	Summary of Events and Information	Remarks and references to Appendices
MOYENNEVILLE	1/8	1pm	Commenced work of clearing MAMELINCOURT of lines not now in use & likely (Sheet 51B S29a)	
			been on new route collected. Jobs & remaining cable to make	
			cable in left Bury. Line as per die No 11 (att's July war diary)	
			Telephone working to Artillery Brigades unchanged.	
	2/8		Airline system completed and lines tested. From early be greater	
			attacks 6 Hqrs & Brigade in Telephone communication with the	
			nearest offices & 20 words per minute after 10 days trial	
	5/8		51st Bde R.F.A. relieved by 29th Bde R.F.A. at Sheet 51B T28c 99 Sheet 57c G19 4	
			R.H.Q. not prepared to B.T.B. Telephone	
	7/8	12noon	III Corps relieved (at BRETENCOURT) by IV Corps (at BIHUCOURT). No Sheet 57c R26.b	
			difficulty with line change	
	8/8		291st Bde move to new position at T.20a.0.2. Sheet 51B	
		10am	" " open in 9th Bde H.Q. at B.M. app " 57c	
		1pm	Violent Thunderstorm. No damage done	
		11/30p	hrt on line change Div chart No 2 shows lines after change	
	9/8	6pm	63 Bde closed T.11.6.2.3 and reopen at MOYENNEVILLE (Que 57c Aub)	
		5.30pm	110th " " " " MOYENNEVILLE at T.21.d.6.6 (from Div Bde Tuesdays)	

(2) 21 Signal Co RE.
(No 1 W or 1 Section)

Army Form C. 2118.

WAR DIARY
or
INTELLIGENCE SUMMARY.
(Erase heading not required.)

Instructions regarding War Diaries and Intelligence Summaries are contained in F. S. Regs., Part II. and the Staff Manual respectively. Title pages will be prepared in manuscript.

Place	Date	Hour	Summary of Events and Information	Remarks and references to Appendices
MOYENNEVILLE	9/4/17		Telephone pair torn through to 55 H.A.G. Work continued on party. Test Boxes being fitted. Weather - very heavy showers	
	10/4		Lieut A E COLLIS R.E. transferred to Fifth Army Signals. Lieut J.A.S SYKES joined from Third Army Signals. Through telephone pair to 62 - D.A. A Corps working party of 10 men was attached for several days in changing up spare cable at HAMELINCOURT	
	13/4	2pm	9th Bde HFA moved to 00d Left Bde HQ T16b 2.3. Line changes carried out without hitch. (T 14B.50) Stewart B Away active route some reaction from SOS Left Bde HQ YUR T94.63	
	14/4		Spokesmoke training given on meaning of gas Respirators and recently issued reinforcements given practice in flag and infantry drill	
	15/4/ 16/4		Work - Polling M.V. routes and completing work on "Army" at Test Boxes A.P, O, P and N. Iron collected materials for Weather - heavy showers	
	17/4/17	6pm	Army Signals and Horse Standings. 62nd H.A. Bde closed MOYENNEVILLE. Opened Signal Station relieving 18th Bde. 118th Bde moves to MOYENNEVILLE (Red area)	

WAR DIARY or INTELLIGENCE SUMMARY

Army Form C. 2118.

3) Signal C.R.E. (No. 1 Section)

Place	Date	Hour	Summary of Events and Information	Remarks and references to Appendices
MOYENNEVILLE	19/4		Corps Horse Show — Fine throughout the R.A.	
	23/4		4 prs DRs cattle poles completed to Army Lines north the B	
	25/4		Capt PORTEOUS Lieut JACKSON No 1 Section W/T personnel ant Sigs with all horses transport moved to DUISANS (Sheet 51c 29d) 110th Bde relieved by 47th Inf Bde + proceeded to BARLY (Sheet 51b P17d)	
	26/4	11 am	110th Inf Bde opened at the Chateau MANIN (Sheet 51c P16b)	
DUISANS	27/4	6:30 p	63rd + 110 closed MOYENNEVILLE and opened DUISANS	
			65 Bde relieved in line by 48th Inf Bde + proceeded to MOYENNEVILLE	
	28/4	10:30 am	at MOYENNEVILLE by 45th Div and opened at WARLUS (51d)	
	28/4		" in Rgt1 Sectn by 47 Bde + proceeded to BOISLEUX (51a S14)	
	29/4	2 p	" in proceeded to BERNEVILLE (Sheet 06d)	
	29/4/11/4		Cleaning up etc afterwards	
			Casualties during month 1 nco (lorry driver) evacuated sick	
			replacement received.	
			Strength of Unit 8 Officers 2/2 OR 47 Riding 77 L.D Horses (including 2th Bde Sig Sectn and Anti Air Bde Subsection)	

A Moore
Maj R.E.

O.C. 21st SIGNAL Co R.E.

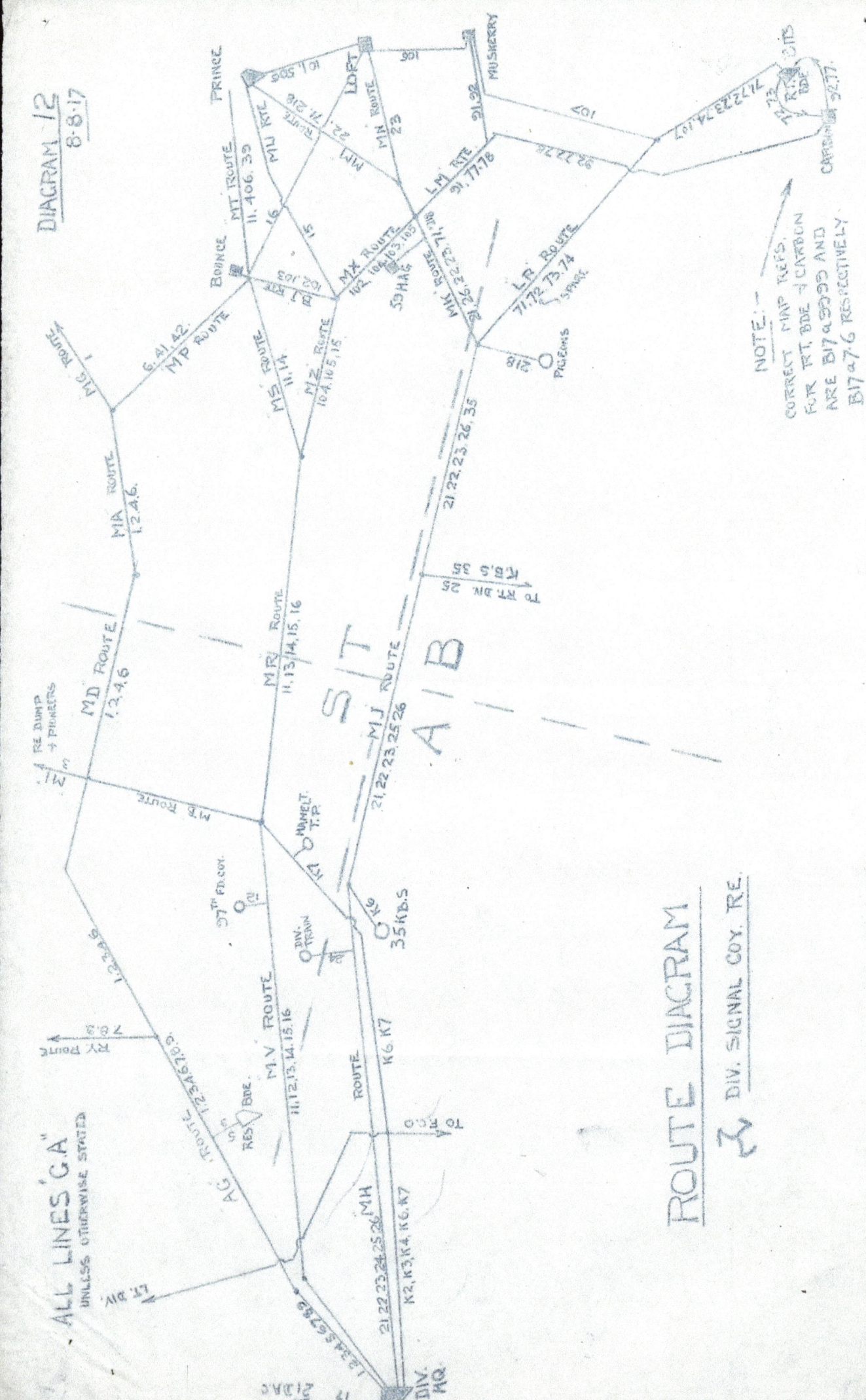

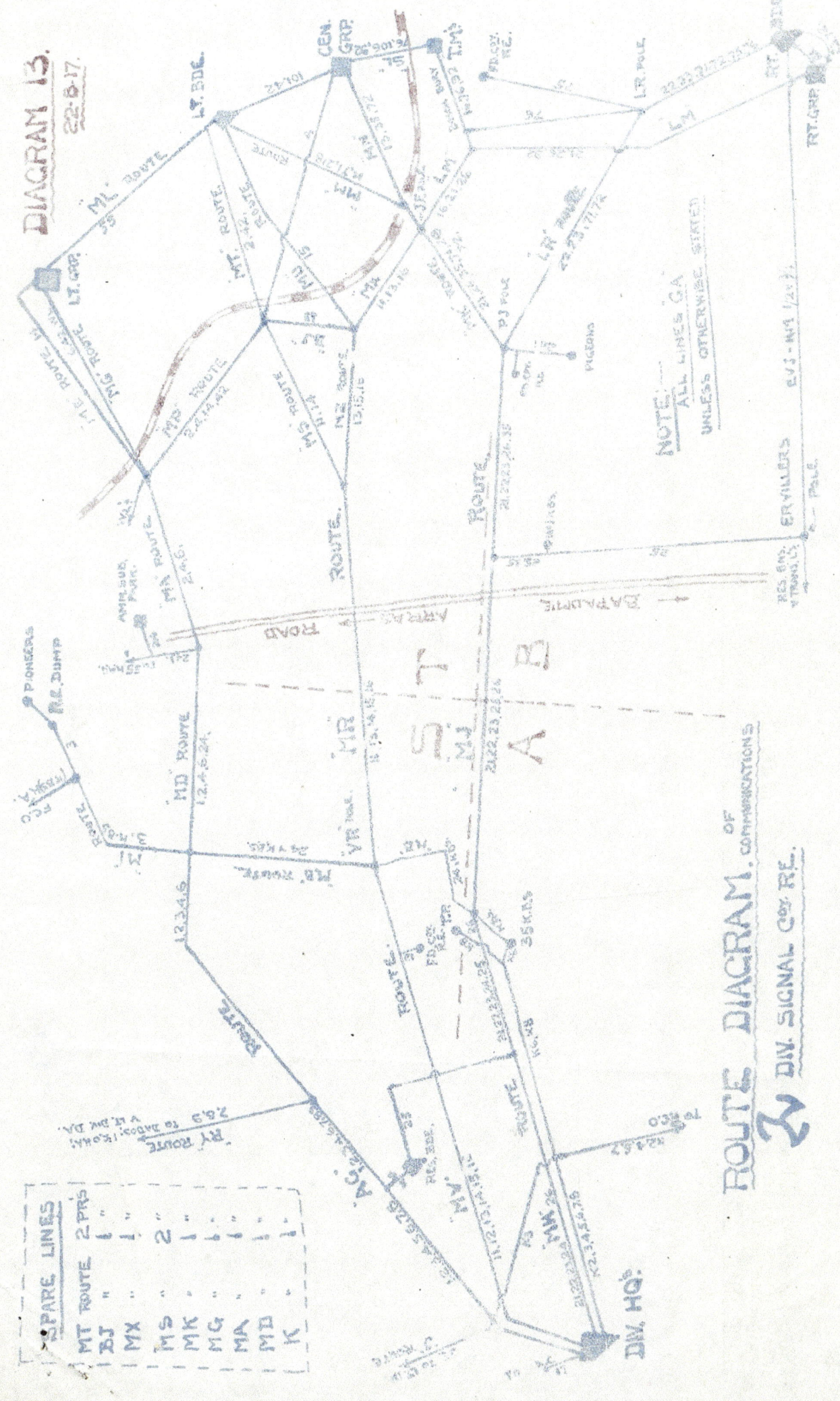

Army Form C. 2118.

WAR DIARY or INTELLIGENCE SUMMARY.

2nd Signal Coy RE O (No & No 1 Section)

(Erase heading not required.)

Place	Date	Hour	Summary of Events and Information	Remarks and references to Appendices
DUISANS	1/9/17		Whole Company; also Bathurst and Battam completed took full establishment of Fullerphones.	
	13½/9/17 5-9 6/9/17		Occupied in training, recreation and sports. Capt PORTEOUS, Lieut JACKSON and No 1 Section and orderlies) left by train from AUBIGNY for X Corps. Camped at BOESCHEPE (R10 A11 Sheet 27) 2/Cpl Robbins and 21st Div Arty HQ. operator left for BERTHEN (R12 d 59) with 21st Div Arty HQ.	
	7/9/17		Lieut JACKSON and NCOs of No 1 Section moves to VIERSTRAAT (Sheet 28 Wheat) by X Corps lorry, for Corps work. NCOs & Sappers of No 1 Section employed on Corps buried lines. Airline party of HQ Section employed on Corps airline work.	
	7/9/17 2/9/17		2/Lieut F.H. GREATREX joined from 19th Corps Signals. WT detachment proceeds to X Corps WT School at BOESCHEPE. Lieut J.H.S. SYKES left for 35th Div Signals.	
	8/9/17		Sergt Cooper took one Office relief and instruments left by lorry for CAËSTRE. (W 3 a Caut Sheet 27)	
	15/9/17		62nd Bde Sigs Supn Sec closes MARCUS (Sheet 21c K36d) opens MONDEGHEM (N26 b Sheet 27)	

2353 Wt. W2544/1454 700,000 5/15 D. D. & L. A.D.S.S. Forms/C 2118.

WAR DIARY
or
INTELLIGENCE SUMMARY.
(Erase heading not required.)

21ˢᵗ Signal Coy RE (2)
(HQ & No I Sect.)

Army Form C. 2118.

Place	Date	Hour	Summary of Events and Information	Remarks and references to Appendices
	15/9/17		64ᵗʰ Bde Signals closed BERNEVILLE (Sheet 51C 06d) opened BORRE	
			110ᵗʰ " " MANIN (Sheet 51C ZIP6) " CAESTRE	
			Direct communication by telephone sent forward superimposed toward positions	
	16/9/17		2/Lieut F.A. GREATREX with 30 OR left SAVY Station by train as 5.30pm for CAESTRE	
			Lorry leaves from II Corps to convey heavy stores to SAVY Station	
CAESTRE	17/9/17	10 am	HQ closed DUISANS Noon opened CAESTRE	
			HQ 21ˢᵗ Div Coy moved to RENINGHELST (Sheet 28 G34b3) also where Sappers attaches from No 1 Section	
			4 reinforcements (2 Pioneers, 2 Drivers) joined from Signal Depot. Company up to strength	
			2 motor cyclist DRs and 1 Tele Station opened bonus to X Corps Sgnls.	
	18/9/17		2/Lieut GREATREX to BOESCHEPE vice Capt PORTEOUS to CAESTRE	
	18/21/9/17		Routine work - nothing to report.	
	22/9/17		Sergt Cooper with one officer relief; drivers + two horses + to METEREN by Lorry. LCpl Yeomans to ABBEVILLE for Wireless course.	
			Capt N. PORTEOUS to officers Rest Station METEREN.	

(3)
21st Signal Coy RE
(HQ & No 1 Section)

WAR DIARY
or
INTELLIGENCE SUMMARY.

Army Form C. 2118.

Place	Date	Hour	Summary of Events and Information	Remarks and references to Appendices
METEREN	23/7/17	10am	Regro closed CAESTRE (W3a C.4.) opened METEREN (X15d.15) Same service. Sheet 27	
			62nd Brigade at X1d.3.2 Sheet 27	
	24/7/17		64th " " THIEUSHOOK (Q35 b.4 Sheet 27)	
	26/7/17		110th " " BERTHEN (R22 c.5.9 Sheet 27)	
			Communication by telephone to 62nd and 64th Bdes through Pt Corps Exchange	
			" " " " 110th " X Corps Exchange.	
			Lieut JACKSON to 63rd Field Amba WESTOUTRE (M9a Sheet 28)	
	28/7/17	7.30am	" C.C.S GODESWAESVELDTE. 110th Bde closed BERTHEN (R22 c.5.9) and opened HALLEBAST Corner (Sheet 28 H32d.5.4)	
			2 OR of Gd Bde Signal Section wounded in action.	
			Capt N. PORTEOUS evacuates to C.C.S. GODEWAESVELDTE.	
	29/7/17	3.0pm	110th closed METEREN opened SCOTTISH WOOD (Sheet 28 H35 c. 5.3)	
			110th Bde closed HALLEBAST Corner opened SCOTTISH WOOD	
			Kopernem Farm & Lotress wounded at BOESCHEPE by enemy bomb	
	30/7/17	2pm	Div Arty HQ closed RENINGHEAST and opened SCOTTISH WOOD	
			2/Lieut MALINS H. joined from X Corps Vice Lieut JACKSON.	

WAR DIARY 21 Signal Coy RE
INTELLIGENCE SUMMARY. (No 7 Section)

Army Form C. 2118.

Place	Date	Hour	Summary of Events and Information	Remarks and references to Appendices
SCOTTISH WOOD	30/9		Lce Cpl Reilly H. and Pioneer Green J wounded by shell fire. Pioneer Green died in hospital same day. Work commenced on found communication to Clapham Junction and Shirley Cole to Pop. Box and to Yeomanry Post and Dormy House for Artillery Brigade. Casualties during month 5 OR evacuated wounded 2 officers sick 6 OR " "	Pri Re.

W Robertson Capt RE
for O.C. 21st SIGNAL Co R.E.

WAR DIARY
or
INTELLIGENCE SUMMARY

Army Form C. 2118.

21 Signal Coy RE
HQ / No 1 Section

Vol 26

Place	Date	Hour	Summary of Events and Information	Remarks and references to Appendices
SCOTTISH WOOD	2/9/17		Capt H. RICHARDSON posted from 8th Divl Sigl Coy Vice Capt PORTEOUS evacuated sick	
	3/9/17		3 other ranks of No 2 Section wounded in action	
			1 OR of No 2 Section as 1 of RD action wounded in action	
			62nd wd Sec Bn at J15a F.7 Sheet 28	
	4/9/17		110th Brigade relieves Anzac Brigade	
	5/9/17		2 OR of 110 wireless section wounded in action	
			4 OR reinforcements joined from Signal Depot	
BLARINGHEM	8/9/17	8a	Div HQ closes SCOTTISH WOOD opens BLARINGHEM (Sheet 36a B23d)	
			P.E.L. Coy as at with 20 OR remains at SCOTTISH WOOD with Div Arty (Sheet 36a B23d)	
			2 OR reinforcements joined from Signal Depot	
	9/9/17		62nd Bde opens at WALLON CAPPEL Sheet 27 U23c	
	10/9/17		64th " " EBBLINGHEM " 27 T24a	
			Telephone lines to each Brigade with secondary superimposed. Telephone pairs to HAZEBROUCK EXCHANGE. Sounder direct to Army.	Div Sigl
			Letter received from GOC complimenting Sig Coy on work in late operations.	
	11/9/17		110th Bde. opened at WANDREQUES Sheet 36a A6d.	

WAR DIARY or INTELLIGENCE SUMMARY

Army Form C. 2118.

(2) 21 Signal Coy RE

Place	Date	Hour	Summary of Events and Information	Remarks and references to Appendices
BLARINGHEM	10/7/17		Cpl MILWARD (mot. cyclist) awarded Military Medal.	
	10/7/17		Major GOULD proceeded on leave to UK.	
	16/7/17		Training and recreation whilst down in rest area.	
	17/7/17		111th Bde moves to MICMAC CAMP (Sheet 28 H 31 b) communication via X Corps RE Exchange and FC 2.	
	19/7/17		A/SSt SKINNER and L/Cpl BROWN awarded Military Medals for work on machine gun lines during late operations.	
ZEVECOTEN	20/7/17	3pm	Sig HR closes BLARINGHEM and opens ZEVECOTEN (Sheet 28 G 3 and 7.3)	
		7am	6th Brigade to H 30 C 5·7 (Sheet 2C)	
		7pm	62nd " G 3 and 5·4 do	
			Lines :– 1 pair to RENINGHELST. Ex ink Sounders superimposed direct to Corps. 62nd Bde via R.E. Ex.) 6th Bde via 23rd Divn, 111th Bde via R.E. Exchge and FC 2.	
	21/7/17		Wireless personnel and Linesmen to Chan. SEGARD (Sheet 28 H 30 C cent.)	
	22/7/17		Wireless stations and Linemen's posts taken over from 23rd Divn.	
Chan SEGARD	23/7/17	11am	Div HQ closes ZEVECOTEN and opens Chan. SEGARD Signal Coy transport and horses Camped near WESTOUTRE	

Army Form C. 2118.

WAR DIARY
or
INTELLIGENCE SUMMARY.

(Erase heading not required.)

2⟨ᵈ⟩ Signal Coy R.E. (3)

Instructions regarding War Diaries and Intelligence Summaries are contained in F. S. Regs., Part II. and the Staff Manual respectively. Title pages will be prepared in manuscript.

Place	Date	Hour	Summary of Events and Information	Remarks and references to Appendices
Arm: SEGINI	23/9/17		Cpl TURNBULL (Motorcyclist), 2/Cpl ROADHOUSE and Spr KIRKMAN (Norfolks) awarded Military Medals. 7 OR reinforcements joined from Signal Depôt. 2 Brigades in line ext 17A at HOOGE Craters I.18.1.6 Sheet 28. Communication as in Diagram attached — 5 pairs from dSD 17A to Double BN HQ. 4 gr Phone pairs and poled cable from XT to I to RC and ground cable thence to Craters. One pair on the Buried route from XT to BX and then ground cable to Craters. The Buried route gave a lot of trouble and was very early. The overland routes were much more satisfactory; good speaking and although frequently cut, were easy to repair and maintain. 5 OR loaned to Corps Area Officer for work on Corps Buried System.	Dia No 1
	26/9/17		Major GOULD reporting from leave to UK.	
	27/9/17		2 OR reinforcements joining from Signal Depôt. A/Sgt STEELE and A/2 Cpl ELLIOT awarded Military Medals.	
	30/9/17		2/Cpl HOLBROOK awarded Military Medal for work on Divl Artillery Lines.	

WAR DIARY
or
INTELLIGENCE SUMMARY
(Erase heading not required.)

21 Signal Coy RE (4)

Army Form C. 2118.

Place	Date	Hour	Summary of Events and Information	Remarks and references to Appendices
	31/7		Strength of Company Officers 8, Other ranks 273. Wanting to complete 6. O.R. During the month 12 NCOs & men were wounded in action. 1 " " reported Missing 15 " " " been evacuated sick 16 NCOs & men were received from Signal Depot 5 NCOs & men rejoined from Hospital 9 NCOs & men were awarded Military Medals	

Major RE
O.C. 21ST SIGNAL Co R.E.

Dec' No

- HAZEBROUCK EXCHANGE
- 2 ARMY HQ.
- 62nd Bde WALLON CAPPEL
- Div HQ BLARINGHEM
- 1st Bde EBBLINGHEM
- 110th Bde WARDRÈQUES

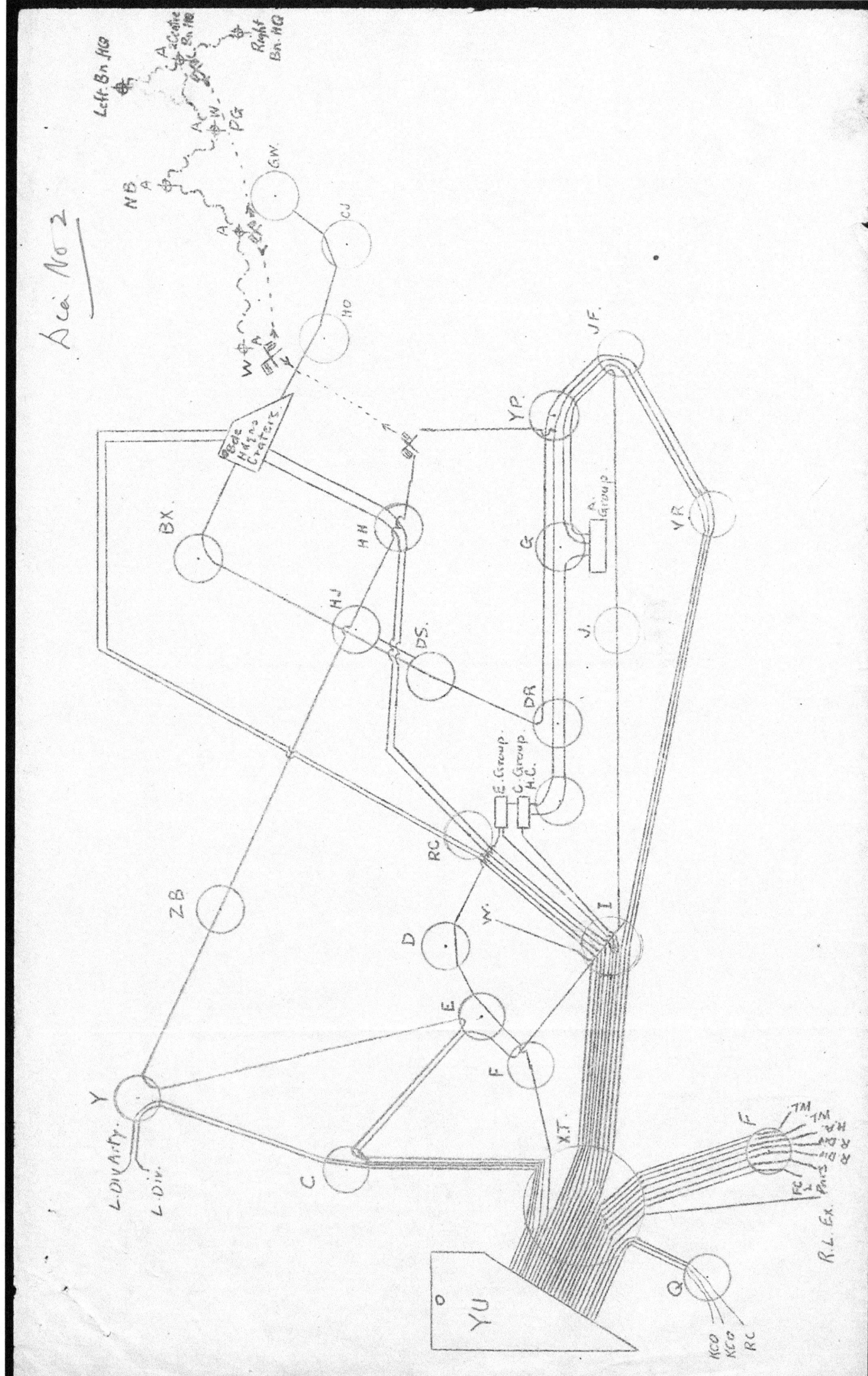

WAR DIARY or INTELLIGENCE SUMMARY

Army Form C. 2118.

21 Signal Coy RE ① November
HQ (No 1 Section)

Vol 27

Place	Date	Hour	Summary of Events and Information	Remarks and references to Appendices
CHAU: SEGARD.	1st/17		Two Brigades in line at HOOGE CRATERS, Two Brigades in reserve at CHAU: SEGARD.	Lewis in on dia not October diary.
	3/17		Work commenced on Bury Line from HQ to CRATERS.	
	4/17		Sergt Fudge (No 2 Section) wounded and evacuated to England.	
	5/17		2 OR to hospital (sick). I driver to hospital (measles)	
	6/17			
	11/17		Work continued on Bury and improvement of Aire lines.	
	12/17		3 OR reinforcements joined from Signal Depot.	
	14/17		Lieut CARTER (QVS Rgt) and 11 OR proceeded to VIEUX BERQUIN E24aSh28Bnk Lorry load of instruments and men to fit up new office.	
	15/17		Transport proceeded to VIEUX BERQUIN, 2 lorry loads stores and men of No 1 Section to VIEUX BERQUIN. E29a Sheet 36A	
VIEUX BERQUIN	16/17	11.30am	Office closed CHAU: SEGARD opened VIEUX BERQUIN same time. 1 Brigade La COURONNE E30a Sh 3A, 1 Bde XXXXX BERQUIN, DOULIEU L5L Sh 36A 1 Brigade BUSSEBOOM G16c Sh 28. Direct lines to DOULIEU and La COURONNE and I ANZAC Corps. Via X Corps to BUSSEBOOM.	
BARLIN	18/17	10.30am	Office closed VIEUX BERQUIN opened BARLIN K27a Sh 36B same time. 1 Brigade DOULIEU, 1 Bde VIEUX BERQUIN, 1 Bde GONNEHEM. V18a Sh 36A Communication via I Army.	

Army Form C. 2118.

WAR DIARY
or
INTELLIGENCE SUMMARY.

21 Signal Coy RE
(D)
HQ & No 1 Section
November

(Erase heading not required.)

Place	Date	Hour	Summary of Events and Information	Remarks and references to Appendices
BARLIN	15/11 19/11		Clean up arms, equipment & checking and cleaning wagon stores.	
	20/11		3 OR to hospital sick.	
VICTORY CAMP	23/11	Dawn	Office closed BARLIN opened VICTORY CAMP (A28c R15SB)	
			1 Bde Trafalgar Camp (A28c R15SB) 1 Bde CHELERS (U23b S17SB) 1 Bde Mt St ELOI (Fsd S21.5/C) 1 Bde Mt St ELOI	
			Direct lines to all Brigades and XIII Corps.	
	24/11		6 OR reinforcement joined from Signal Depot.	
	25/11		Office closed VICTORY CAMP opened VILLERS CHATEL (W8d S11SB) same time.	
VILLERS CHATEL			Div Artilly remained VICTORY CAMP. 8 men left to work Signal Office.	
			Brigades remain as above. No 1 Section remained at VICTORY CAMP	
			2 OR to hospital sick.	
	26/11		All surplus kit disposed of & unserviceable clothing and stores replaced.	
	29/11		PEL 1 KW set, Lorry BSO an personnel replaced by 3 KW set	
			3 ton lorry and new personnel.	
	30/11		Orders received for Div to move to VII Corps area immediately.	
			Brigades entrained evening 30th. Adv party Div signals left Derict	
			by Lorry for TINCOURT. (N24c Sheet 62C)	
			Strength of Company 8 officers 274 OR, 147 Riding & 71 LD Horses - deficiency 5 OR	

O.C. 21st SIGNAL Co R.E.

WAR DIARY
or
INTELLIGENCE SUMMARY

Army Form C. 2118.

2 Signal Coy R.E. ① HQ & No.1 Section

December 1917

Vol 2.

Places	Date	Hour	Summary of Events and Information	Remarks and references to Appendices
TINCOURT	1/12/17	8.30am	Div HQ closed VILLERS CHATEL opened TINCOURT J.13.c.90 (about 6.c) HQ Section moved by lorry (2 lorries from Corps) No 1 Section transport by road.	While in ?
VILLERS-FAUCON	2/12/17		Div HQ closed TINCOURT opened VILLERS FAUCON Two Brigades in line, one Brigade at LONGAVESNES. "LL" Cable section attached. Sub Offices left at TINCOURT for rear Div HQ communications. Line handed over by 55th Div to Right Bde in St EMELIE E.24.a.82.63c. Left Brigade communication on 16th Div Forward Exchange Reserve Brigade communication via Cavalry Div LONGAVESNES.	
	3/12/17		One pair laid to St EMELIE for Right Brigade	
	4/12/17		One pair laid to HEUDECOURT W.21.6.51.35g for Left Brigade One pair laid to W.D.S. and spare to St EMELIE for 2 Arty Brigade 3 OR to hospital sick	
	5/12/17		One pair laid to SAULCOURT E.10.a.52.6 c for Arty Brigade	
	6/12/17		Work on poling cable and maintenance of lines	
	7/12/17		Two terminal cct to E.28.6.1.9 for 2 Arty Bde and one pair to ARP at E.2.d.3.8	

Army Form C. 2118.

WAR DIARY
or
INTELLIGENCE SUMMARY.
2 Signal Coy RE
HQ No 1 Echelon
December 1917

(Erase heading not required.)

Place	Date	Hour	Summary of Events and Information	Remarks and references to Appendices
LONGAVESNES	8/12/17	11.0a	Div HQ closed VILLERS FAUCON opened LONGAVESNES E.20.a.7.4 ambulance	
	9/12/17		All lines extended to new Theatre	
	31/12/17		Lateral laid and all cable poled	
	10/12/17		7 OR reinforcements joined from Signal Depot	
	11/12/17		LL Cable section left	
	13/12/17		Right Brigade moved from ST EMILIE to FAUCOURT	
	8/12/17 16/12/17		4 OR admitted to hospital sick and one wounded	
			3 OR reinforcements joined from Signal Depot	
			TINCOURT office closed. Rear Div HQ rejoined Div.	
			No 1 Section with Company transport moved from BUIRE to HQ Camp	
	20/12/17		Weather very bad with deep snow and blizzards. Little work	
	22/12/17		possible beyond maintenance of present lines	Vide Ap 2
	27/12/17		Sergt Cooper (11Q) Revd Berry (No 2 Sec) and Sergt Jones (No 3 Sec Army)	
	31/12/17		were mentioned in despatches pub London Gazette 21/11/17	
			During month 7 men were evacuated sick and 1 wounded	
			15 OR reinforcements were received from Signal Depot	
			Strength of Coy 10 Officers and 295 OR (Appendix N°1)	

[signature] Major RE
OC 2 Signal Coy RE

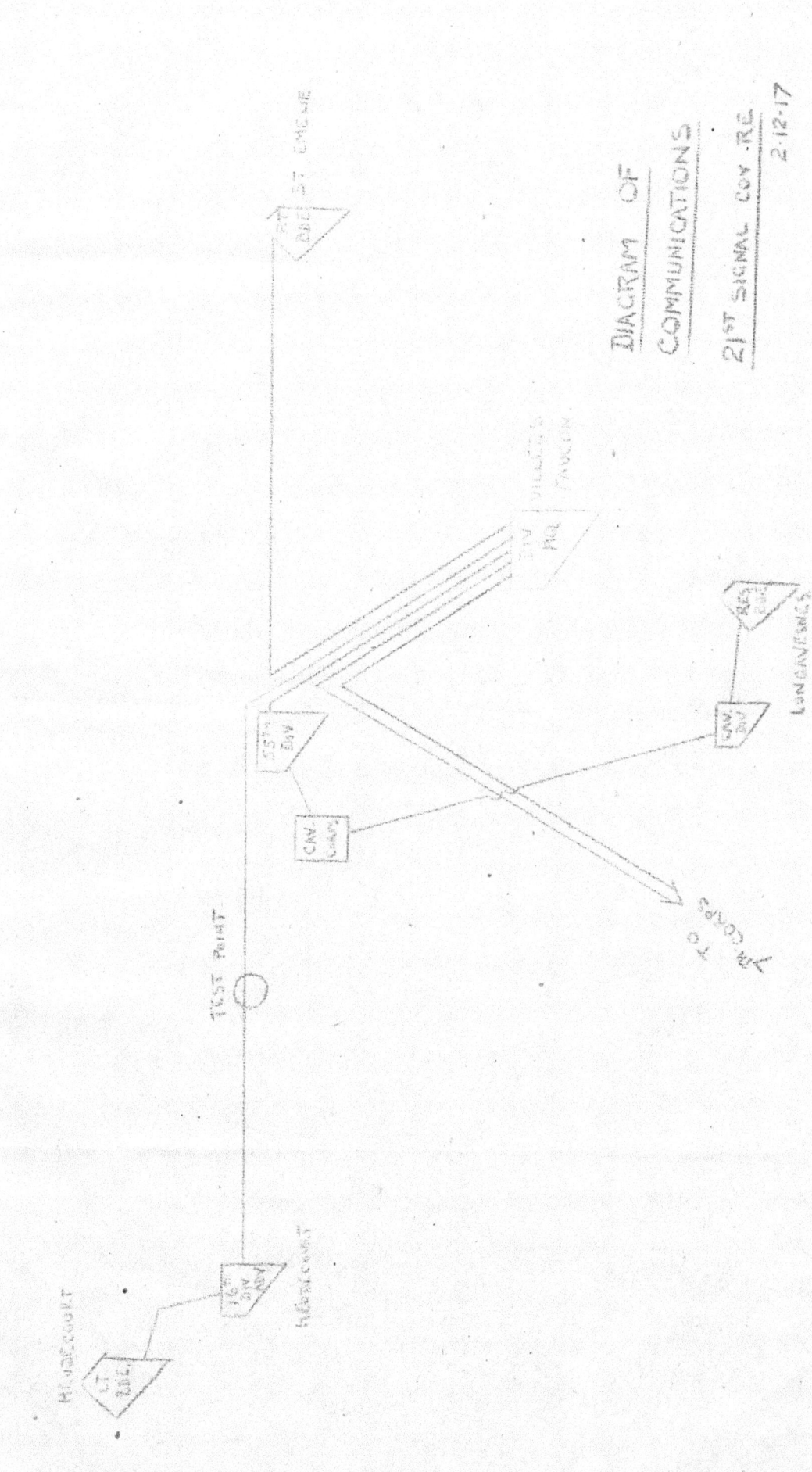

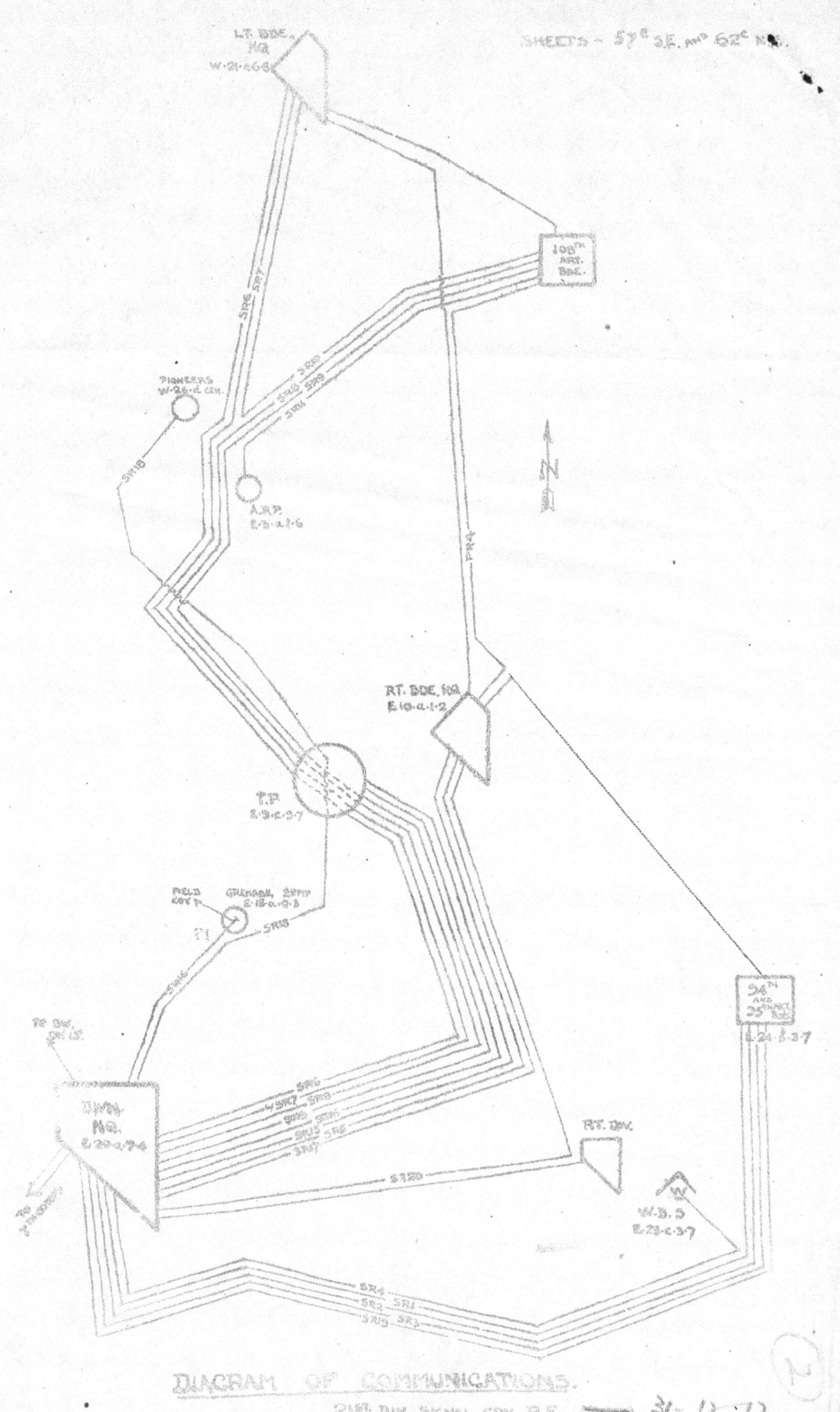

WAR DIARY
or
INTELLIGENCE SUMMARY

Army Form C. 2118.

21 Signal Coy R.E. January 1915

WO 29

Place	Date	Hour	Summary of Events and Information	Remarks and references to Appendices
LONGUENESSE	1/1/15		Very severe weather, hard frost & snow. Work on construction here standing by. NCO's & men detailed to defend if DRs & WO nearer Camp Const. Men instructed in duties, detailed to posts and went prepared on these posts & made them secure.	
			Lives as shown in diagram not been done.	
			Following award published in New Year Honours List:—	
			Major A. E. GOULD MC RE — DSO	
			M/Capt A. I. WALKER RE — MC	
			Lieut F. J. D. MONTGOMERIE RE — MC	
			66535 Sergt JOHNSON F. — DCM	
	6/1/15		Two Bgpsm in line with two direct pans to each. On Refugee in Reserve at LONGUENESSE with on direct pair. 2 motor Cyclist DRs and Desp Repair Coy RE with Corps of instruments required from 5th DIV (in ITALY) and 2nd Supply Col respectively. Reserve Brigade moved to HAUT ALLAINES — Comm: through III Corps.	
	11/1/15 to 14/1/15		207 reinforcements joined for Signal Depot. No 75846 Driver KEAN. J. died of heart trouble.	

Army Form C. 2118.

WAR DIARY
21 Signal Coy RE (2)

INTELLIGENCE SUMMARY.
January 1918.

(Erase heading not required.)

Place	Date	Hour	Summary of Events and Information	Remarks and references to Appendices
	19/1/18		One Junior NCO & 4 OR to attend for 4 weeks course in Signal Work at OR to Fifth Army School for wireless Course.	Vide app. 1.
	20/1/18		"Silent Day" — All telegrams by visual, wireless, DR or runner. No telephonic or telegraphic communication allowed forward of Div HQ. Being repeated for 24 hours from 6am to 6am twice weekly. Comparatively few messages handed in and no delay, weather conditions suitable for visual.	
	22/1/18		Major H.E. HEBBERT. NC RE posted for I Corps Signals as 2 OR on Command of Company.	
	23/1/18 24/1/18		Major A.E. GOULD DSO. MC. RE left for Signal Depot BEDFORD. Silent day repeated. Traffic disposed of successfully. Fair to warm too foggy for visual.	
	30/1/18		Sergt and 4 OR proceeded to new Div HQ at HAUT ALLAINES for work on local lines & Camp wiring. 1 Corps Brigade relieved by 117th Bde and moved to MOISLAINS. Connect via III Corps. Sheepshank Coy 10.19pm 230 OR. 50 R erected and during month. 70 R reinforcements joined from Signal Depot	

M. Walker
2/Lt OC 21 Signal Coy RE
Capt RE

Orders etc for Silent Day.

Circulation

62nd Bde. Wireless via W.O.S
    or Visual via 64th Bde (later 110th Bde)

64th Bde.
    Until relief — Visual direct.
    After relief — Telephone.

110th Bde.
    Until relief — Telephone.
    After relief — Visual direct.

94th & 95th Arty Bdes.
    Wireless via W.O.S.
    or Visual via 64th Bde (later 110th Bde)

108th Army Arty Bde
    Visual via 64th Bde (later 110th Bde)

Note. In the event of a block of messages, they will be sent by runner.

Very long messages will always be sent by runner.

Office copies of all messages sent by Visual or Wireless will be forwarded to H.Q. Div Signals by first D.R.

All telephones to be tested frequently during the day, to see that lines are OK.

All messages for transmission by Wireless must be handed in "in code", or signed to be sent "in clear" by the commander of a formation.

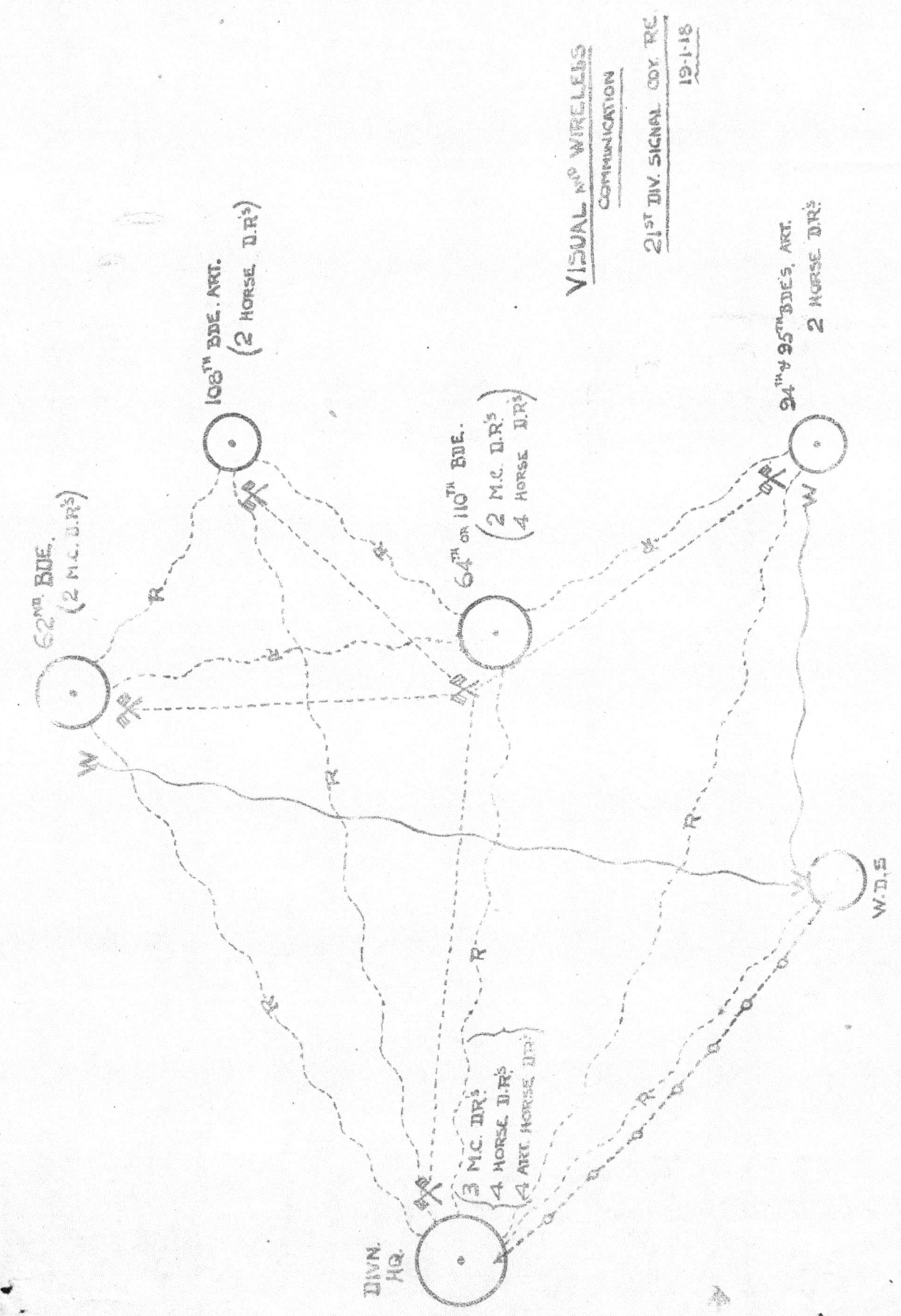

WAR DIARY
or
~~INTELLIGENCE SUMMARY~~
(Erase heading not required.)

Army Form C. 2118.

Vol 30

21ˢᵗ SIGNAL COY.

FEBRUARY 1918

Instructions regarding War Diaries and Intelligence Summaries are contained in F.S. Regs., Part II. and the Staff Manual respectively. Title pages will be prepared in manuscript.

WAR DIARY
or
INTELLIGENCE SUMMARY.
(Erase heading not required.)

2 1st Signal Coy. R.E. Army Form C. 2118.

February 1918

Place	Date	Hour	Summary of Events and Information	Remarks and references to Appendices
LONGAVESNES	1/2/18		Office relief, instruments and lorry load of stores sent to Reserve Div. Hy. HAUT-ALLAINES to fix up local wiring	
HAUT-ALLAINES	2/2/18		Hy. closed LONGAVESNES 10 a.m. opened HAUT-ALLAINES same hour. One Bde left on the line under 16= Div One Bde in old Div Hy. Camp LONGAVESNES One Bde MOISLAINES Communications One pair superimposed to Coys Hy One pair superimposed to MOISLAINES One pair Coys Hy to old Div Hy LONGAVESNES Power Buzzer class of 20 infantry O.R. exemplified at Div Hy. Div Signal School of 12 Officers 146 O.R. opened at HAUT ALLAINES. Staff :- One R.E. Officer	

WAR DIARY
21st Sig. Coy R.E.
February 1918

Date	Hour	Summary of Events and Information	Remarks
24 hrs contd.		two R.E. operators, one Infantry Officer, instructors, three Infantry N.C.O. instructors, one C.Q.M.S., four Cooks.	
		School — 1 Officer, 2 N.C.O. or B.O.R. for Butts 3 O.R. for Beoty M.G. 6 O.R. M.G. Beoty	
		Course 6 weeks	
4/2/18		5 O.R. reinforcements join from Signal Depôt went cleaning up transport, clothing store	
		2 O.R. evacuated sick	
6/2/18		Training (1) Cable Wagon Drill (2) Spelling Word (3) Visual (4) Jointing cable	

(3)

WAR DIARY
or
INTELLIGENCE SUMMARY.

21st Sig Coy R.E.   Army Form C. 2118.
February 1918

(Erase heading not required.)

Place	Date	Hour	Summary of Events and Information	Remarks and references to Appendices
	6/2/18 contd.		(5) Riding + Driving Drill (6) Map Reading (7) Wireless (8) Signal Drill + Physical Drill (9) Recreational Training	
	13/2/18		Div. Signal School moved to BOUCHAVESNES one N.C.O. to course at Corps Gas School	
	15/2/18		G.O.C. inspected the company Bde left in line under 16th Div, rejoined Bde	
Hav̂t-Allaines				
	18/2/18		6 O.R. reinforcements joined from Signal Depot (including two drivers for increase in establishment of R.F.A. Bde Sections)	
	28/2/18		One N.C.O. to Junior N.C.O's Course at Signal Depot One office relief, one cable section, and Army Level of stores moved to Div HQ LONGAVESNES	

Army Form C. 2118.

21st Sig. Coy R.E.

February 1913

WAR DIARY
or
INTELLIGENCE SUMMARY.
(Erase heading not required.)

Instructions regarding War Diaries and Intelligence Summaries are contained in F. S. Regs., Part II. and the Staff Manual respectively. Title pages will be prepared in manuscript.

Place	Date	Hour	Summary of Events and Information	Remarks and references to Appendices
	28/2/18 Contd		One Bde moved to Heudecourt under 39th Div	
			One Bde " " SAULCOURT " 16 Div	
			One Bde " " LONGAVESNES	
			Following lines laid from our Div H₁	
			1 Pair to Bde in LONGAVESNES	
			2 Pairs to "A.W." Bde, thence on permanent to HEUDECOURT	
			One pair on semi-permanent L-G route to GUYENCOURT thence cable to 108" A.F.A. Bde W.23 & 1.8 also 5.7.C	
			One pair on semi-permanent L-G route to GUYENCOURT thence cable to Bde in HEUDECOURT	
			Strength of Company 11 Officers 288. O.R.	
			2. O.R. evacuated sick during month	
			11. O.R. joined from Signal Depot " "	

H. Richardson Capt R.E.
for O.C. 21st Signal Coy. R.E.

21st Div.

WAR DIARY

21st DIVISIONAL SIGNAL COMPANY, R.E.

MARCH

1918

Attached:-

Appendices A, B & C.

Army Form C. 2118.

WAR DIARY 21st Signal Co., R.E.

or

INTELLIGENCE SUMMARY.

(Erase heading not required.)

March 1918.

Vol 31

Place	Date	Hour	Summary of Events and Information	Remarks and references to Appendices
HAUT ALLAINES LONGAVESNES	1st		Det 140 moved from HAUT ALLAINES to LONGAVESNES as I.O.R. as command of the two Brigades in the line at SAULCOURT and ST HEUDECOURT. Recce of the LONGAVESNES Artillery Bde at STEMELLE, CARRON COPSE and W2 d 1.0 (about 57c) Commencement as in appendix 'A'.	
	2nd		took on company line	
	4th			
	5th		2/Lieut R.W. LOWMAN R.E. joined as experienced from Fifth Army Sig Co. 1 O.R. admitted to hospital.	
	7th		Brunos scheme as in appendix 'B' started. Working parties of 600 per day supplied, trench after up into 1 NCO and 10 men, tasks of 23 yards first day then to dig a trench 4ft 6 - deep 3ft wide at top at each to be known as one side. Second day that trench to be completed to 8/1 deep 1ft wide at bottom. 1 O.R. admitted to hospital.	
	11th			
	12th		Ten par part trench in tacey from SAULCOURT to FISHERS KEEP and one from SAULCOURT to PEIZIERE	
	15th		Communication Cables - The General Principle in the area is the establishment of Coment cables to serve all units between which Comment is not dependent on Cable.	

WAR DIARY (2) 2 Signal Coy RE

or INTELLIGENCE SUMMARY.   March 1918

Army Form C. 2118.

(Erase heading not required.)

Place	Date	Hour	Summary of Events and Information	Remarks and references to Appendices

There are at Bde H.Q. each Inf'y Bde H.Q. and one forward station per Bde front. The Arm is in communication by Visual & Wireless with each Bde Centre.

Left Bde Centre is in comm'n by Visual & Wireless with its forward centre at Right Bath H.Q. W15 d 4.2 and with the Right Bde Centre; also by Phone with Bde on left.

Right Bde Forward Centre at W15 d 4.2 is in comm'n by Wireless & Visual with the Left Bde Centre, by P.B. and Amplifiers with the Right Bde Fwd centre, and by P.B. & Amplifiers with the Baths on the left.

Right Bde Centre is in comm'n by Visual & Wireless and Left Bde Centre, by P.B. & Amplifiers & Visual with the Right Bde Fwd centre & with the Bdes on its right by Wireless & Visual.

Right Bde Forward Centre at F1 a 1.5 is in comm'n by P.B. & Amplifiers, Wireless with the Right Bde Centre, by P.B. & Amplifiers with the Left Bde Fwd centre & by P.B. & Amplifiers with a Bath station on the right. It can also be reached by Visual from the support Baths & by gp Bde R.F.A.

In addition the Left Fwd station can receive by Visual & P.B. & Amplifiers from Chapel Hill   MARTINPUICH Farm.

The Right Fwd station can receive by P.B. from both Baths.

(2) On the adm "Main Bath Stations" each Bath is on the line with ans 2 runners

WAR DIARY (3) 23rd Signal Coy RE

March 1918

INTELLIGENCE SUMMARY.

(Erase heading not required.)

Place	Date	Hour	Summary of Events and Information	Remarks and references to Appendices
	5/-d		to their nearest centre. The Artillery wire and runner in the counter measures including or mounted or mounted orderlies from the 93rd Bde RFA to the Right Bde centre. No messages can be accepted for delivery at these centres unless there are orderlies from the addressee. For normal times the forward centres are being connected to Batt HQ & OP Stations by telephone. If telephone communication was available a pair would be laid to each forward centre. The Left Right Bde Bn will each detail an officer and despatch at each of the Bn Sec centre. They should be detailed at once to report to O.C. Signals for preliminary instructions. The latter will give them sufficient information to enable them to take charge of the station.) IOR admitted to hospital.	
	21st		7 pairs through [?] to each main in EPEHY & PEZIERE always left through at night in spite of enemy attentions during the day. German attack commenced 4.30 am, attack launched 9.20 am Lines to Bdes cut continually. Chance of ground cable line on 21st Appendix C. maintained as far as possible. All other lines abandoned. Brigade lines through intermittently throughout the day.	

WAR DIARY (4) 31st Signal Coy RE
INTELLIGENCE SUMMARY
March 1918

Army Form C. 2118.

Place	Date	Hour	Summary of Events and Information	Remarks and references to Appendices
			travel now only possible for a very short period during the day, even to meet. Capt Rds was destroyed by shellfire early in the day & a station was established at Div Hortly to the right of Capt Lty Hdr and works well. The buried cable route from the Bde at SAULCOURT to EPEHY kept through the whole time. Left (front) Comm's cable was captured at about 9.30am. About a dozen messages has been received by PB from CHAPEL HILL & VAUCELETTE FARM transmitted to the Bgt Bde code. The other Comm's cables worked perfectly the whole time. During the night maintenance of lines became even more difficult because messages were dealt with, pointing to the fact that enemy lines cannot be communicated by day, they should be laid by night by Brigades at least.	
TEMPLEUX LA FOSSE	22nd	10am	Div HQ closed at LONGAVESNES, opened at TEMPLEUX LA FOSSE. 12th Bde HQ closed HEUDECOURT about 12 noon, reopened at LIERAMONT. No Comm to Div except by horsehm. Lines were laid to LIERAMONT but shelling was too heavy for maintenance. By Bde closed at LONGAVESNES village about 10am + reopened at Div HQ Camp LONGAVESNES. 110 Bde closed SAULCOURT about 11.30am + reopened Div HQ Camp LONGAVESNES (closing Office with 6th Bde)	

WAR DIARY or INTELLIGENCE SUMMARY

Army Form C. 2118.

(5) 2 Signal Coy. R.E.

March 1918.

Place	Date	Hour	Summary of Events and Information	Remarks and references to Appendices
HAUT ALLAINES	2nd		1 Cable pair was laid from Div HQ. (Camp) LONGAVESNES to TEMPLEUX LA FOSSE. The pair was kept through continually with the fde honed. Great difficulty was experienced in working to the Corps at CLERY. Afternoons were got through by sounder, but the reports were by D.R. About 4.0 pm the buzz North Bde HQ had to retire from Div HQ. (Camp.) LONGAVESNES but the fde moved to cherry behind LONGAVESNES and North fde to AIZECOURT LE BAS. Div. was then ordered to fold the Green line, Bde HQ being bz/a North AIZECOURT LE HAUT and buzz at BUSSU. At 7.0 pm Div HQ closed at TEMPLEUX LA FOSSE and reopened at HAUT ALLAINES Spring back 39th Div. 1 Cable pair was laid from HAUT ALLAINES Div Bde HQ at AIZECOURT LA HAUT to the fde at BUSSU, two single cable lines were also laid by Cable wagons from the HQs of the centre & each fde area for forming. These were afterwards extended by fde to Battns.	
CLERY	3rd	8.30 a.m.	Div HQ closed at HAUT ALLAINES and moved to CLERY. Owing to shortage of transport a Divisional Serial Coy. some stores had to be dumped at HAUT ALLAINES. Test panels, two damaged motor cycles and part of the N.C. Artificers kit had to be left. The pair was laid from ALLAINES to CLERY ready for the Brigades before they moved back. Communication was maintained to the Brigades by A.T.R. About 2.0 pm Div HQ moved back to	

WAR DIARY / INTELLIGENCE SUMMARY

Army Form C. 2118.

C. 21 Signal Coy R.E.
March 1918.

Place	Date	Hour	Summary of Events and Information	Remarks and references to Appendices
MARICOURT.			MARICOURT, which had then the Corps H.Q. and remained so until about 8.0 p.m. when the Corps retired to CORBIE. During the afternoon all the horse back gear. (?) could not be found. but reopened at CLERY. Communication to Division by air on the permanent route running alongside the MARICOURT-CLERY road. Visual was impossible owing to mist. During the day the 6th & 110th Brigade Section lost all their transport and stores. We have buried Signal Stores for the Divisional Signal Section was also lost. It was impossible to lay a cable line along the MARICOURT-CLERY road, owing to the block of transport cross-country work was impossible owing to the nature of the ground.	
	26th	3.30 a.m.	About 3.30 a.m. a Cable pair was laid from the G.H.Q. Salvage Dump, HEM, to Divisional H.Q. rear for half an hour when they moved back. About 6.0 a.m. a trench wireless set has established on the W. edge of CLERY, working to a Wilson Set at the G.H.Q. Salvage Dump. At least one important message was got through by this means after the permanent route had gone. About 7.0 a.m. all Brigades horsed back to the G.H.Q. Salvage Dump using the Cable pair for Communication back to Division, the pair was put on to DM telephones at each end and pairs & buzzers hooked every 1000 yards along the line level, a DM tapped in its heels.	

Army Form C. 2118.

WAR DIARY
or
INTELLIGENCE SUMMARY.
(Erase heading not required.)

(1) 2/ Rqt at Coy R.E.
March 1918

Instructions regarding War Diaries and Intelligence Summaries are contained in F. S. Regs. Part II. and the Staff Manual respectively. Title pages will be prepared in manuscript.

Place	Date	Hour	Summary of Events and Information	Remarks and references to Appendices
			of Ambulance worked very satisfactorily. 1 Case Fair Los tree from Qrt. 8.95th	
			Arlen fac at Crossroads in A 30 b to Div HQ in T in to 118th Arthur	
			Ide that H.Q. MAUREPAS. Visual (heliograph) has established from Divisional	
BRAY	25th		HQ to a forward Visual Station at BIQ. c.15. Div. HQ. closed down at	
			2.15 pm having now command to 35 Division and billetes to BRAY.	
			A Composite Brigade has formed in the Division and all stores parties to	
			supply the same and Brigade Section of this Brigade. He signals to the	
			Brigade have been put in charge of Lieut Montgomerie who has returned from the	
			Divisional Cyclist Coy.	
SAILLY LAURETTE		8.0 pm	Divisional HQ. closed BRAY and reopened at SAILLY LAURETTE.	
BRESLE	26th	6.30 am	Divisional HQ closed SAILLY LAURETTE and reopened at BRESLE. Division	
			Withdrawing to the of River from Probable HQ of	
			Brigade at BUIRE and RIBEMONT to Division. Cable Fair laid from HQ of	
			Division and laying out a reeling up Lines, Brigades eventually supped	
			at HEILLY and RIBEMONT and have been laid to them. Several visual schemes	
			were worked out, and stations posted, but none were actually used owing	
			to changes of HQs. Lines also laid to 9th & 95th Artillery Bdes.	

Army Form C. 2118.

WAR DIARY
or
INTELLIGENCE SUMMARY.
(Erase heading not required.)

(B) 2 Corps Coy R.E.
March 1918.

Place	Date	Hour	Summary of Events and Information	Remarks and references to Appendices
BAVELINCOURT	29th		Division relieved by 3rd Australian Division and moved to BAVELINCOURT. Corps Troops Brigade left to the line. Nucleus of Brigade grouped round Div. HQ. Clearing up.	
	29th			
ALLONVILLE	30th		Advance HQ moved to ALLONVILLE. 61st Bde & ALLONVILLE and 10th Bde to POULAINVILLE. Visual established from ALLONVILLE to Poulainville.	
			POULAINVILLE.	
	30th		Clearing up. 61st Brigade moved to ALLONVILLE.	
	31st		Clearing up. 63rd Brigade moved to HANGEST. Communication established via PIQUIGNY RAILWAY Exchange.	

Major R.E.
OC 2nd Corps Coy R.E.
23rd April 1918.

APPENDICES A, B & C.

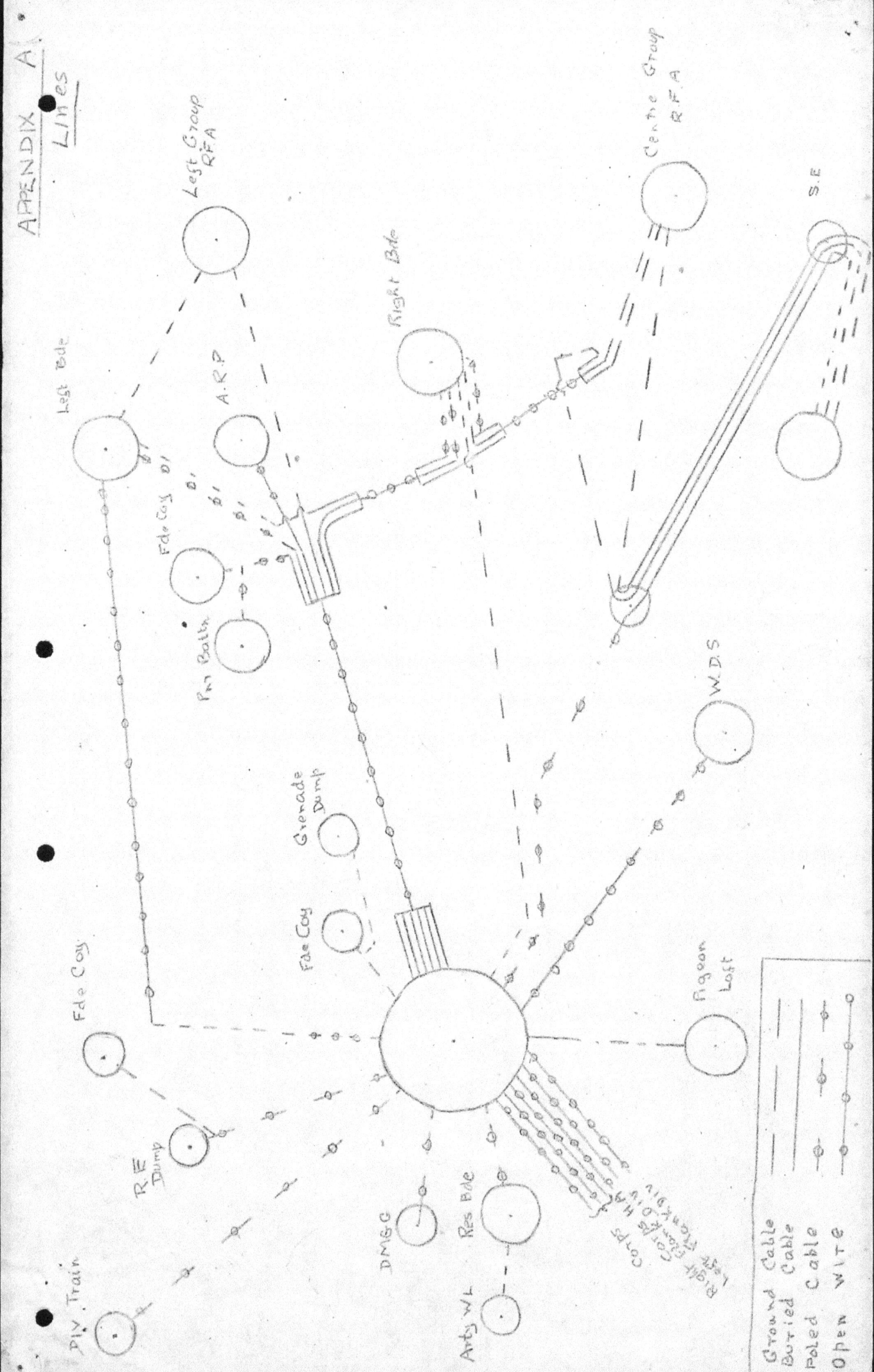

APPENDIX "A"
Visual

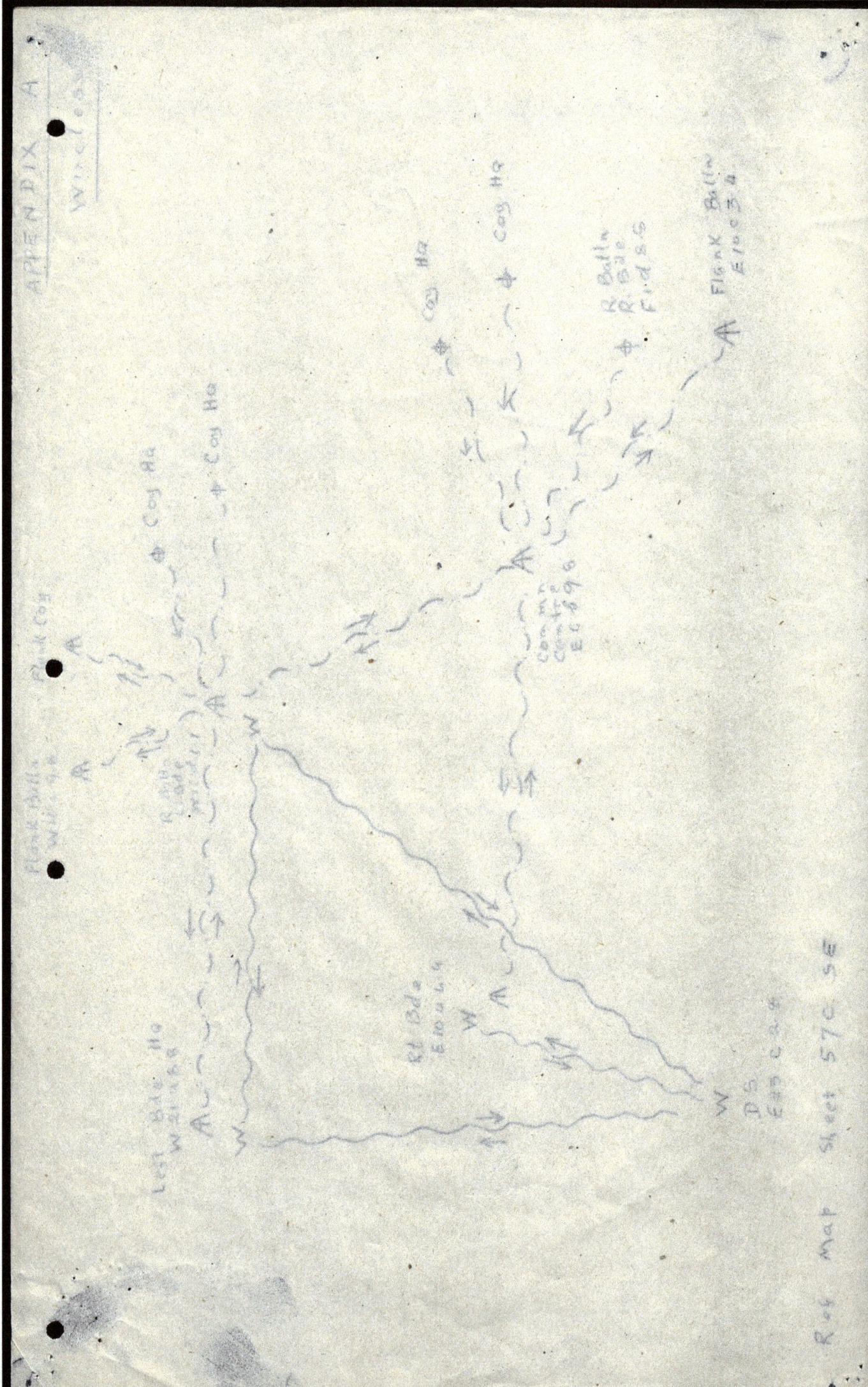

APPENDIX B
BURY

EPEHY

Part 57° SE4
1/20,000

O.P. Ex4
Fisher's Keep

Peiziere

E5	E6
E11	E12

Saulcourt

Appendix "C"

NOTE:— THESE LINES ARE THE MOST IMPORTANT COMMUNICATIONS, AND MUST BE KEPT THRO' AT ALL COSTS

21st. DIV. SIGNAL COY. RE

21st Divisional Engineers

21st DIVISIONAL SIGNAL COMPANY R.E.

APRIL 1918.

21st Signal Coy. RE.
April 1918

Army Form C. 2118

WAR DIARY
INTELLIGENCE SUMMARY.
(Erase heading not required.)

Place	Date	Hour	Summary of Events and Information	Remarks and references to Appendices
ALLONVILLE	1/4/18		Div HQ closed ALLONVILLE and reopened into Australian Corps at CAESTRE. Advr. party with instruments sent to CAESTRE by lorry. Company entrained at AMIENS.	
CAESTRE	2/4/18		Div. HQ closed CAESTRE and reopened DRANOUTRE. Company detrained at HOPOUTRE at 11.0am and marched to DRANOUTRE. Communication via LOCRE test point.	
DRANOUTRE	3/4/18 4/4/18		All Brigades in LOCRE area. Div. transferred to IX Corps. Two Brigades move into the line, one Brigade into reserve. 62nd Bde on Right, but on Left, 110th in Reserve.	
	5/4/18 7/4/18		1 Serjeant and 1 OR wounded in return to hospital. 110th Sig Bn relieved by a Brigade of 19th Div, and moves to LA CLYTTE. Communication via LA CLYTTE exchange. But HqBde relieved by Bde of 19th Div and moves to LA CLYTTE. 110th Bde moves to WESTOUTRE area. Communication via RENINGHELST Exchange.	
	9/4/18		Div. relieved by 19th Div and comes under orders of 22nd Corps.	

Army Form C. 2118.

WAR DIARY

21st Signal Coy R.E.

April 1918.

INTELLIGENCE SUMMARY.

(Erase heading not required.)

Place	Date	Hour	Summary of Events and Information	Remarks and references to Appendices
	9/4/18		146th Inf Bde moved into 49th Div reserve HQ. Bedford House. 110th Inf Bde moved into Reft Sector 49th Div. HQ ZILLEBEKE BUND. Adv. Party and 10 49th Div HQ.	
CHATEAU SEGARD	10/4/18		Div HQ closed BRANOUTRE & opened CHATEAU SEGARD in relief of 49th Div. 146th Inf Bde in Left sector came under orders of 31st Div. 62nd Inf Bde moved to PARROT CAMP & came under orders of 6th Div. Communications to all Bdes by the Corps lines & cable schemes.	
	11/4/18		Corps HQ. moves to STEENVOORDE. Corps lines very bad. 64th Inf Bde moved to PARROT Camp & came under orders of 7th Div. 39th Compostie Bde moved into 31st Div Reserve at BEDFORD House	
	14/4/18		Div HQ closed CHATEAU SEGARD, reopened WALKER CAMP (H.27.C) Sheet 28 Communication to Brigades by buried cables. Two pairs to each	
WALKER CAMP	15/4/18		Brigade in turn. One pair to the Reserve Brigade. 39th Composite Bde relieved 146th Bde. 110th Bde moved back to WALKER CAMP Bdx HQ WALKER CAMP P at CORNWALL CAMP OUDERDOM. 46th Bde to Div reserve One OR Killed by shellfire near WALKER CAMP P	

WAR DIARY

21 Signal Co, R.E.

April 1918

Army Form C. 2118.

(3)

INTELLIGENCE SUMMARY.

(Erase heading not required.)

Place	Date	Hour	Summary of Events and Information	Remarks and references to Appendices
HOOGGRAAF	18/4/18		Div. HQ. moved to HOOGGRAAF. Two Cable pairs laid to WALKER CAMP. One permanent train to WALKER CAMP. Two Power Bds. wires to Corps. 21 OR reinforcements joined from Signal Depot. Lieut A. LAZZELL Actg. Adjt. RE joined from T. Corps Signal. Adjutant for Wireless Section joined from Signal Depot.	
	19/4/18		Div. HQ. moved to G.15.a S.E. Sheet 27	
GISA S.E. Sheet 27	19/4/18		21st Composite Brigade came under orders of 21st Div. but the line on right of 110th Bde. HQ. near WALKER CAMP. Pair Cable laid to WALKER CAMP. Connection as in Appendix A.	
	20/4/18		Corps moved back to ZUYTPEENE. 90 minutes delay on cable to Corps.	
	23/4/18		Visual established from Div HQ to Brigades.	
	24/4/18		2 OR wounded in action and evacuated.	
	25/4/18		Bgd. Rds. Came under orders of 21st Div. HQ HALIFAX CAMP. Lines being Cut considerably by shell fire. 6th Bde moves to WALKER CAMP. 2/Lieut R.W. LONGMAN RE. Rd. One OR wounded in action & evacuated.	
	26/4/18		1 Sergeant and 1 OR wounded and evacuated.	

Army Form C. 2118.

WAR DIARY
21 Signal Coy RE
INTELLIGENCE SUMMARY. April 1918

(Erase heading not required.)

Instructions regarding War Diaries and Intelligence Summaries are contained in F. S. Regs., Part II. and the Staff Manual respectively. Title pages will be prepared in manuscript.

Place	Date	Hour	Summary of Events and Information	Remarks and references to Appendices
	27/4/18		21st Brigade moved to WALKER CAMP. Great difficulty with Brigades there owing to shelling.	
	28/4/18		89th Brigade relieved 21st Brigade. 62nd Brigade moved to G Wd 2.5. 58th and 59th Brigades came under orders of 21st Div. Cable pair run out to 56th Bde.	
	29/4/18		Very heavy bombardment. All forward lines down at 6.0am. Lines maintained throughout the day. Luminous posts along the two main routes to Brigades. 62nd Bde moves to Bush area. 1 OR killed in action, 1 OR wounded.	
L.W.a.2.0 Sheet 27	30/4/18		Div HQ moves to L.W.a.2.0 Sheet 27 Croix au Bac. Decorations awarded:- Sgt ELLIOT MM	DCM
			Cpl SIMPSON MM	Bar to MM
			" Brethast	MM
			" Clark	MM
			" Collins	MM
			Sgt Yorston	MM
			Pio Harris JT	MM
			" Thomson	MM
			H Dickerson	MM

OC 21 Signal Coy RE

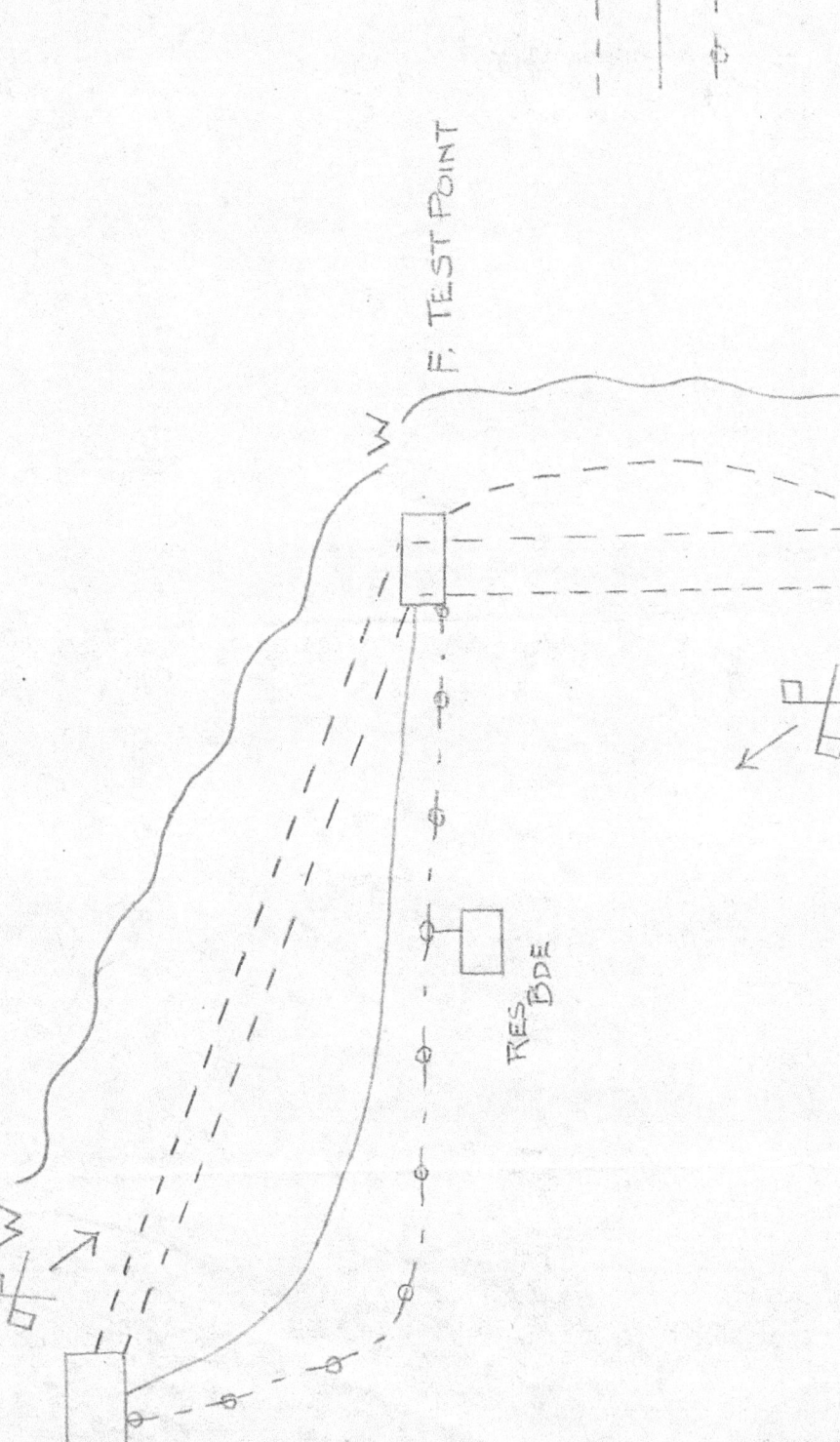

APPENDIX B

— — — GROUND CABLE
++++++ ARMOURED CABLE
———— BURIED CABLE

DIV HQ

2 LINEMEN
P TEST POINT

FTP
3 LINEMEN

21 DOS
DMGC
ATP
2 LINEMEN

B.TP
2 LINEMEN

C.TP
6 LINEMEN

PIONEER EXCHANGE

WALKER CAMP

ADV CORPS
2 LINEMEN

T.P
G.15 A 5.2
2 LINEMEN

Army Form C. 2118.

May 1915
21 Signal Coy, RE

WC 33

WAR DIARY
or
INTELLIGENCE SUMMARY.
(Erase heading not required.)

Instructions regarding War Diaries and Intelligence Summaries are contained in F.S. Regs., Part II. and the Staff Manual respectively. Title pages will be prepared in manuscript.

Place	Date	Hour	Summary of Events and Information	Remarks and references to Appendices
LHAZO	1/5/15		Brigades in position as follows:— 62 Inf Bde G15a 4.8 Sheet 27, 64 Inf Bde G8a 8.8 Sheet 27, 110 Bde WATOU, 21 Div G24a 5.5. 59 and 58 Bdes WALKER CAMP (M27C SK128) 39 Bde near BRANDHOEK	
RUBRUCK	2/5/15		Div relieved by 19th Div. Div HQ moved to ROUBRUCK. Communication — one pair to ARNEKE Exchange. 62 Bde — G15a 4.8 Sheet 27, buble — G8a 8.8 Sheet 27, 110 Bde M6a 8.6 Sheet 27.	
	4/5/15		Div HQ closed ROUBRUCK. Two lorry loads of stores and one officer relief left by road for new HQ. Company entrained STOMER at 7.30pm	
ROMIGNY	6/5/15		Div HQ opened ROMIGNY 12 noon. Company detrained at BOULEUSE at 10am and marched to ROMIGNY. 62 Inf Bde at LHERY, 64 Bde ROMIGNY, 110th Bde LARGERY. Communications - One pair to French Ex ROMIGNY. One pair from 62 Bde to French Ex LHERY, One pair from 110 Bde to FRENCH Ex at LARGERY. One pair to but by Bde	
	7/5/15		Training	
	10/5/15		62 Inf Bde moved to VAUX VARENNES. Comm: La Vaux Varennes French Ex.	
	12/5/15		" " " " PROUILLY. " PROUILLY PEVY.	

110.

Army Form C. 2118.

WAR DIARY
or
INTELLIGENCE SUMMARY.   21 Signal Coy RE
(Erase heading not required.)   May 1915

Instructions regarding War Diaries and Intelligence Summaries are contained in F.S. Regs., Part II. and the Staff Manual respectively. Title pages will be prepared in manuscript.

Place	Date	Hour	Summary of Events and Information	Remarks and references to Appendices
ROMIGNY	13/5/15		Advanced party sent to 74th French Div to take over communications	
	14/5/15		63rd and 64th Inf Bde moved into line under 74 French Div.	
			62 Bde HQ PC. SIDI-BRAHIM.	
			but " PC CENOBITES	
CHALONS LE VERGEUR	15/5/15		Div relieved 74th French Div	
			Arty HQ PC ADELE CHALONS LE VERGEUR	
			110th Bde move into line Bde HQ PC SAVOIE Comms as in Appoint A.	
			The change over was very simple. Everything was taken over exactly	
			as it stood. All the main central exchange were left in position	
			and two French telegraphists at each. A French "Chef de Poste"	
			was left at each Comms cable test point. English signallers were	
			sent to each exchange and test point to get to know the lines	
	16/5/15		One direct pair put through to each Brigade	
	17/5/15		62 Inf Bde moved to PC JUNIOR.	
	18/5/15		Training. Testing out the forward lines. MT Coy, Div Mop,	
			Pigeon Loft, RE Dump, & AADOS put on the phone	

Army Form C. 2118.

WAR DIARY
INTELLIGENCE SUMMARY.
(Erase heading not required.)

(3) May 1918
21 Signal Coy RE

Place	Date	Hour	Summary of Events and Information	Remarks and references to Appendices
	27/5/18	1am	Enemy bombardment commenced. Jam Attack launched. Brigade Hrs Rec very well. Owing to the numerous exchanges through which it was possible to get Brigade, we were never completely cut except to the 9yd Arty Bde which was dis for about four hours.	
PROUILLY	27/5/18	7pm	Div HQ closed CHALONS reopened PROUILLY. It was intended that Bde HQ should fall back to CHALONS, as the exchanges were left there. About F.15pm the enemy reached CHALONS. The exchange were destroyed and abandoned. Two men with a W/T set were sent to BOUVANCOURT about 10pm. This set had to be abandoned and destroyed. Eventually the but. + 110th Bde settled at CHAMPIGNONIERES and there through to Div on the buzz. 62nd Bde took up a position near VAUX VARENNES. Communication by DR. 7th Bde attached to Div.	
ROSNAY	28/5/18	7am	Div HQ closed PROUILLY reopened ROSNAY. Bdes establishing report centre at PROUILLY. One pair laid by Callington from PROUILLY to ROSNAY. 7.30am Enemy entered PROUILLY	

Army Form C. 2118.

WAR DIARY

May 1918   2 Signal Coy R.E.

INTELLIGENCE SUMMARY.

(Erase heading not required.)

Instructions regarding War Diaries and Intelligence Summaries are contained in F. S. Regs., Part II. and the Staff Manual respectively. Title pages will be prepared in manuscript.

Place	Date	Hour	Summary of Events and Information	Remarks and references to Appendices
SARCY	28/5/18	6pm	62nd, 110th & 7th Bdes with 93rd Bde RFA on Tile Works near SAPICOURT. PROUILLY – ROSNAY line diverted to them. 6th Bde at TRIGNY. No communication.	
	29/5/18		Div HQ closes ROSNAY reopens SARCY. All Bdes retired to ROSNAY. Cable pair laid from ROSNAY to SARCY. 5th Div moved SARCY and shared office. Communication good to all Bdes of ROSNAY, including Artillery Bdes. Direct wire "Coryon". Div HQ closes SARCY reopens LA NEUVILLE. Visual cut to Bdes. Cable pair tied on to the forward line at SARCY and out to LA NEUVILLE. Test point and visual transmitting station left at ROSNAY.	
LA NEUVILLE		2pm	All Bdes moved to MERY PREMACY.	
		4pm	Forward cable pair from LA NEUVILLE diverted to MERY PREMACY. Visual established to Brigades.	
	30/5/18		Div relieved by the French. Div HQ moved to CHALTRAIT-AUX-BOIS. 6th Inf Bde – VAUCIENNES, 62nd and 110th Bde midway between ST MARTIN D'ABLOIS and VAUCIENNES. All communication by D.R.	
CHALTRAIT AUX BOIS				

WAR DIARY
or
INTELLIGENCE SUMMARY.

Army Form C. 2118.

May 1917 (3) 21 Signal Coy RE

Place	Date	Hour	Summary of Events and Information	Remarks and references to Appendices
CHALTRAIT AUX BOIS	31/5/17		62 Inf Bde at SOULIERES, 64 Bde CHALTRAIT. 110" " " MARIE ETRECHY. All communication by D.R. Decorations — 65871 2/Cpl Stephens T.H.S. awarded Military Medal. 50660 Dvr Jackson E. Casualties — 1 OR killed in action. 10 OR wounded " " 9 OR missing " " 4 OR evacuated sick 8 OR reinforcements joined from depot. Strength of Coy. 12 Officers 290 OR. 35 R and 71 LD Horses	

N Kellick Major RE
O.C. 21 Signal Coy RE

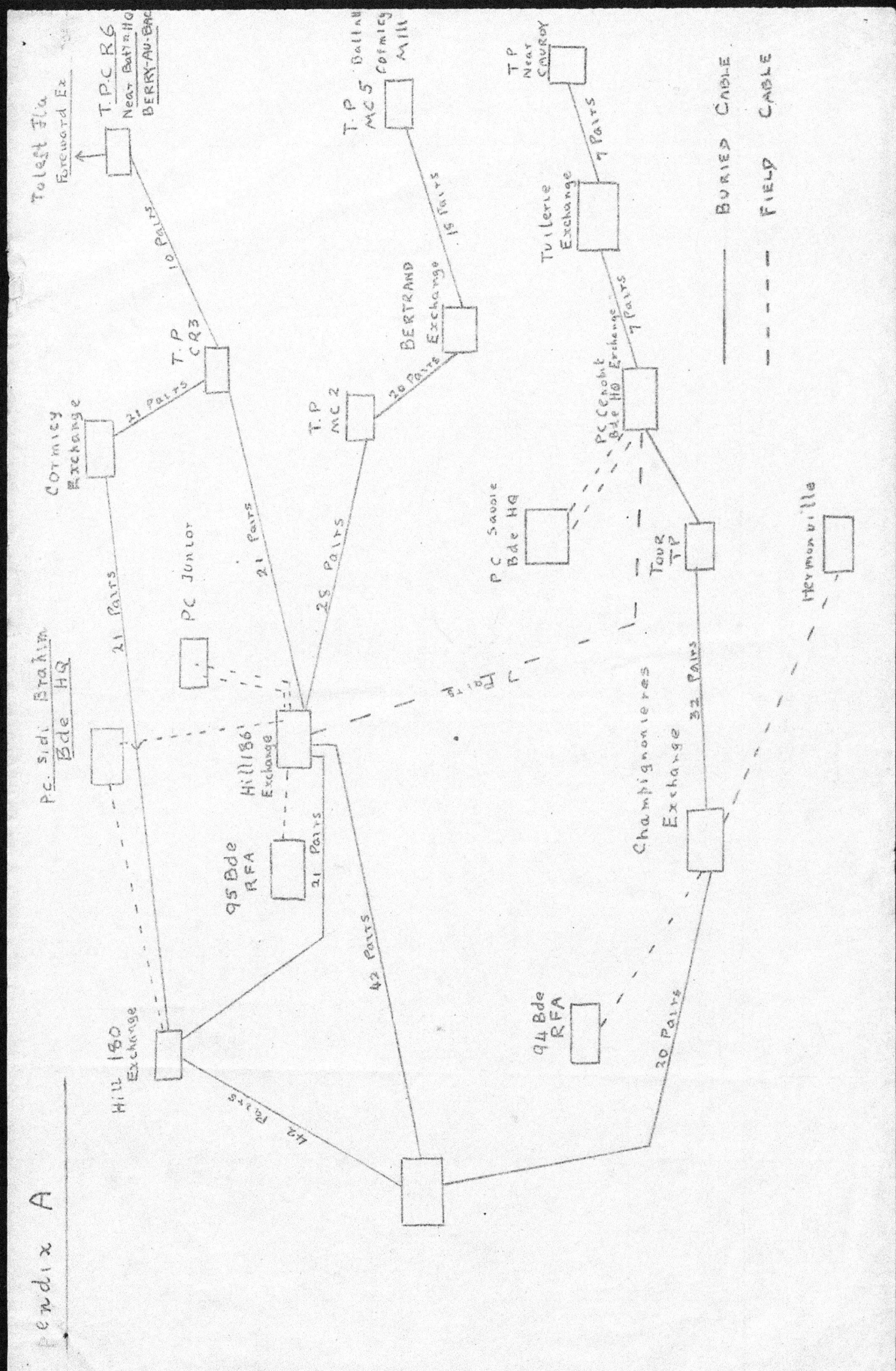

WAR DIARY or INTELLIGENCE SUMMARY.

(Erase heading not required.)

Army Form C. 2118.

① 21st Signal Coy R.E.

Vol 34

Place	Date	Hour	Summary of Events and Information	Remarks and references to Appendices
CHALTRAIT	1/6/18		Divl Independent Bde unit 62nd Infy Bde Signals, 7 OR of No 1 Section, and 3 OR of 1st/T section moved to COMBLIZY - DORMANS area (Map SOISSONS No 2s)	
	3/6/18		8 NCO reinforcements joined from Signal depot	
	4/6/18		Independent Bde at BOUQUIGNY, 64 Bde at CONGY, 110 Bde - COURJONNET, 62 Bde - VILLENART, 21st DA St MARTIN d'ABLOIS, Communication by D.R.	
	6/6/18		A/Capt A.G. RITCHIE joined from 3rd Divl Signal Coy	
	6/6/18		21st Indep Bde moved to COMBLIZY. 12 OR of Power Buzzer Pool sent to Indep Bde	
LA NOUE	9/6/18	2.30pm	Divl H.Q. opened LA NOUE	
			64 Bde - Les ESSARTS, 110 Bde - PECHARD, Communication by D.R.	
	10/6/18		A/Capt H. RICHARDSON left for Third Army Signal Coy and A/Capt A.G. RITCHIE assumed duties 7 2nd Command of Company	
	12/6/18		Cable pair laid to ESTERNAY Exchange	
			Lieut W.G. JACKSON left for 8th Divl Signal Coy	
	14/6/18	8am	Divl HQ closes LA NOUE. Company proceed by train, entraining SEZANNE, detraining LONGPRE les CORPS SAINTS. (Map ABBEVILLE No 14)	
OISEMONT	15/6/18	12noon	Divl HQ opened OISEMONT. One line to 8th Divl (62 Bde not here) HALLENCOURT Army Ex, 64 Bde - BEHEN, 110 Bde HANGEST, communication by D.R.	

Army Form C. 2118.

(2) 21 Signal Coy RE

WAR DIARY
INTELLIGENCE SUMMARY.
(Erase heading not required.)

Place	Date	Hour	Summary of Events and Information	Remarks and references to Appendices
OISEMONT	17/6/18		62nd Inf Bde move to BERNAPRÉ	
	18/6/18		64th " " " " BEZINCOURT	
	19/6/18		The Company less 2 OR to man Div Signal office. Mtr Cyclist & PBL personnel proceeded by road to BOURBEL.	
	20/6/18		Company training. Personnel of No 5 Section, MTT & PS Posts rejoined from Cpy less Sec.	
	21/6/18		62nd Inf Bde at GLANCOURT. Comm by DR. 1st OR reinforcement joined from Signal Depot, 2 OR admitted hospital sick	
GAMACHES	22/6/18	10 am	Div HQ opened Chateau LA HAIE near GAMACHES. Motor Cycle - BARONESVILL 1 Cable pair to ABBEVILLE Ex, 1 to GAMACHES Civil Ex. Cable detachment required from 21st DA signals	
	23/6/18		The Company less personnel at OISEMONT marched from BOURBEL. 64th Bde at GAMACHES - direct line laid	
	26/6/18		4 OR to hospital - sick	
	28/6/18		3 " " " "	
	30/6/18	3.30 pm	Company transport less 2 cable detachments left by road for OISEMONT area One cable detachment left by road to join HQ 21 D.A.Sigs in MARTAINNEVILLE area	

Army Form C. 2118.

21ˢᵗ Signal Coy. R.E.

WAR DIARY

INTELLIGENCE SUMMARY.

(Erase heading not required.)

Instructions regarding War Diaries and Intelligence Summaries are contained in F. S. Regs., Part II. and the Staff Manual respectively. Title pages will be prepared in manuscript.

Place	Date	Hour	Summary of Events and Information	Remarks and references to Appendices
GAMACHES	23/5/18		Company training.	
	30/5/18		Strength of Company – 12 Officers, 310 OR, 112 horses	
	30/5/18		Decorations awarded during month	
			N.C.O awarded Bar to M.M.	
			5 OR " M.M.	
			3 NCOs " M.S.M.	

N.P.Abbott
Major R.E.
O.C. 21 Signal Coy. R.E.

21st Signal Coy, RE
July 1918

Army Form C. 2118.

WAR DIARY
INTELLIGENCE SUMMARY
(Erase heading not required.)

Vol 3

Place	Date	Hour	Summary of Events and Information	Remarks and references to Appendices
BEAUQUESNES	1/7/18	8.0am	Office closes GAMACHES and reopens BEAUQUESNES (N 2 b Sheet 57d) Div HQ at Chateau VAL VION (N 4 D Sheet 57d)	
		5.0pm	Dismounted party (about 60) left by train from BLANGY. 1 cable detachment and RA HQ signal detachment left in R MARTAINVILLE area with H.Q 21st D.A.- Lines to BEAUQUESNES and TALMAS Exchange (4th Corps) 62nd Inf Bde at BEAUQUESNES 110th Inf Bde at RAINCHEVAL (N 12 c Sht 57d) but Inf Bde at PUCHVILLERS (N 22 a Sht 57d) 63rd Division at " No communication other than by D.R.	
	2/7/18		Telephone party to all three Inf Bdes. All trunks complete & connected to Exchange	
	3/7/18		Signal Company transport, proceeding by march route, arrived. Lieut G.E. Ruberts left for months leave to UK.	
	4/7/18		Lieut H. Carter and 3 N.C.O's left for six weeks course at Fourth Army Signal School	
	5/7/18 to 12/7/18		The Company in training at BEAUQUESNES	
	13/7/18		2/Lieut J.M. Baxter joined from Third Army Signal Company. I.N.C.O. left for Junior N.C.O. Signal Course at Signal Depôt	
	14/7/18		62nd Inf Bde close BEAUQUESNES opens TOUTENCOURT (U 1 b Sht 57d) Line to ECO	
	15/7/18		62nd Inf Bde on direct line to Signal Coy HQrs	

Army Form C. 2118.

21 Squad (or) RE.
July 1918

WAR DIARY
INTELLIGENCE SUMMARY
(Erase heading not required.)

Instructions regarding War Diaries and Intelligence Summaries are contained in F.S. Regs., Part II. and the Staff Manual respectively. Title pages will be prepared in manuscript.

Place	Date	Hour	Summary of Events and Information	Remarks and references to Appendices
	16/7/18		2/Lieut E.S. Abbott joins from Third Army Signal Coy.	
	18/7/18	11am	62nd Inf Bde closed TOUTENCOURT	
		4pm	opened RAINCHEVAL same hour	
		4.15pm	" " " ACHEUX	
	19/7/18		Communication via 63rd Divn and ACHEUX Exchange, but speaking very faint. Direct sounder circuit to 110 Inf Bde. Telephonic communication with the 63 RN Divn and ACHEUX Exchange.	
	20/7/18		5 OR reports from Field Ambulance	
	23/7/18		7th Bde RHA Group close BEAUQUESNES and report 1st Cavalry Div at BEAUVAL. 2/Lieut BAXTER left for 3 Army Signal Coy.	
		3pm	2/Lieut D.A. arrive BEAUQUESNES.	
			2/Lieut A.F. PLUMMER joins from 3 Army Signal Coy.	
	24/7/18	4.30pm	110 Inf Bde close ACHEUX and reopen Belle HQ ENGLEBELMER (P24d 3.4 Sh 57d)	
		6.0pm	62 " " RAINCHEVAL. Left " BEAUSSART (P15d 3.4 ") to centre Bde BEAUSSART, Rt Bde ENGLEBELMER, L ACHEUX. W/T sets sent to relieve 63rd Division's sets at these places.	
RAINCHEVAL	25/7/18	6pm	Div HQ with DA closes BEAUQUESNES and reopens RAINCHEVAL same hour.	
		7.30pm	61st Inf Bde closes PUCHEVILLERS and reopens centre Bde in line. A party of 1st OR sent forward to take over the 3 visual stations viz:- RAINCHEVAL (O13a 25.25 7K15 7d) BELLE EGLISE (O16 05.05 Sh15 7d) ACHEUX (P11c 9.2 7K157 7d)	

Army Form C. 2118.

21st Signal Coy R.E.
July 1918

WAR DIARY
INTELLIGENCE SUMMARY.
(Erase heading not required.)

Instructions regarding War Diaries and Intelligence Summaries are contained in F.S. Regs., Part II. and the Staff Manual respectively. Title pages will be prepared in manuscript.

Place	Date	Hour	Summary of Events and Information	Remarks and references to Appendices
	25/7/18		Visual communications taken over as in Appendix.	I
			Weather	II
	26/7/18		21st Div Train on to 63rd Div Exchange at BEAUQUESNES.	
			3 N.C.Os. left for branch Signal course at Third Army School.	
	25/7		A party of 1 N.C.O. and 8 men sent to take over the Cdr. Exchange in ACHEUX from Signals 63rd R.N. Div.	
			The following units of 63rd Div remained on 21st Div Exchange.	
			63rd DAC 63rd Div Train 63rd Employment Coy	
			190th Bde move to ACHEUX and come on ACHEUX Exchange	
	27/7/18		A party of 2 N.C.Os and 4 men sent forward to be billetes in MAILLY MAILLET for work on returning Arms lines and disposing that horses.	
	29/7/18		63rd Div Train off our Exchange, 190 Bde off ACHEUX Ex, 63rd DAC & Employed Coy off our Ex. Somme evened to 42nd Div on left. 21st Div Train on phone as above.	
			63rd Div close at BEAUQUESNES.	
	30/7/18		Cable lie to 63rd Div goes through to 21st Div Train	
			64th Fd. Amb. on RAINCHEVAL–TOUTENCOURT Road joins through to 21st Div Exchge	

(4) 21st Signal Coy RE.
July 1918

WAR DIARY
INTELLIGENCE SUMMARY.
(Erase heading not required.)

Army Form C. 2118.

Place	Date	Hour	Summary of Events and Information	Remarks and references to Appendices
	30/7 31/7		Party at work poling cable between RAINCHEVAL and LEALVILLERS.	
			Wilson det: from Div HQrs moved to Adv. Div. HQ near LEALVILLERS.	
			Trench set from ACHEUX moved back to Div HQrs RAINCHEVAL.	
	31st		15 N.C.O's & men evacuated to hospital sick during month chiefly with influenza;	
			11 reinforcements joined from Signal depot during month.	
			Sergt Davies D.H. and L.e Corpl Anderson F.J. awarded D.C.M's.	
			Strength of Company 12 Officers, 301 OR, 122 Horses. 16 OR, 1 Riding Horse deficient	

[signature]
Major RE
O.C. 21 Signal Co RE.

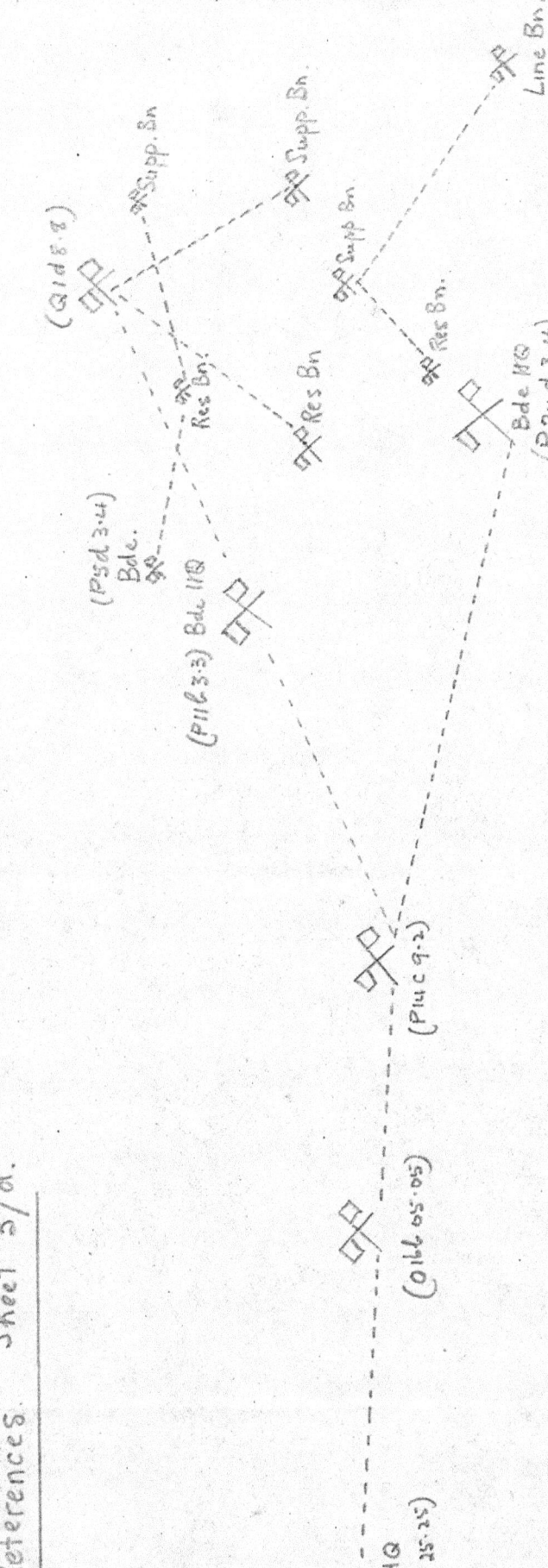

Wireless & P.B. Communications. 26.8.18.   21st Signal Co. RE.   Appendix II.

Map References. Sheet 57d.

Wireless ～～～
P.B. & A. ― ― ―

Div. HQ
N.11.d 6.3

T. △ Adv. Ex.
(P.19 & 9.9)

T. △ Centre Bde. (P.5.d.3.4)

Line Bn.
Left Bde.
(Q.3.d.0.1)
⊕ Coy.

(Q.2.d.5.5)
⊕ Coy.

T. △ Right Bde.
(P.24.d.3.4)

△ Line Bn.
Right Bde.
(Q.22.c.6.2)

21 Signal Coy RE.
August 1918

WAR DIARY
or
INTELLIGENCE SUMMARY.

Army Form C. 2118.

Place	Date	Hour	Summary of Events and Information	Remarks and references to Appendices
RAINCHEVAL	1/8/18		Work continued on forward lines and emergency ground to lines & cables	
			5 OR reinforcements joined from Signal Depot, 3 OR to hospital (2 gassed, 1 sick)	
	4/8/18		21 Air Train line to BOUQUESNES split as connects to 63rd Div. HQ Advd.	
	5/8/18		9 OR reinforcements joined from Signal Depot	
	7/8/18		RV visual detached and BL station moved to front near Advd Div HQ	
			Fullerphone working to latter station	
	13/8/18		6 OR reinforcements joined from Signal Depot. 1 OR wounded on active service	
			64 Inf Bde move to AUCHONVILLERS to follow enemy withdrawal. Fullerphone	
			working to new HQrs. Visual direct from AUCHONVILLERS to Div. Forwarding	
			station at ACHEUX. Wireless from D.S. at ACHEUX to 64th Inf Bde.	
			64th Bde also in communication with 62nd and 110th Inf Bdes by wireless	
			and cable and also by visual to 62nd Inf Bde.	
			From 25.7.18 to 13.8.18 practice was carried out daily by Brigade and	
			Battns (except front line Battns) with Popham Panel Message received	
			by plane being dropped at Div. HQ. Practice very successful	
	16/8/18		64th Inf Bde close AUCHONVILLERS open BEAUSSART	
	17/8/18		" " " move to ARQUEVES	
	18/8/18		5 OR reinforcements join from Signal Depot	

WAR DIARY

21 Signal Co R.E.
August 1918

INTELLIGENCE SUMMARY

Army Form C. 2118.

Place	Date	Hour	Summary of Events and Information	Remarks and references to Appendices
	20/8		64th Inf. Bde move to ACHEUX, 62nd & 110th Inf Bde at AUCHONVILLERS. Adv Div HQ opened ACHEUX. Cable parties from cable head at DA hutspoel. Counter working to both Brigades. Enlelephone to 42 Div on left, 42 Div having no sounder available. 63 Bde through on buried cable from DA testpoint to Brigade on left. 110th Bde through to Bde on right and to ENGLEBELMER. WT DS erected at MAILLY MAILLET replying to 62nd and 110th Bdes and to BF set at ACHEUX. Div Power transmitting station at ACHEUX became temp. alarm working to Brigades at AUCHONVILLERS and 94 Arty Bde at ENGLEBELMER.	X
ACHEUX	21/8		Div HQ moves to ACHEUX. 62 Bde in hot trench Q6d 0.0. 64th Bde Adv HQ Q12 B.1.8. Two cable pairs laid by cable wagon from cable head to Bde. HQrs. 62 Bde also extended both lines to new HQ. Over 900 messages dealt with, the majority between 2pm and midnight. Maximum delay 15 minutes. 4 OR admitted to hospital (2 gassed 2 sick)	
MAILLY-MAILLET	23/8	7am	Div HQ. opened MAILLY MAILLET. Rear exchange remaining at HOMEUX. Smooth working between Adv and Rear. 62 Bde now at AUCHONVILLERS receiving messages for their Adv HQ and for 64 Bde and transmitting via transd. arr established at AUCHONVILLERS receiving from Bde and transmitting by phone from cable head	

WAR DIARY or INTELLIGENCE SUMMARY

Army Form C. 2118.

21st Signal Coy RE
August 1916

Place	Date	Hour	Summary of Events and Information	Remarks and references to Appendices
	24/8		62 hy Bde R16 c.0.1, 6t hy Bde R9d 4.7, 110 Bde R16a 6.4 and 94 FA Bde BEAUSSART all on cable line. 110 Bde Office opened at Q.12.c.1.9 at 12.30am. This Bde worked on manned exchange with two direct call pairs on ringing exchange to Div and Cable to 62 and 6t Bdes. Double also working to hy Bde which received from other hy Bdes and 9t arty Bde. Single D's cable laid to Bridge tent on MICHE at GRANDCOURT. All three Bdes moves along exchange Single D's to extension. All 3 Bdes working on one line. 110 hy Bde moves during night to M.B.C. D's ample extended	Appendix A
GRANDCOURT	25th	6am	Adv Div opens GRANDCOURT Communication on Pilot line Single D's cable in twos during early morning from GRANDCOURT via MIRAUMONT and PYS to serve 62 Bde who are advancing on LE SARS. Bde enable to get into LE SARS until 11.0am. T. is run into 110 Bde from PYS — LE SARS. Line is run from 110 Bde to 62 Bde. 62 Bde move to BUTTE LE SARS. D's cable is extended along PYS – LE SARS Road to WARLENCOURT. Communication with arty is obtained through hy Bde in to Bde HQ. Div Visual Stn is established Arty Bdes are moving with Infy Bdes. Div Visual Stn is established at R.11.6 working to Bde at BUTTE and 110 Bde at M.B.C.	

WAR DIARY 21 Signal Coy RE

INTELLIGENCE SUMMARY. August 1916

Army Form C. 2118.

Place	Date	Hour	Summary of Events and Information	Remarks and references to Appendices
	26/8		In addition to Cable detachment already with R.A., another detachment with personnel for 2 forward centres & visual station and 2 M'cers to be sent forward. Forward cable exchange to open at R.8.d. One cable pair on land from Corps to GRANDCOURT to this exchange. All Bde, Arty Bdes and M.L. H.Q. Bde have lines to this exchange.	
	27/8		In anticipation of forward moves, second forward exchange opened at BUTTE de WARLENCOURT. Exchange at R.8.a is now known as "A" exchange, at BUTTE as "B". Single D3 lines to Lus & LUSENHOF Farm and later D8 pair to same place. Visual Terminal Visual station remains at R11.b. otri Transmitting station to be towed with Brigades on right and left moved to LE SARS.	Appendix B
LE SARS	30/8	Noon	From H.Q. moved to LE SARS. Strength of Company 12 Officers 311 OR, 118 Horses September 6 OR	

[signature]
OC 21 Signal Coy RE

Major RE
OC 21 Signal Coy RE

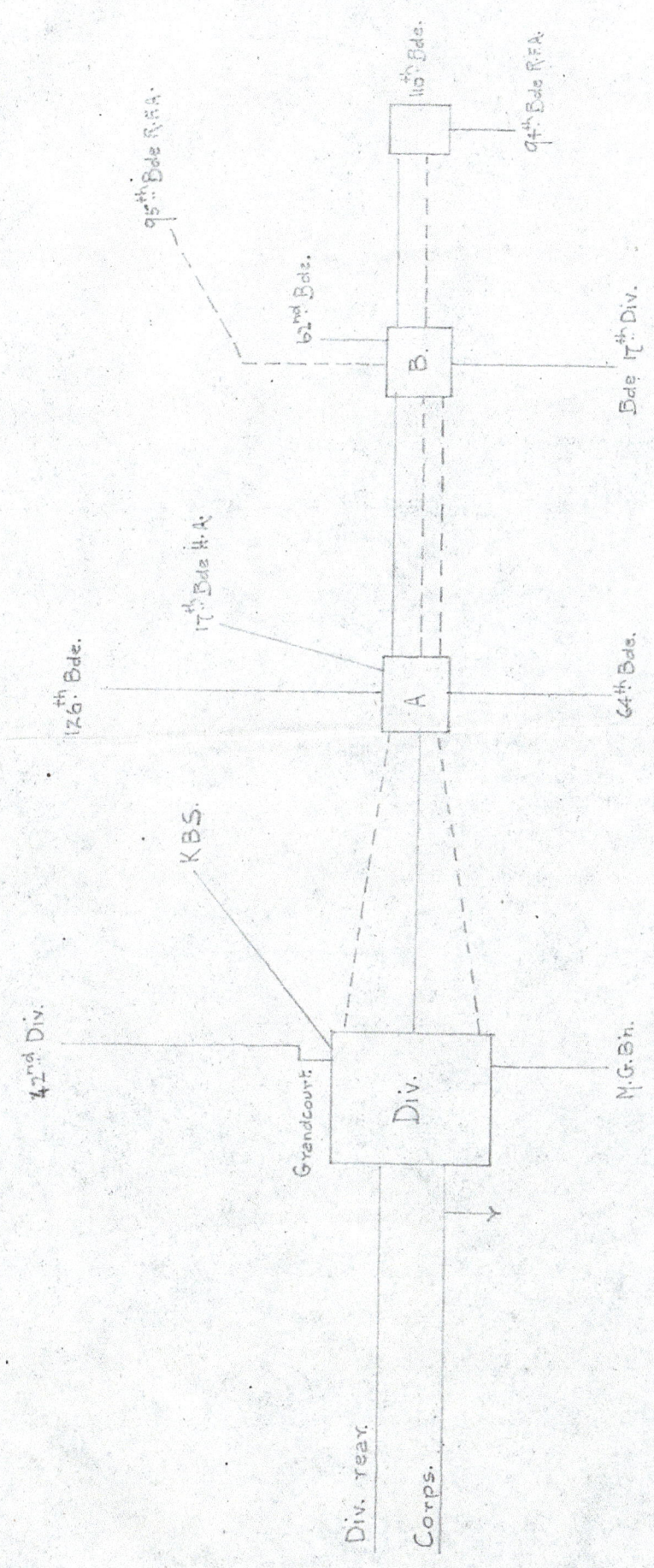

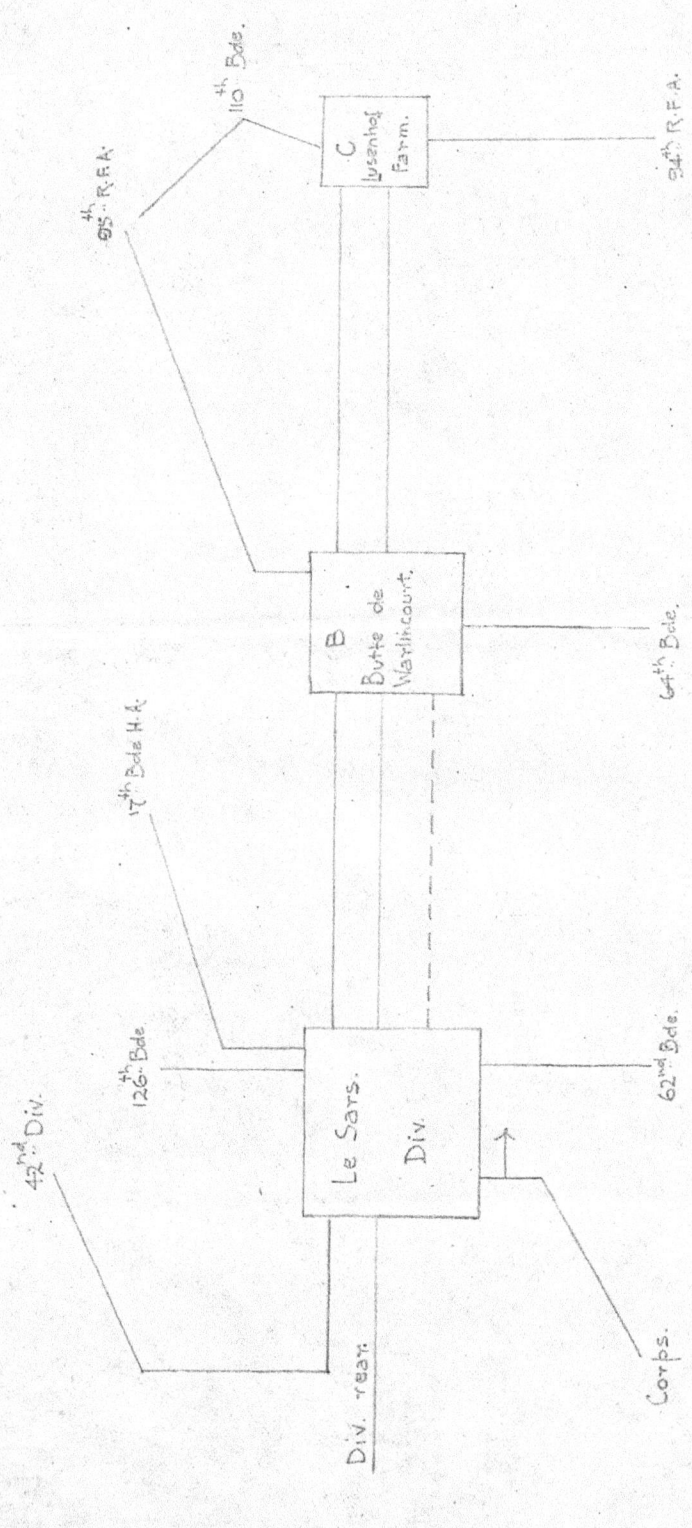

Army Form C. 2118.

WAR DIARY
or
INTELLIGENCE SUMMARY.

(Erase heading not required.)

Instructions regarding War Diaries and Intelligence Summaries are contained in F. S. Regs., Part II. and the Staff Manual respectively. Title pages will be prepared in manuscript.

Place	Date	Hour	Summary of Events and Information	Remarks and references to Appendices

Army Form C. 2118.

WAR DIARY
or
INTELLIGENCE SUMMARY.
(Erase heading not required.)

Place	Date	Hour	Summary of Events and Information	Remarks and references to Appendices

WAR DIARY or INTELLIGENCE SUMMARY

Army Form C. 2118.

21st Signal Coy R.E. (5)

September 1916

(Erase heading not required.)

Instructions regarding War Diaries and Intelligence Summaries are contained in F. S. Regs., Part II. and the Staff Manual respectively. Title pages will be prepared in manuscript.

Place	Date	Hour	Summary of Events and Information	Remarks and references to Appendices
	15/9/16		a direct line to Bde HQ exchange. 19th Brigade 33rd Division have a line to No 62nd Inf Bde exchange. 2 OR to hospital sick. 33rd Division opened cable work on entering cable station to II Corps. 110th Inf Bde has a line from its new post. 110th Inf Bde had a line from V Bde to 62 Inf Bde. 19th Division orders have to 98th 33rd Division orders have to 58th Inf Bde. 33 Div. orders.	Appendix VIII
	16/9/16		Their line and take over from others exchange. Two wires are late out from D. Centre to Railway cutting at H.23.a.6.11. Laid a line from 110th Inf Bde HQ. 2 OR killed, 3 OR wounded (2 depts) Bombs on Ninnsunk at 11 PM. D Depot to Lahone out (someone about) forward. O Depot Laid 2 lines.	
	17/9/16		98th Brigade joined forward. Moved W. to 33rd Division Z cable relaid. 33rd Division HQ to Bde HQ exchange - Ras N.28.F.8.9. The two lines on the new line to H.22.a.6.2 are out on account of Z cable. A cable from D Centre to Z centre Two OR slightly wounded from H.23.a.62 to D Batt HQ's at NR closed. Two OR slightly wounded on this line (carried in cart). Our only cable no line from Z Centre to the Lowne Bath. All Are laying a line to back from D Centre to HQ. Let us know to Foreshe Coy exchange at W.9.c. 47 Bde exchange.	

Instructions regarding War Diaries and Intelligence Summaries are contained in F. S. Regs., Part II. and the Staff Manual respectively. Title pages will be prepared in manuscript.

WAR DIARY
or
INTELLIGENCE SUMMARY.
(Erase heading not required.)

21st Signal Co R.E. (6)

September 1918

Army Form C. 2118.

Place	Date	Hour	Summary of Events and Information	Remarks and references to Appendices
			The Sig. Directing station is moved to C centre. Trench sets are erected at D centre and Z centre. 62nd and 19th Inf Bdes relieve one another. 64th Inf Bde move to W22 d and have a line to Z centre. BC 2 is joined through from B centre to C centre at 64th Inf Bde Hdqrs EQUANCOURT. 95th, 315th, 2nd NZ RFA Bdes lay lines to Z centre. 72nd & 94th RFA Bdes and 62nd 110th Inf Bdes move to D centre and connect [illegible] to Bde exchange at D centre. 37th and 17th [illegible] lay lateral lines to D centre. Main [illegible] of [illegible]	Appendix IX
	18/9/18		64 Inf Bde moved to near F centre. 110th Inf Bde moved to F centre + [illegible]. A Trench set is erected at F centre. A Loop set at F centre is in communication with 2 loop sets at W13 b and W21 c. A wireless receiving station is established at D centre in communication with transmitting station at V4 b, north of EQUANCOURT and with a Bde stn at F centre.	
	19/9/18		100th Inf Bde relieve 19th Inf Bde and come on to B centre. 19th and 98th Inf Bdes move to near C centre and have lines to C centre exchange. 72nd and 94th Bdes R.F.A. move to near F centre and have lines to [illegible] exchange. A third pair DZ 4 is laid between D centre and Z centre exchange. DZ 2 and DZ 3 are poled from D centre to Z centre. 62nd Inf Bde remain at D centre. 19th and 78th Inf Bdes move to F centre.	

D. D. & L., London, E.C.
(10340) Wt W5300/P713 750,000 5/18 E 2688 Forms/C2118/16.

WAR DIARY
INTELLIGENCE SUMMARY

Army Form C. 2118.

Place	Date	Hour	Summary of Events and Information	Remarks and references to Appendices
	20/9/18		[illegible] moved back to [illegible] to BF from [illegible] to [illegible] attached have been by 33rd Division Coy. See rendezvous and personnel [illegible] 10.B.N MQ Communication [illegible]. The Div'l Centre Bns over to 38 Div. Signal Engineers sent to arrange for a [illegible] Bn HQ. [illegible] and cable [illegible] from D. Centre taken on by Bde HQ [illegible] as follows: 1. LES BŒUFS - HQ and Sig. [illegible]. B2 Left at LE MESNIL and HQ Sig Bde at ÉTRICOURT. [illegible] in time to [illegible].	
	21/9/18		The Company [illegible] at LE MESNIL EN ARROUAISE	
	22/9/18			
	23/9/18		Bn L Sp Bde moved to NANANCOURT area and [illegible] 64 [illegible] and connected up by 7 pair heavy cables up to B HQ. A Bn at LECHELLE. Brick Stack also connected up to [illegible].	
	24/9/18	10.19	Lieut F. H. GREATREX to hospital wounded Gas. [illegible] about	
	25/9/18		[illegible] built up [illegible] 64 L Sp Bde at LECHELLE [illegible] received from B down the line to [illegible] by [illegible] and brickstack and forward to A in the forward exchange at WHC1 4. 62 Inf Bde now at WHC W3 C1 73 HQ. Lf Bde to WeB C1.15B [illegible] dropped 25 [illegible] not received to 110 Bde. 5 Div Arty 525 Artlly miles BOEUFS on WHC C12c [illegible] ten 170 [illegible] for 110 Bde from A to W [illegible] and MOB 1 [illegible] at LES BŒUFS or [illegible] no to B HQ + [illegible] Russ and at MANANCOURT Fwd [illegible] arranged at WHC 79 and B HQ at W B5	

Army Form C. 2118.

WAR DIARY
or
INTELLIGENCE SUMMARY.
(Erase heading not required.)

Place	Date	Hour	Summary of Events and Information	Remarks and references to Appendices

Strength of Company 12 Officers 312 OR 137 horses
                                    5 OR   2 Riding horses

Major RE
OC 21 Airline Coy RE

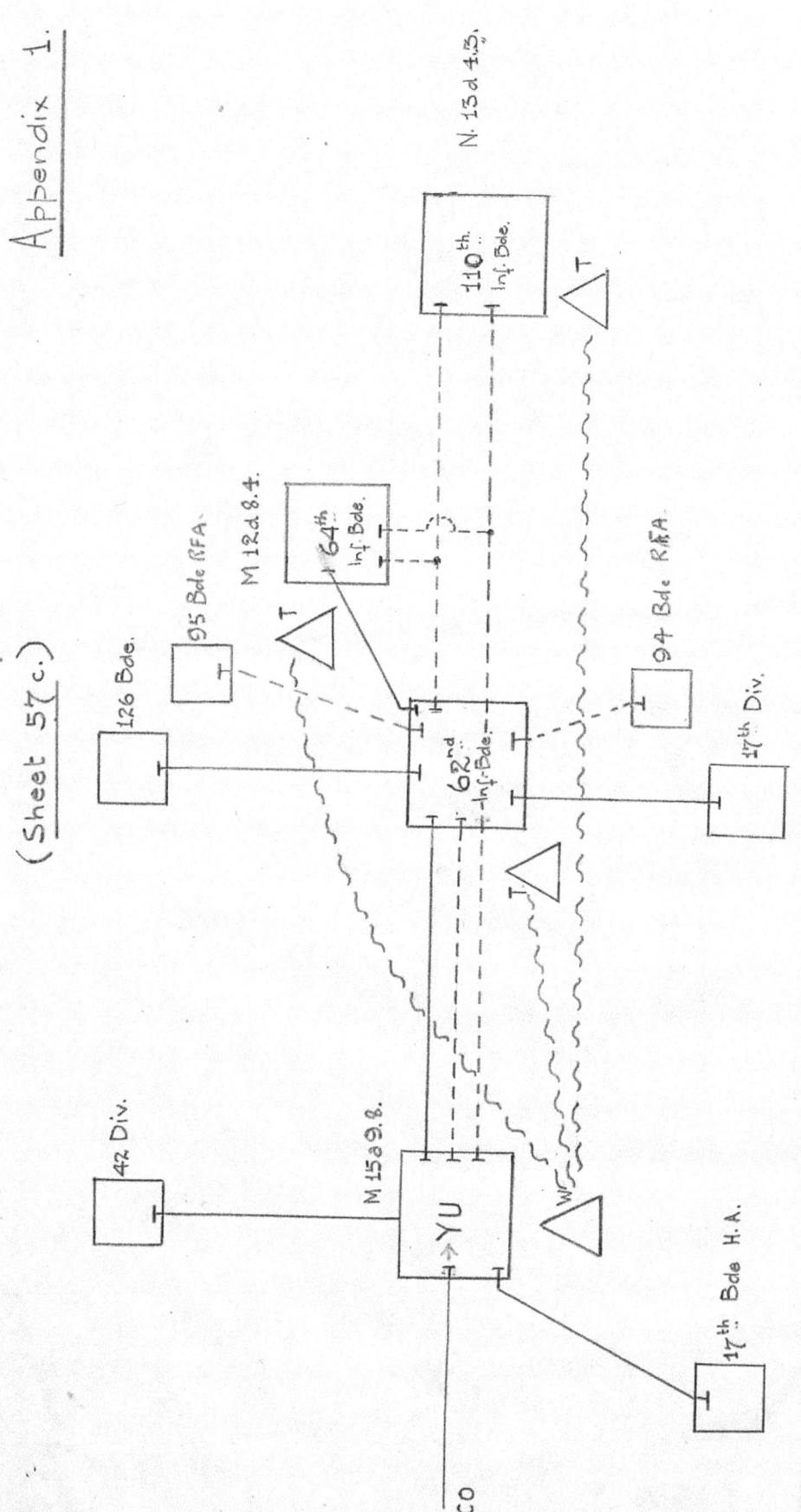

Appendix 1.
(Sheet 57 c.)
1st September 1918.

Appendix II

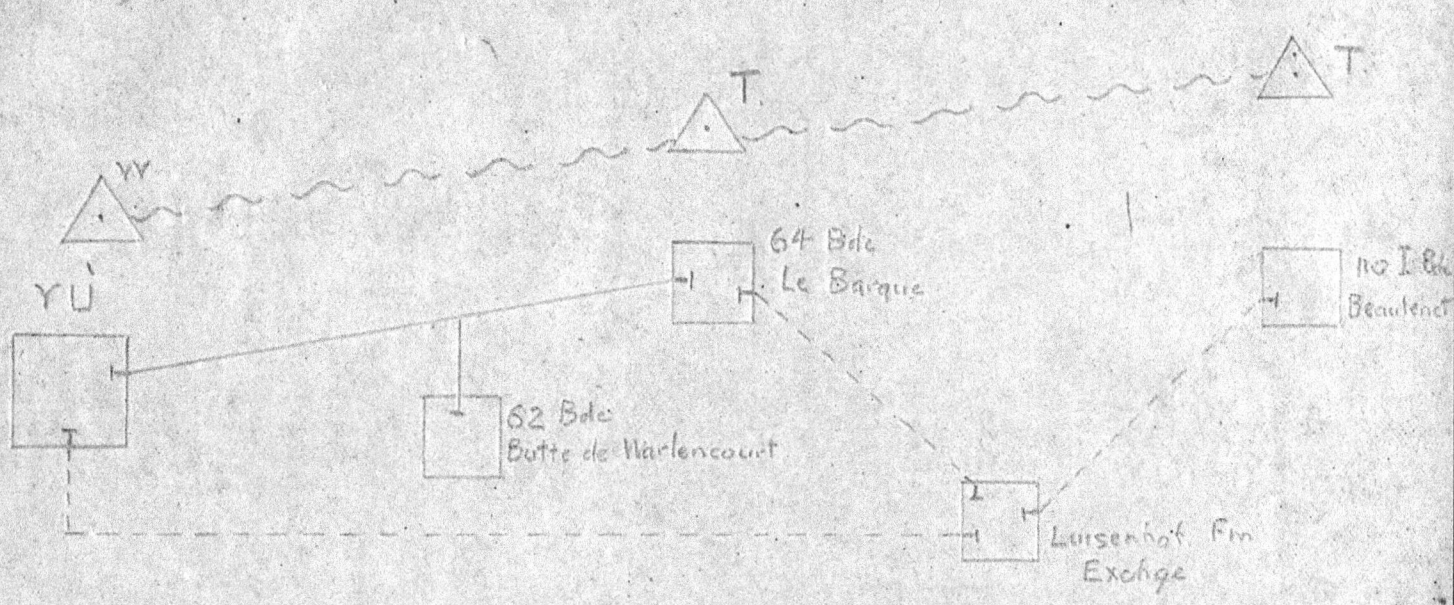

Communications 3-9-18.

Appendix III

Communications — Night 5-6/9/18.   After completion of relief of 38 Division

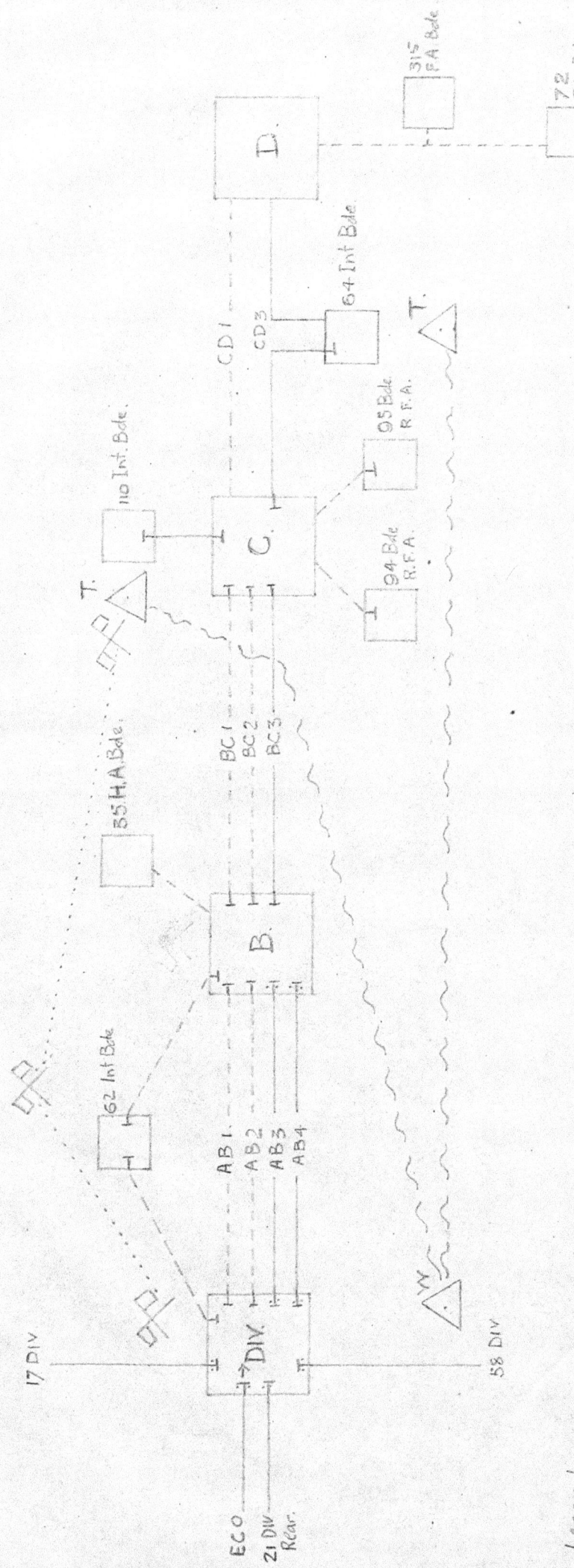

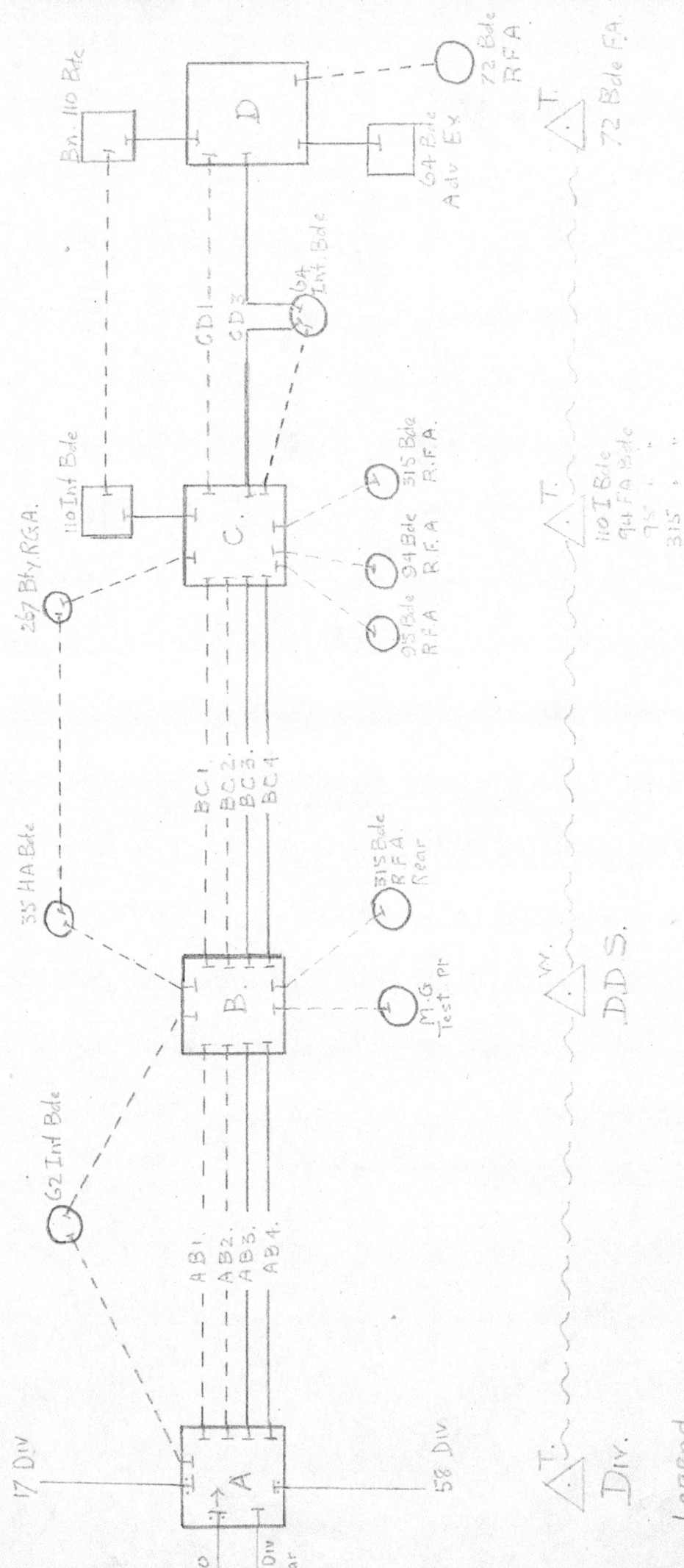

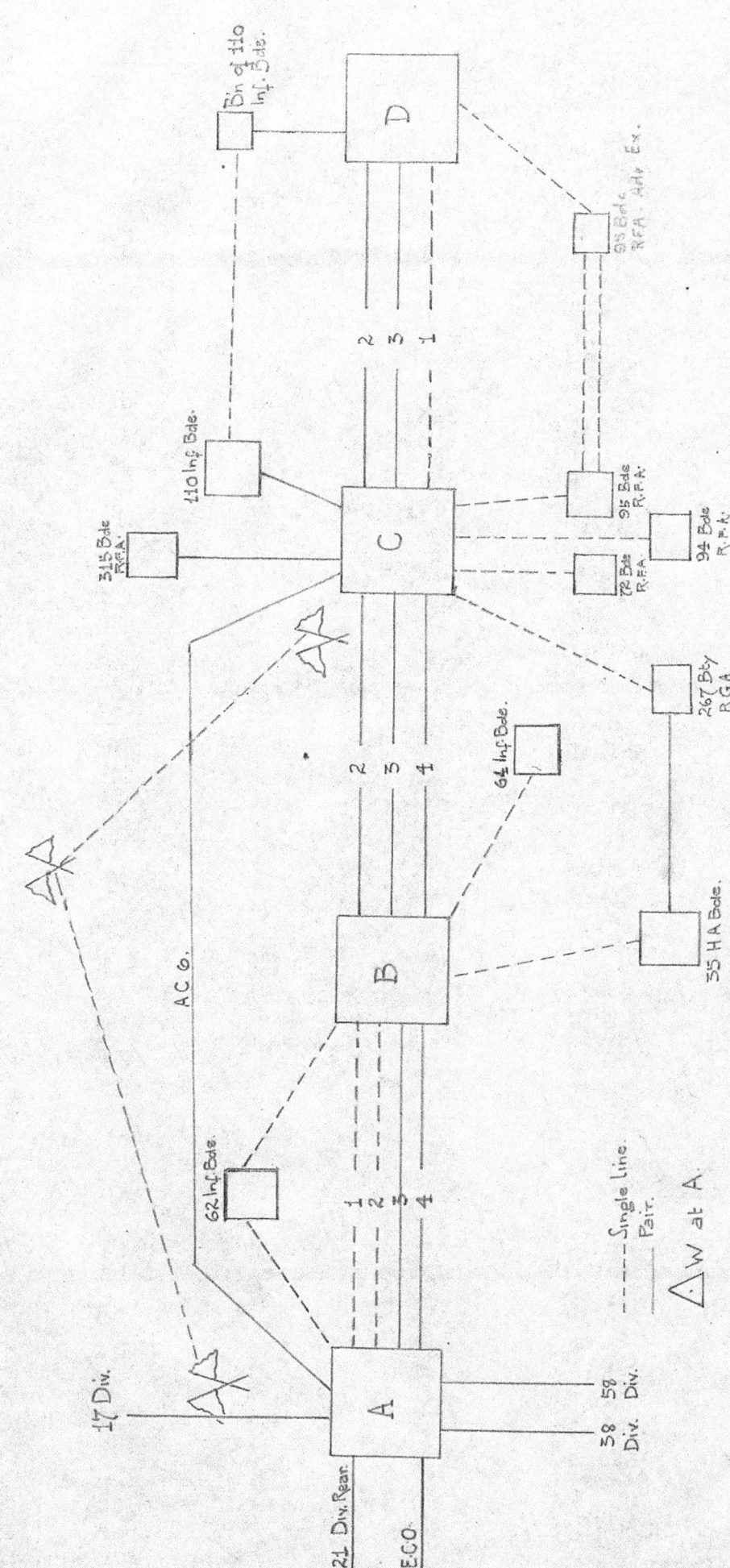

21st. Div'l Signal Coy, R.E.   Appendix VII

Trench Sets

△ T — R9 → ← — △ W — R9 → ← — △ T
Div H.Q.   "B" point   Front Bde
                Div. D.S.   and Art'y Bdes.

Loop Sets

△ L (Bde H.Q.) — R5 → ← R7 — △ L (1st Wilts Reg't)
     ↘ R9 ↔ △ L (6th Leicester Reg't) ↔ R9 ↗

13th Septem. 1918.

Communications. 14.9.18.   Appendix VIII.

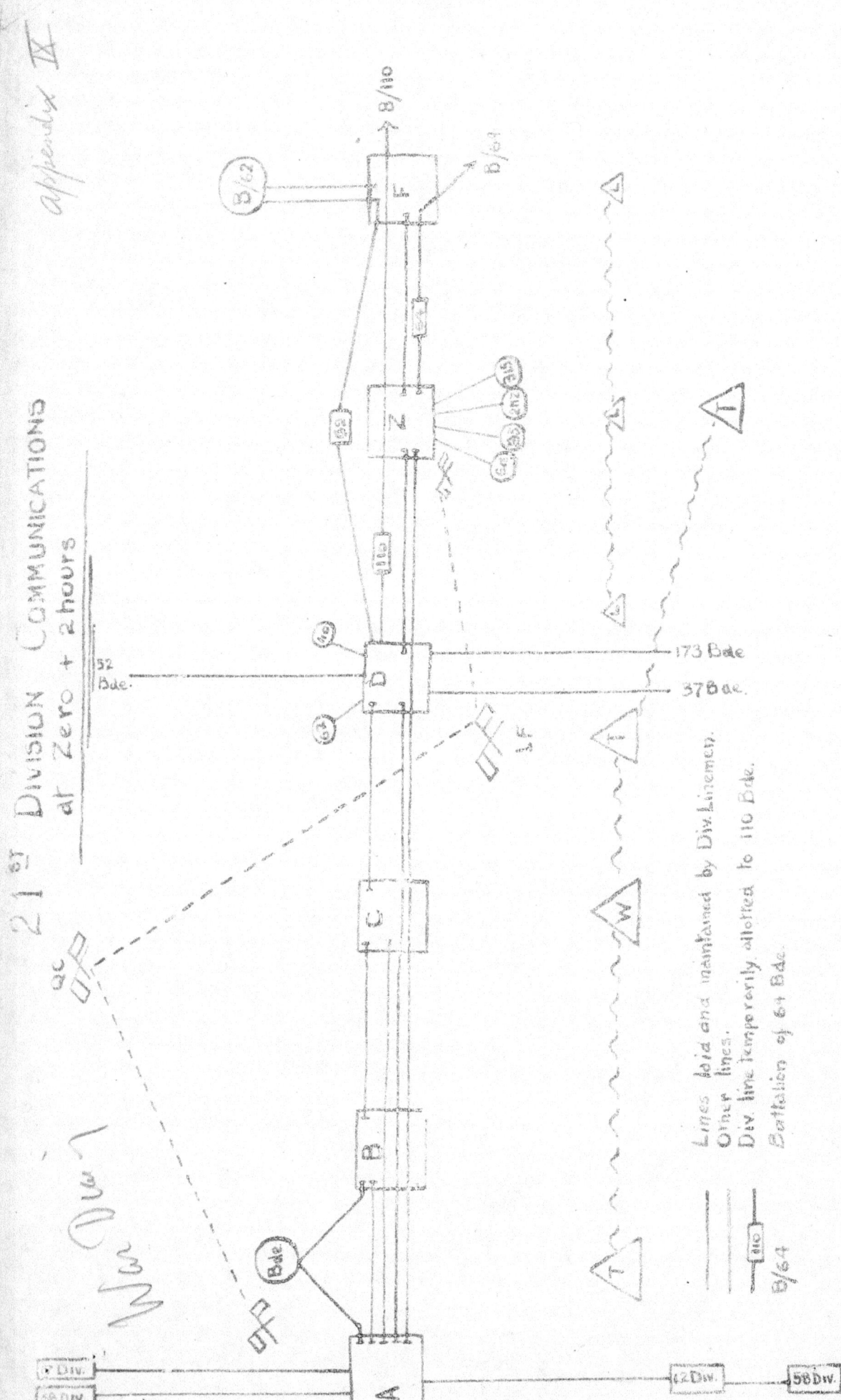

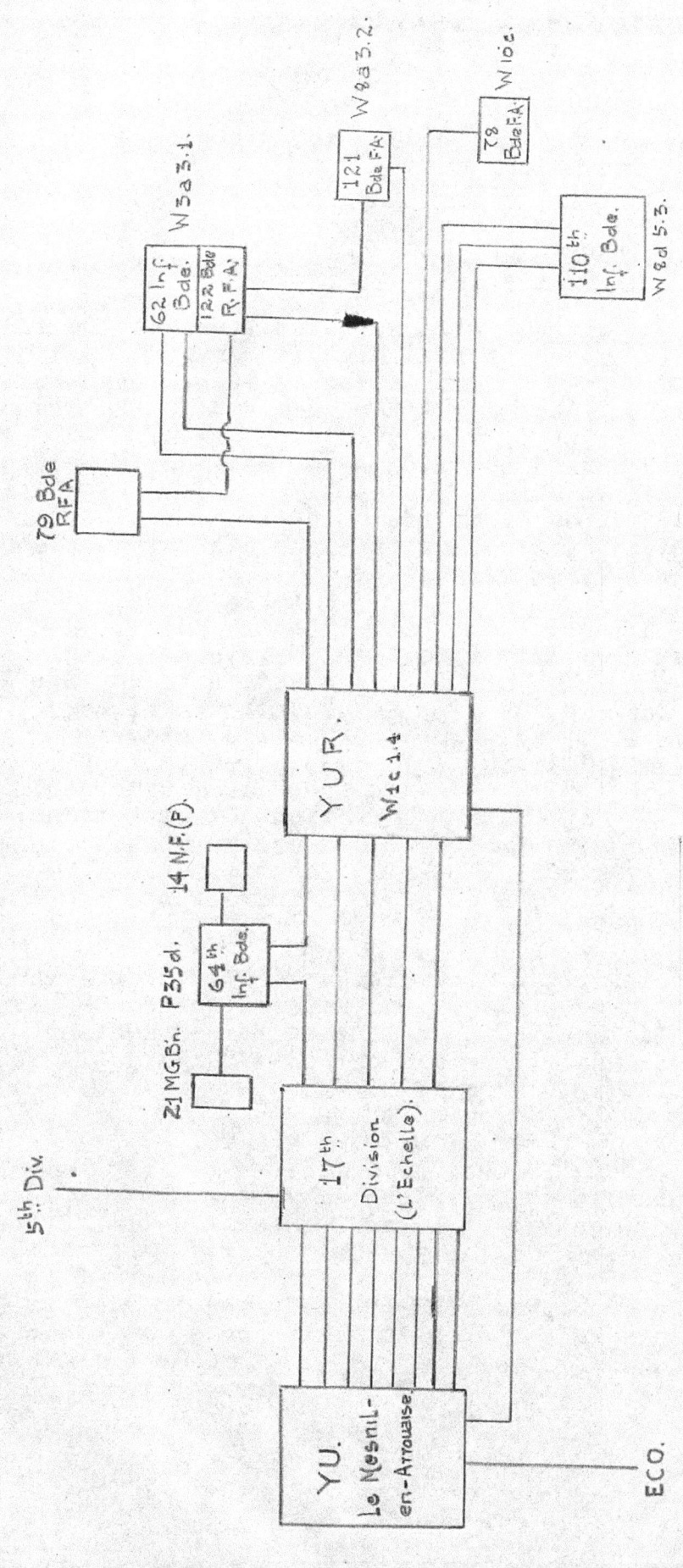

21st Divisonal Signal Orders for Divisional
Communications.

(Ref. 21st Divisonal O.O. No. 237).
Ref. Map 57c. S.E. 1/20000.

(1) <u>Communication Centres</u>. will be established at the following
YUR at W.1o13 manned by Div. Signals.
FB (62 Bde H.Q.) at W.3a40 manned by 62 Bde Signals.
LK (110 Bde H.Q.) at W?d52 manned by 110 Bde Signals till
  Bde moves forward, when by Div. Signals.
CH at W.18a40 manned by 110 Bde on arrival, if they go there
  instead of to CC.
CC at X.7c07 manned by 64 Bde on arrival.

(2) <u>Divisonal Lines</u>. The following lines are being arranged by
the Divisional Lines Officer.

YU - YUR.	5 cable pairs.
YUR to 62 H.Q. at	3 cable pairs.
(FB) 62 Bde H.Q. to 62 R.C.	1 pair and 1 single in addition to any Bde lines.
YUR to 110 Bde H.Q. at	3 cable pairs.
LK (110) Bde H.Q.) to CH.	3 cable pairs.
LK (110 Bde H.Q.) to CC.	2 buried cable pairs if possible, with cable extensions at either end.
CH to CC.	3 cable pairs.
YUR to each Arty Bde.	1 cable pair.
LK (110 Bde H.Q.) to M.G. Coys at W.9c73.	1 cable pair.

(3) <u>Lateral Lines</u>.
(a) The 33rd Division are arranging a Divisional lateral
to YU, and, if possible, a Bde lateral to CC.
(b) The 62 Bde are laying a line to Bde on left at Q.26b76.
(c) The Divisional Lines Officer is arranging the following
Divisional laterals from YU to YE.
                from YU to YER.
                from YU to YE via YQ.
Bde lateral from 110 Bde to 62 Bde.
Arty Bde laterals between each Arty Bde.
He will also arrange with the Officer i/c D.A. Signals
to connect up to FB exchange the two Arty Bdes which move
forward.
The complete communications are as shewn in diagram 1; the
Lines Officer will dispose his linemen to maintain the
above keeping sufficient personnel at CC to extend at least
one Div. pair if Bdes move forward from there.

(4) **Divisional Wireless.**
  (a) The D.S. (H.Q. basic call) is at YUK.
  (b) A trench set (basic call no. 2) is at 62 Bde H.Q. The 62 Bde will erect this set at their report centre when they move there.
  (c) A trench set (basic call no. 3) is at 110 Bde H.Q. This will not move with 110 Bde.
  (d) A trench set (basic call no. 4) will be in the dug-out at CC by mid-day on 27.9.18. 64 Bde will erect this immediately on their arrival.
  (e) The D.S. and H.Q. visual station will be connected to YU by a specialline to be laid by the visual party under instructions from the Lines Officer.

(5) **Divisional Visual.**
  (a) The Divisional Terminal station (call DV) is established at V.12b19.
  (b) The 62 and 110 Bdes will arrange to obtain visual communication with DV by 9.0. pm reporting by visual to Division that they have done so. They will maintain continuous watch until they obtain permission from Division to close down.
  (c) All Arty Bdes will arrange to obtain visual communication with D.V. by midnight, reporting by visual to Division directly they have done so. They will only man visual when their main Divl. line fails.
  (d) When 110th Inf. Bde. moves forward, a visual station (Call C.H.) in communication with D.V. will be established on CHAPEL HILL. The Brigade will report to Division by visual directly communication has been established. Messages to and from 64th Inf. Bde. will be received and sent by this Station.

(6) **Traffic.**
  (a) While lines permit the allotment of lines for the three phases will be as shown on diagrams 2 and 3.
  (b) During phase 1, the 78th and 121st Artillery Bdes. will attach orderlies to the 110th Inf. Bde. for the delivery of messages in accordance with technical Instructions para A.5. Messages to 79th and 122nd Arty. Bdes. will be dealt with over the telephone.
  (c) During phases 2 and 3, all four Arty. Bdes. will attach orderlies to the 62nd Inf. Bde. if they are manning a fullerphone at the H.Q. in W.3.a.4.0. If fullerphone is at the report centre, messages will be dealt with by telephone direct.

- 3 -

(d) All Priority messages to Arty. Bdes. will be dealt with by telephone direct to the H.Q.

(e) During phase 1, the M.G.Coys. in W.9.c.7.3 will attach an orderly to 110th Inf. Bde. for messages. When the 110th Inf. Bde. moves forward, messages to these Coys. will be dealt with direct over the telephone.

(f) During phase 1, a D.R. from Division will be posted at 62nd Inf. Bde. Rear H.Q. for the delivery of messages to the report centre if lines fail.

(g) Officers or N.C.Os will be detailed by all Signal Offices in accordance with para A.7 of Technical Instrns.

(h) Visual will be used as much as possible to relieve traffic. Wireless will only be used for important messages so as to avoid jamming other Divisions.

(i) Attention is called to paras E.1 and F.8 of Technical Instructions.

(j) One pair to the 5th Division will be super-imposed for sounder.

(k) Messages for Q.Rear and C.R.E. will be by telephone to the 17th Division exchange at LE MESNIL and by orderly from there.

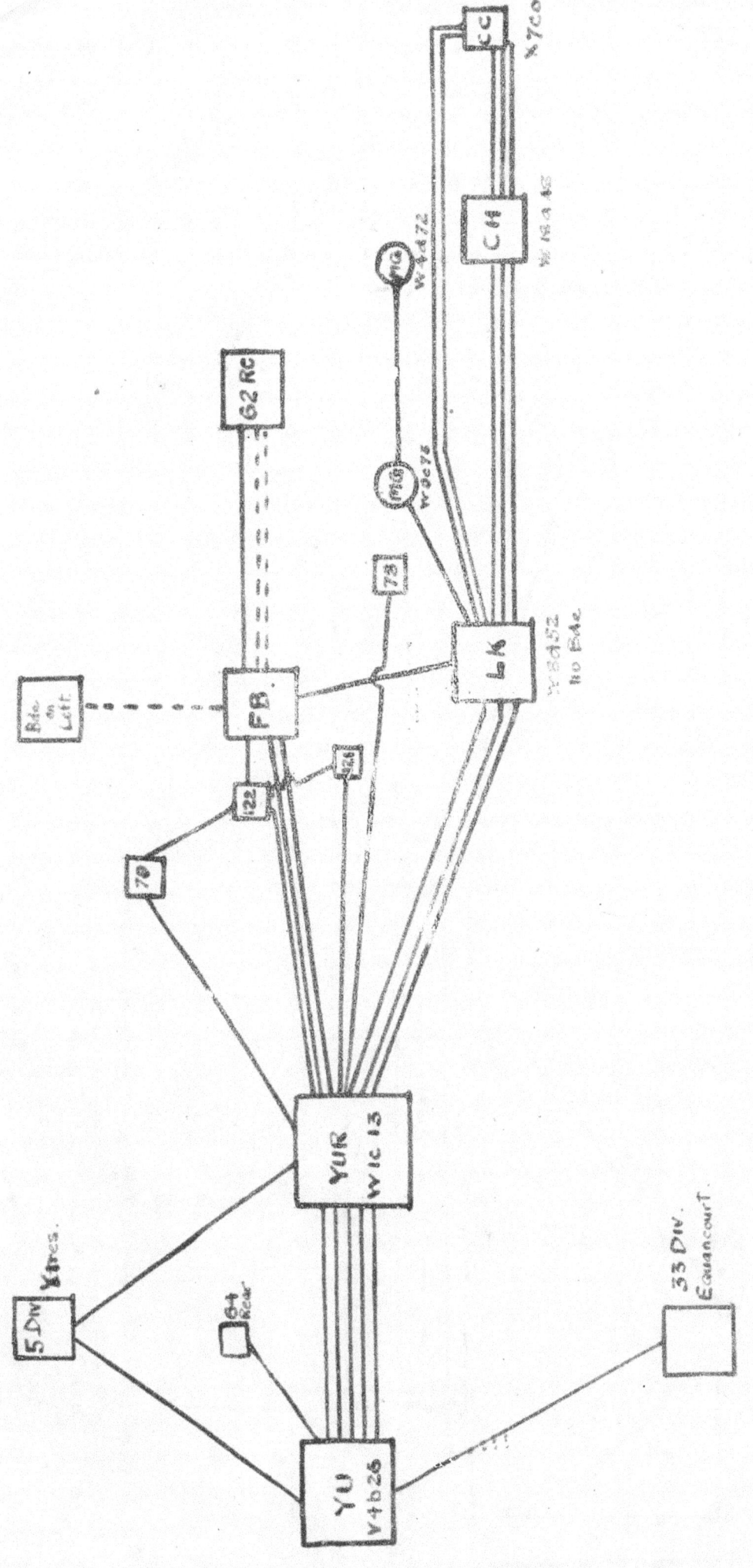

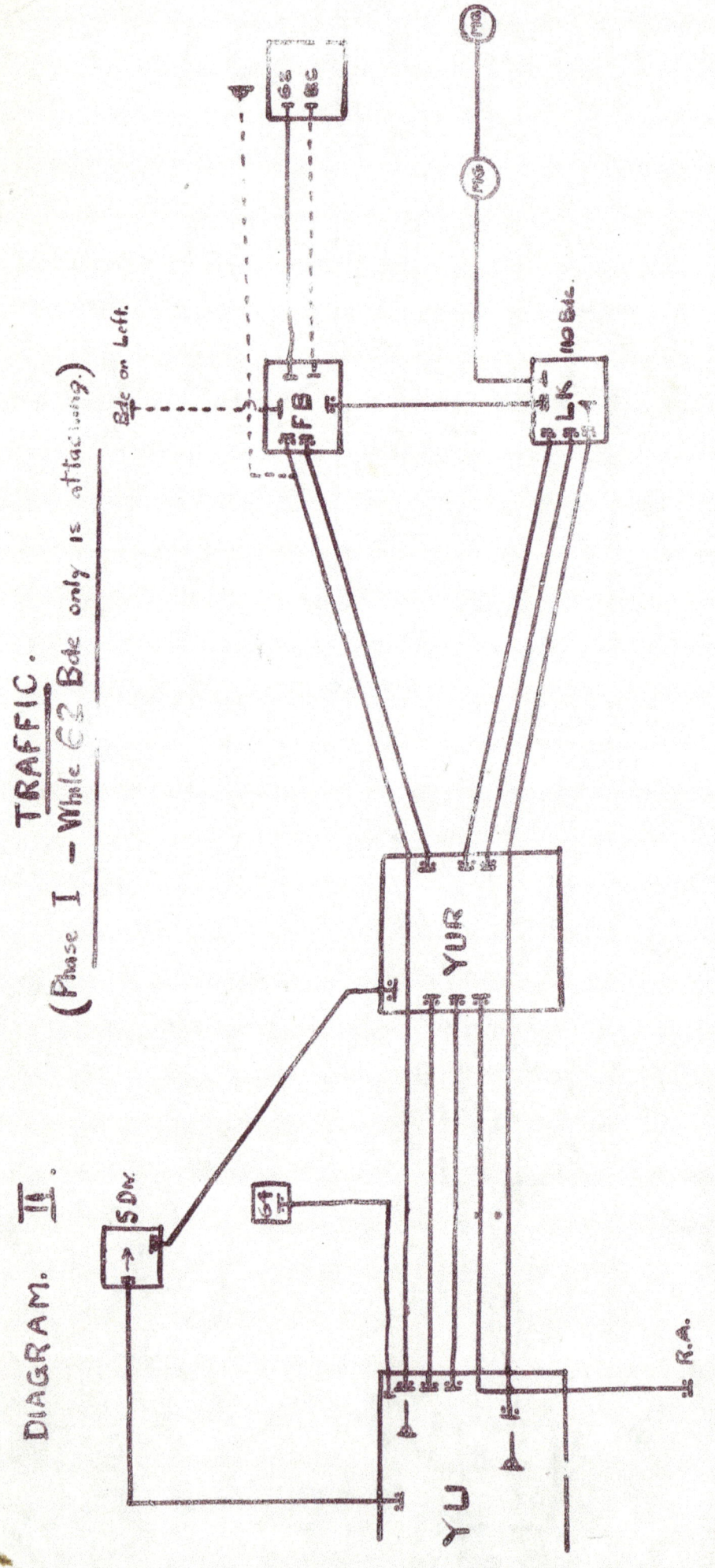

CONFIDENTIAL.

WAR DIARY

21st Divl. Signal Coy., R.E.

October 1st - 31st 1918.

Army Form C. 2118.

WAR DIARY
or
INTELLIGENCE SUMMARY.
(Erase heading not required.)

① 2 Signal C.R.E.

October 1918

Instructions regarding War Diaries and Intelligence Summaries are contained in F. S. Regs., Part II. and the Staff Manual respectively. Title pages will be prepared in manuscript.

Place	Date	Hour	Summary of Events and Information	Remarks and references to Appendices
EQUANCOURT	1/10		Dispositions of Brigade as follows – 110th in Army res at GOUZEAUCOURT, 62nd at Chapel Crossing and S.62d N. of Ry stn at GOUZEAUCOURT. Line communication in Army appears 1. Visual station at Windmill N. of REVELON FARM. Comm established with all Infantry and H.Q. Bdes. WT Dets at REVELON. BF at 62⅔, T 110th Bde, Loop set at 110th Bde. HQ	Appdx. 1
	2/10		S.Balm HQ x 2B.SW in 62nd Bde closes at Chapel Crossing and reopens W11a. 3 new pairs opd. but Bde closes at Chapel Crossing and reopens W11a. Three pairs are picked up on OEd5 Armed cable route W.11.a to QUENTIN Redoubt and extends to the Army Exchange (QY) all new pairs are led into 62nd Bde Sig Off. Preparatory moves of 2nd Signal Off. by 62nd Bde Hdqrs on pair into B.SW ✓ one pair to L.K. ✓ on pair to QY. Telephones working from B.SW to 62nd Bde.	
	3/10		Cable frame established in the of the cable frame from A L.K. Return. Leeds from 62nd Bde to 336 Div as Cept BF not at 62nd Bde changes to erected at D2 Bde RCA on R21.C.	
	4/10		62nd Bde moves back from R.21.A.9.7 to N.3.a.3.1. Direct Pair run through LK exchange. WT Loop set at 110th Bde. 2nd 110 moves to GONNELIEU.	
			1 Perm of 1 Lance Corp reinforcement posted from Signal Depot.	
REVELON W11a.5.8	5/10		Bde HQ moves to REVELON with 62 Bde at Quarry (or to QY exchange) 110 Bde and 62 Bde in Tione. Army Exchange which is now opened at HINDENBURG Line. Army offensive are cable from in the Area F.M. HINDENBURG Line.	Appdx 2

WAR DIARY or INTELLIGENCE SUMMARY

Army Form C. 2118.

(3) 2nd Signal Coy RE
October 1917

Place	Date	Hour	Summary of Events and Information	Remarks and references to Appendices
	5-6/10		Rain fell the whole day over air POWER frequent as established between Bde. Artillery Bde. & Divn. Stations in WHA and 62nd and 61st Bde. Bowers wanting & unstable are obtained through TC exchange. WT RF at 122 Bde & FA was unstable and Telephone to 62nd Bde at times to the Army. GOUZEAUCOURT Turner Gate for 110th Bde. to 64 Bde. and M32 and laid line to 6 GRATTS	
	6/10		One cable waggon proceeded to 64 Bde. for new exchange or reinforcing a divisional (HQ) PANCHE FARM, 64 Bde. Bde. for TC to HL on New Centrales 6 GRATTS. Second pair in use for 64 Bde. closed down at HL at 9.20 & meeting PANCHE FARM (GP), 64 Bde. closed down at TC at 9.30h and opened at Al 62.3 to GP, 110th Bde. closed down at OY. Gu 4 Bde RFA annex to through HL and 5 99 L Bde Bde remained at OY Gu 4 Bde RFA GP. GP a nuisance. RFA through GP. GP a nuisance at true to be by the above lines Sound sounds worked to PortBle the following were improved to 64th Bde owing to line being damaged by transport to 64th Bde and 76 64 Bde and creates at BLOTTE PANCHE FARM WT BE Set sent to 64 Bde and creates at BLOTTE PANCHE FARM D.S. moved 16 M32 L 9.1. Loop not working at 64 PANCHE M 35E 5.5 to Batn 110 at S56 9.9	
	7/10		Line improved and full phase working to 64 by the 62nd Bde closed down at OY and opened in vicinity of the exchange line laid to 133 Div. (Left) from HL. Branches also formed to the 37th Div.	

WAR DIARY
INTELLIGENCE SUMMARY

(3) 2nd Signal Coy. NE

October 1918

Army Form C. 2118.

Place	Date	Hour	Summary of Events and Information	Remarks and references to Appendices
	7/10		Corps Cav. ev. rct. HL. from where he had extended preparations to move G.H.Q. by Bde move to S52 c95. 110 & Bde go up and move HQ to GP. Somewhere working to HL. for artillery and some work of HQ established at G+ Bde HQ Bn running to G+ & HQ Bde. WT. BF. ad erected at G+ Bd. HQ. Bn at bde at places at G+ Bd. HQ and 13 d. D.29 (S.6.p.75) and at 110 Bde and 30 Bd. M2 c.70 30 Bd expanses.	
M32 c.l.3	8/10		Bn. HQ. moved to HL evening (CM326) Bn to Corps HQ are line. and all Bn and Arty Bde 30 Bd by GP Two lines to fm GP to fm GP to fm Appendix. 62nd Bde. moved to B.P. 110 Bd moves to MONTECOURSZ FM platine Km GP III	Appendix
			WT. BF. 01 moved up. HARDICOURT FM at 0900 km Fm 62 Bd about HQ Looks at at 62 bp Bde established.	
	9/10		M. Bn. Travelled forward. Plan of dummy early morning. Bn runs planned as follows rising to 62 Bd moves to MALINCOURT etc. to N24 d 1.6.1 WT Loops at all outputs are formed.	
WALINCOURT	10/10		Bn HQ. move to G. WALINCOURT line to 62nd Bn to 5th by MALINCOURT and to 110th Bde in CAULLERY at S line to CP. and at SELVIGNY	
	11/10		Work on ebaney of working to transport and works the by to factory.	
	15/10		6+ Inf Bde moves to MONTIGNY with lines on to 19th Div at on surface. C+D cable attached lines to NOYY and bg on.	
	19/10		Preparation for operations at NEUVILLY (ND) Personnel formed escape area.
	20/10		line from the MS SR at NEUVILLY (ND) Personnel formed escape area. L. NOVY

WAR DIARY
of 21st Signal Coys (?)
INTELLIGENCE SUMMARY.

(Erase heading not required.)

Army Form C. 2118.

October 1918

Place	Date	Hour	Summary of Events and Information	Remarks and references to Appendices
INCHY	21/10		Div HQ moves to INCHY. Forms Skel Bank concentrates at NEUVILLY. Line held by C detachment from NV to 37th Div (Reps) Colo Sn at BRIASTRE. 17th Div offshoots via Sig Bde. Right Div (32-2) long line to INCHY. 110th Bde move from CAULLERY to INCHY. 62nd outside Bde also move to INCHY. 62nd and 110th Bde on telephone but Bde move to NEUVILLY. All artillery Bde come in NV exchge. Sounds to NV and other attacks from all units to NEUVILLY. W/T DS erected at NEUVILLY. BF est at Bde HQ INCHY and with Brigade at AMBRUM and V.G.	Line
NEUVILLY	22/10 23/10		Div HQ moves to NEUVILLY. Three poles are laid out from NV and exchange establish NE of AMBRUM (NV). IV experiments sounds to 1 AM. 62 Rf Bde close at INCHY and move forward 1 AM. As above progress Infy and Arty Bde move forward and in obtain through AM exchge Onderbn are attached. In delivery of messages. Three lines are laid from AM and exchange is temporary established about 500 yd West of UCN&EGIES CHAU. Later Div excge (VG) is moved into Chateau. Sounds superimposed to VG. Toward evening all arty Bde and 62 and 110 Ry Bde move to OUILLERS and AM exchge is moved there to suit convenience of Bde. However oderlies are attached to Bde Office, 10 AM and to VG but have little work. Hd and the WT DS moves to OUILLERS. BF est at Div HQ (NV) and 3 Ry Bde at V.G.	Appendix IV

WAR DIARY
or
INTELLIGENCE SUMMARY.
(Erase heading not required.)

Army Form C. 2118.

(3) 21st Divn C60 R.E.

October 1918.

Place	Date	Hour	Summary of Events and Information	Remarks and references to Appendices
	24/10		Three pairs are laid from VG to POIX DU NORD (PX) and centre exchange is established. Sounder working to PX. 6s. Bde close OUVILLERS and is obtained. Pair PX. 6s Hy Bde close at VG and also come on at PX. 110th Bde move to VG. R.F. Sub with Hy Bde at VENDEGIES and POIX	
OUVILLERS	25/10		Divn HQ moves to OUVILLERS. Regtl centre is opened at 8.28 & 4.? Only 78th Arty Bde comes on this exchange. Line laid to this on Regtl 110th Bde move from VENDEGIES to POIX DU NORD. WT DS moves to POIX with R.F. Sub at OUVILLERS and with Hy Bde ready to move forward. Loops are allotted to each Arty Bde.	
NEUILLY	26/10		Divn HQ moves to NEUILLY. 6s Bde move to VENDEGIES. 94 K Bde move to CLARY, 64th Bde to INCHY. 110th to OUVILLERS. All Bde in telephone. All WT station withdrawn to NEUILLY.	Appendix I
	27/10		Div takes over from 17th Div. Call 6s & 110th Hy Bde to POIX and 5th to VENDEGIES Communication at NEUILLY. 2nd WSn Section in operation. Hwe lines Brgt ... direct to 6s Bde from Div and on to 64 & R.PX. Other units on this exchange are put in to 64 Bde. Auto exchange is also opened at OUVILLERS for Div Arty who have moves here. Pairs opened & found working with line to 64 - 110s Bde and 2 Arty Bde. WT DS exch at OUVILLERS with BF gets at Br 110 and 3 at Hy Bde. Loop set at Regtl Bde 110 and 3rd Bn Battn at POIX	Appendix II

WAR DIARY
INTELLIGENCE SUMMARY

Army Form C. 2118.

(2) 21 August 1915
08/16 No 6/9

Place	Date	Hour	Summary of Events and Information	Remarks and references to Appendices
OVILLERS	30/10/16		Bin HQ. move to OVILLERS. Strength of Company 12 Officers 296 OR. 19 OR to hospital during month. (Bombers in action 13 are OK) 1 OR killed in action. 9 reinforcements joined company.	

J.W. Walker
Major RE
O/C 2nd August C.R.E.

Appendix I

Diagram of Forward lines 1-10-78.

- TC
- KC — 79 Bde FA.
  - 122 Bde FA.
  - 78 " FA.
- 62 Bde
  - D/21 inf.
  - C/21 inf.
- QY 110 Bde — A/21 M.C.
  - 79 Bde FA
  - Bn
- CC 64 Bde — B/21 M.C.
- LK

Appendix II

Communications. 5-10-18.

```
                                    ┌──────────┐
                                    │  64 I.Bde│
                                    └──────────┘
                                         │  ┌──────────┐
                                         │  │  78 Bde. │
                                         │  │   RFA    │
                                         │  └──────────┘
                                         │ /
                                    ┌─────────┐
                                    │   TC    │
                                    │110 Inf Bde│
                                    └─────────┘
                                         │       ┌──────────┐
                                         │       │  79 Bde. │
                                         │       │   RFA    │
                                         │       └──────────┘
                                         │
                   C & D Coys            │
                   21 MG Bn              │
                         \    21 MG Bn   │
                          \     │        │
                    ┌─────────┐
                    │   QY    │
                    │62 Inf Bde│
                    └─────────┘
                         │
                         │
              ┌─────┐
              │ YU  │
              └─────┘
                 │
                 │──── 17 Div
                 
   21 Div Rear
   33 Div
   5 Div
   Corps HA
   DADOS
   TRAIN.
```

Appendix III

DIVISIONAL COMMUNICATIONS AFTER 8·0 AM 8/10/18.

Ardissart Farm
N. 26 d.

[A.F.]

Gratte
Panche Farm
M 35 A.

[G.P.] — 62 Inf Bde.
110 Inf Bde.

9.5 FA, 9.4 FA, 9.1 FA, C? FA

64 Inf Bde

CVS — M 36 c.

Visual at AF only manned on arrival of 62 Bde. and if lines fail. CVS visual station can deliver to Gratte Panche Farm or 64 Bde. in case of emergency.

[Div.] — 37 Div, 38 Div, M.G. Battn, Corps.

DV.
AF.

⚐W Wireless Station.
⚑ Visual Station.

Appendix IV

Line Communications 22-10-18

```
37 Div ──┐
         ├──┐
5 Div ───┘  │
            ├──── 37 Div Adv ──┐
            │                   ├──┬── N Y ──┬── 94 Bde RFA
            │                   │   │        ├── 95 Bde RFA
            │                   │   │        ├── 79 Bde RFA
            │                   │   │        ├── 110 I. Bde
            │                   │   │        ├── D.A.C / Bde Adv
            │                   │   │        └── 64 I. Bde
            │                   │   │
50 Bde ──┐  │                   │   │
         ├──┘                   │   │
17 Div ──┘                      │   │
                                │   │
                                └── Y U ──┬── 62 I. Bde
                                          └── B.M. RA
```

Appendix V

Communications 26-10-18

```
                                    [LT]   X 28 b 47.
                                     |
                                     | PX LT 1.
                                     |
                                    [PX]   F 3a 91.
                                    /|\
                                   / | \
                              VG PX 1 do 2 do 3
                                   \ | /
                                    \|/
                                    [YG]   F 13a 8·6
                                    /|\
                                   / | \
                              AM VG 1 do 2 do 3
                                   \ | /
                                    \|/
   37 Div ───────────────────────── [AM] ───────────────── 38 Div
                                      \— CRA
                                     /|
                                    / |
                                21 Div
                                V. Corps
```

△ N

△ T

Appendix VI

Line Communications. 29-10-18.

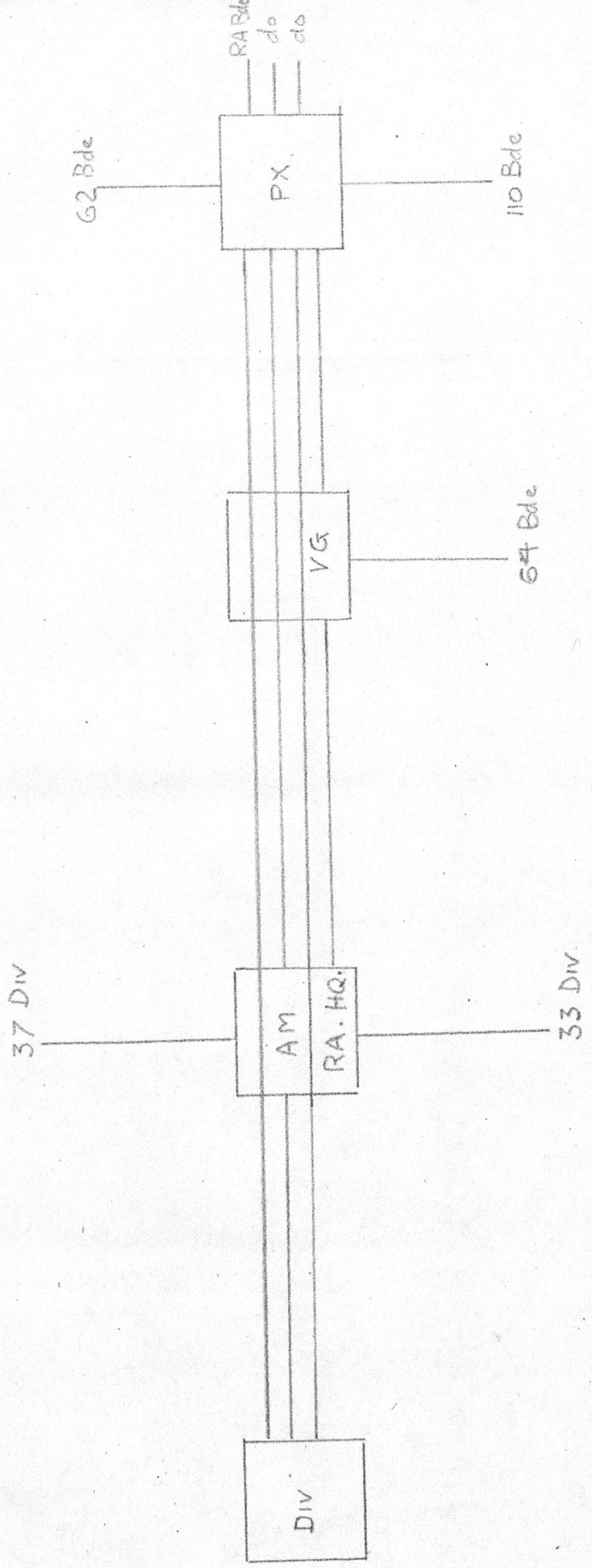

CONFIDENTIAL.

WAR DIARY

OF

21st Divl. Signal Company., R.E.

FROM:- 1st November 1918.   TO:- 30th November 1918.

Army Form C. 2118.

WAR DIARY
INTELLIGENCE SUMMARY.
(Erase heading not required.)

Instructions regarding War Diaries and Intelligence Summaries are contained in F. S. Regs., Part II. and the Staff Manual respectively. Title pages will be prepared in manuscript.

21st Divl Signal Coy. R/6
November 1918

Place	Date	Hour	Summary of Events and Information	Remarks and references to Appendices
OVILLERS	1/11/18	—	Divnl line and sounder to front bg Jde. Divnl line from CRA to PX (forced back) for all army Jdes. See Diagram A.	
NEUVILLY	2/11/18	15.30	Moved from OVILLERS to NEUVILLY. Line to Corps, to br Jde in NEUVILLY, to 110 Jdn at OVILLERS and to br Jde at VENDIGIES through 17 Divn in OVILLERS and 50 Jde in VENDIGIES. Bre cable Sector A & B. thence in OVILLERS.	
POIX DU NORD	4/11/18	15.00	Moved from NEUVILLY to POIX DU NORD. Infantry going through 17 Divn on morning of 5th. Two hours construction from POIX DU NORD to FUTOY. Exchange established there (FT). Three pairs bus from FUTOY to INSTITUTE FORESTER. (IF) See Diagram B.	
		13.00	and endorfm established there at 19.00 hrs.	
		20.00	br Jde move to VENDIGIES	
		15.00	110 " " " FUTOY.	
		10.00	" " " F&a. 5.5.	
S.24d 3.3.	5/11/18		Moved to S.24d 3.3 (IF) Divn move to FUTOY. opens there for one hour, then move to INSTITUTE FORESTER (IF) and at 10.00 hrs to TETE NOIRE (TN). 62 and 110 Jdes and	
		8.30	br Jde there to IF. Three hours air construction IF to TN and all Army Jdes move to TN. See diagram C.	
	6/11/18	07.30	Exchange established that am 8.00 hrs. 110 Jde move to U 20c 2.7. and to BERLAIMONT (B6) and exchange established at 07.30 hrs. Two cable pairs are laid to BERLAIMONT.	
BERLAIMONT.	7/11/18	10.00	Divn. move to BERLAIMONT. Office opens at MARCHIDIE. Line laid to ET. ETREE, 110 Jde at ET. One pair tension from MARCHIDIE, Lun Cable line to ET, 62 Jde home to BERLAIMONT. Two buzzer lines in front of ET for br Jde.	

WAR DIARY
INTELLIGENCE SUMMARY

Army Form C. 2118.

21st Divl Signal Coy R.E.
November 1918
Sheet 2.

Place	Date	Hour	Summary of Events and Information	Remarks and references to Appendices
	9/11/18	10.0.0	62 Bde. move to AMERIES.	
	11/11/18		7) Div. takes over on morning of 9th. Div. Rec. at Mal. V 2 w c 3.9.	
	12/11/18	11.00	Div Std. move to AVLNOYE.	
AVLNOYE	13/11/18	11.00	62 Bde move to BACHANT.	
		13	39/15 Durango Signal Coy at AVLNOYE. Issuing clothing slips, signing cards etc. Kelsey Mr Sergeant Century 18 B/Melts Bore OR, to Joseph during travel (All Said.) 1 in check of wounds. 30 …… yesterdays 15 general Company.	

[signature] Capt RE
O/C 21 Signal Coy RE.

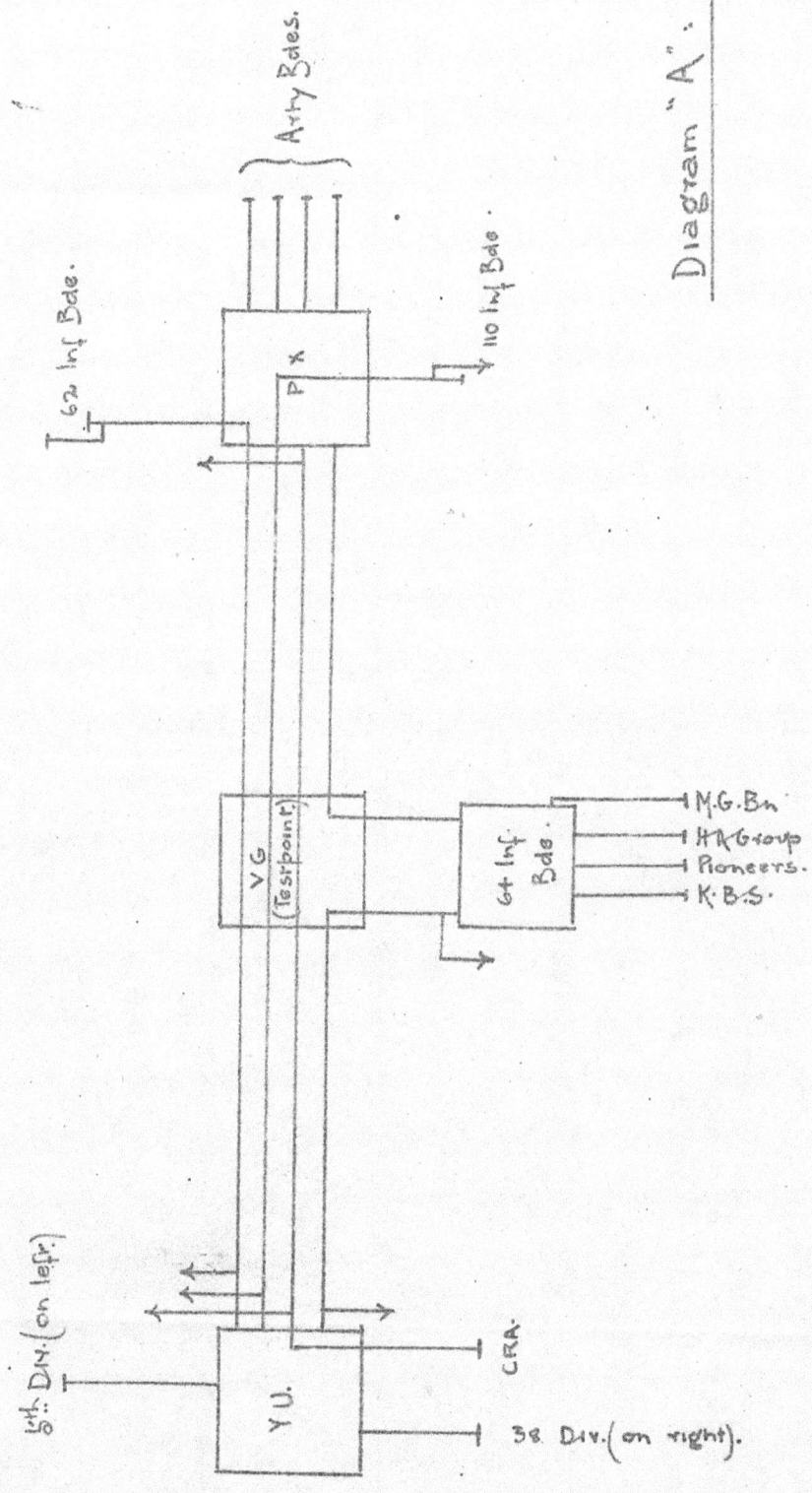

21st. Signal Coy, R.E.

Lines at Lero, 5th. Novem 1918.

```
17th Dn.
   |
 [17th Bde.]
   |
   |                    Arty Bdes.
 5th Dn. (on left)       ↓
   |                   ||||
  [DG]─────────────────[ FT ]───── 17 Bde RGA.
                        │  │  ───── 62 Bde.
                        │  │  ───── 64 Bde.
                        │  │  ───── 110 Bde.
                        │  │
                     [ YU ]
                        │
                     [ IE ]
```

Diagram 'B'.

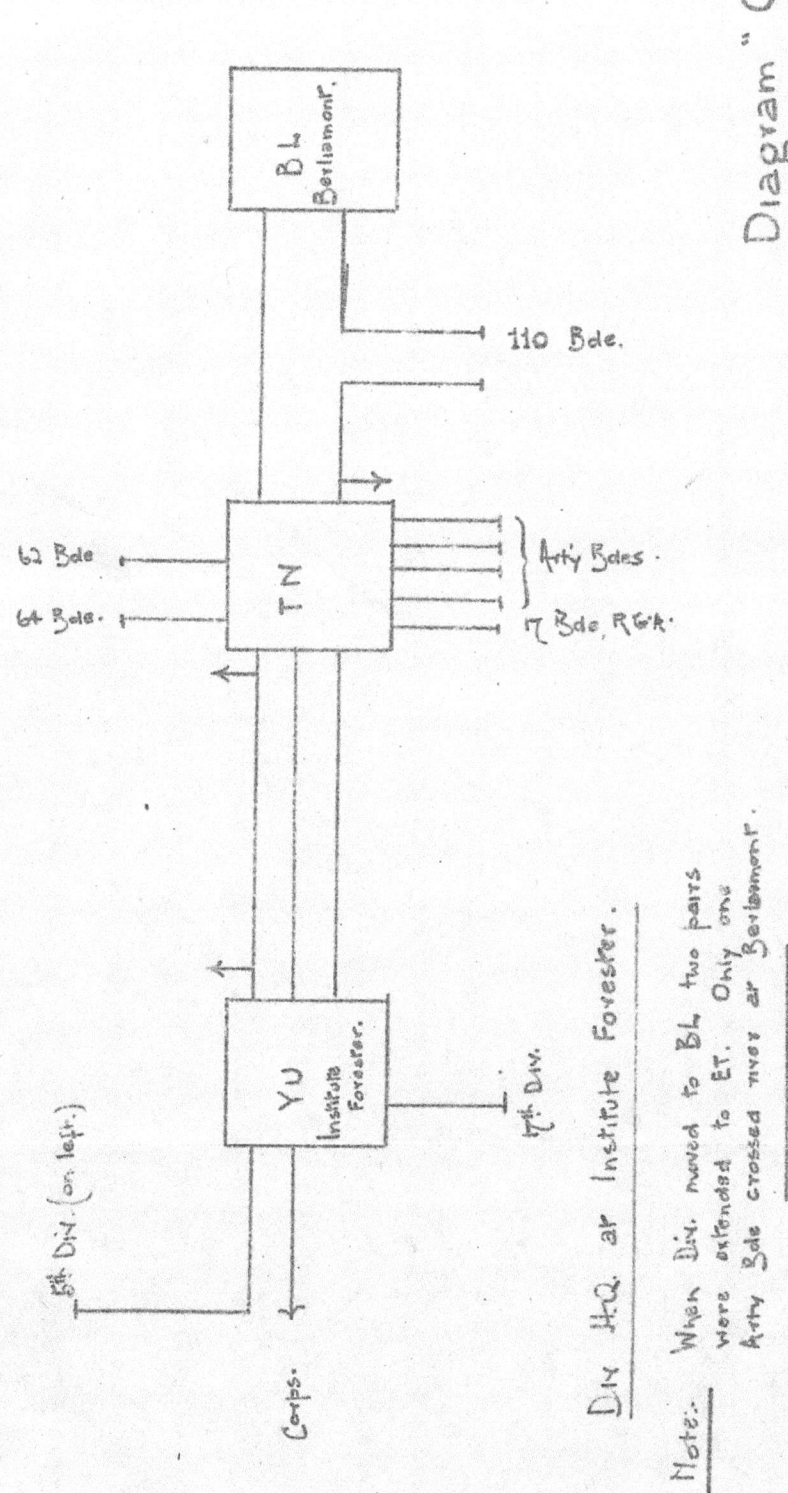

CONFIDENTIAL.

WAR DIARY

OF

21st Divl. Signal Company., R.E.

FROM:- 1st December 1918.   TO:- 31st December 1918.

Army Form C. 2118.

WAR DIARY

21st Divl Signal Cy. V6

INTELLIGENCE SUMMARY.

December 1918.

(Erase heading not required.)

Instructions regarding War Diaries and Intelligence Summaries are contained in F. S. Regs., Part II. and the Staff Manual respectively. Title pages will be prepared in manuscript.

Place	Date	Hour	Summary of Events and Information	Remarks and references to Appendices
AULNOYE	2/12		1 Officer and 2 O.R. to hospital sick.	
	7/12		2 O.R. rejoined from hospital. Lieut A.J. Dockrill left for UK for duty	
	8/12		9 O.R. joined from Signal Depot. 1 Cable Section left by march route attached to 17th Divn and proceeded to the CAVILLON Area	
	9/12		2 O.R. to hospital, sick	
	13/12	10.30	Div HqArts closed BERLAIMONT and opened VENDEGIES. The Company, less M.T. Signal Office personnel proceeded by road to OVILLERS attached to 6th Brigade Group.	
INCHY	14/12	10.00	Div HQ opened INCHY. The company, less M.T. Signal Office personnel proceeded from OVILLERS to INCHY	
	15/12	05.30	Div Brigades closed VENDEGIES and opened PISSI on arrival	
		10.00	Brigades closed BERLAIMONT and opened INCHY. Mounted personnel, less those required for Signal Office at INCHY proceed by bus to MOLLIENS-VIDAME and Signal Office opened at latter place. Horse transport of the Company, less one Cable Section proceeded by march route to bd Bde Group, with transport of by Bde Group to MOLLIENS-VIDAME	

WAR DIARY
INTELLIGENCE SUMMARY.

(Erase heading not required.)

Army Form C. 2118.

21st Div'l Signal Coy R.E.

December 1918.

Place	Date	Hour	Summary of Events and Information	Remarks and references to Appendices
INCHY	17/12	05.00	No Brigade closed INCHY, and opened BOVELLES on arrival.	
		04.30	64 " " " ENGLEFONTAINE.	
	19/12	11.00	62 Brigade opened INCHY.	
MOLLIENS-VIDAME	19/12	10.00	Div'l HQ closed INCHY and opened MOLLIENS-VIDAME same hour. 62 Brigade closed INCHY and opened CAVILLON on arrival. 9 O.R. joined from Signal Depot. Horse transport arrive MOLLIENS-VIDAME. Communications of the Division in the CAVILLON area as in Appendix.	
	22/12		2 O.R. joined from Signal Depot.	
	26/12		5 O.R. transferred to Army Reserve on (Calamets?)	
	27/12		30 attached infantry (Power Buzzer Pool) regained their Units.	
	31/12		10 Officers 284 O.R. deducted 2 Officers 30 O.R. 17 O.R. to Hosp. 5 O.R. during month. 9 O.R. left for sick for demobilisation.	

J.H. Hellat
Major R.E.
O.C. 21st Signal Coy R.E.

21st (DIVISIONAL) SIGNAL COMPANY.

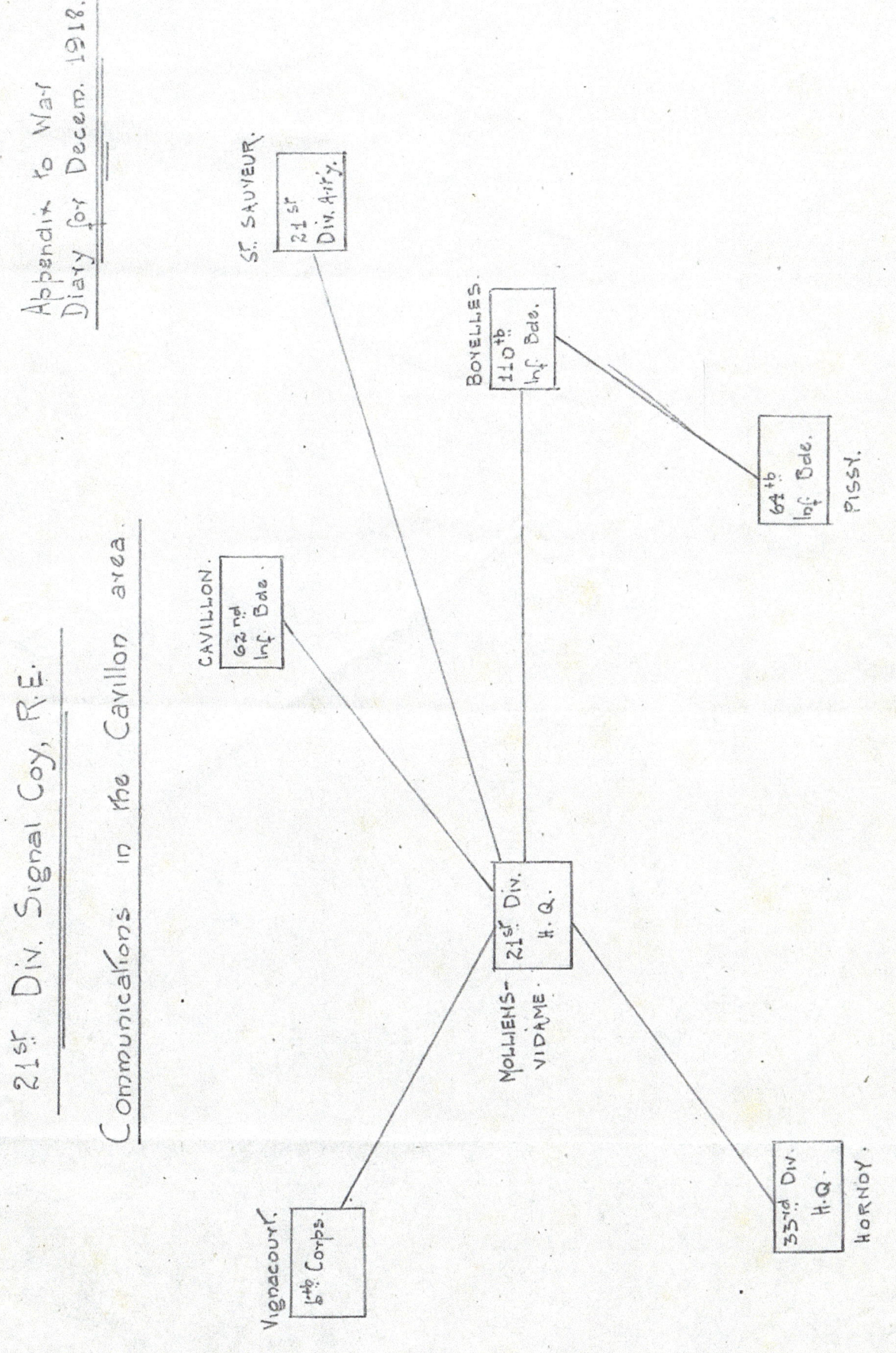

CONFIDENTIAL.

WAR DIARY.

OF

21st Divisional Signal Company., R.E.

FROM:- 1st January 1919.   TO:- 31st January 1919.

Army Form C. 2118.

21st Divisional Signal Coy R.E.

WAR DIARY
INTELLIGENCE SUMMARY
(Erase heading not required.)

January 1919.

Instructions regarding War Diaries and Intelligence Summaries are contained in F.S. Regs., Part II. and the Staff Manual respectively. Title pages will be prepared in manuscript.

Place	Date	Hour	Summary of Events and Information	Remarks and references to Appendices
NOMENY - VIDAYE	1/1/19	—	No change in locations of Div H.Q. or H.Q.'s of Sections and sub-sections during the month of January 1919. The Communications existing throughout the month are as shown in appendix 1.	
	2/1	—	1 O.R. rejoined from hospital	
	5/1	—	1 " joined from Signal Depot	
	7/1	—	1 Offr & 1 O.R. joined from 30 Army Signal Coy.	
	8/1	—	O.R. admitted to hospital	
	9/1	—	1 " " "	
	10/1	—	1 O.R. joined from Signal Depot	
	11/1	—	1 " left for demobilization	
	12/1	—	1 " admitted to hospital	
	13/1	—	2 " left for demobilization	
	14/1	—	2 " " " "	
	15/1	—	2 " " " "	
	16/1	—	1 " rejoined from hospital	
	17/1	—	1 " left for demobilization	
			1 " admitted to hospital	

WAR DIARY
INTELLIGENCE SUMMARY

Army Form C. 2118.

21st Divisional Signal Coy. R.E.

January 1919.

Place	Date	Hour	Summary of Events and Information	Remarks and references to Appendices
MOLLIENS-VIDAME.	20/1/19	—	1 Offr. & 10 O.R. left for demobilisation	
	24/1	—	70 O.R. left for demobilisation	
		—	1 Offr. left for Clacton (Course of Instruction) (O.C. Coy) (Capt. A.P. Ritchie acting O.C. from 24/1 – 31/1/19)	
		—	1 O.R. admitted to hospital	
	26/1	—	1 Jones from Signal Depot	
	27/1	—	2 left for demobilisation	
	29/1	—	2 admitted to hospital	
	30/1	—	8 obtained demobilisation A/c on leave to UK	
		—	3 Re-engaged under A.O. IV of 1918.	
		—	Strength of Company attached to march. 9 Offrs. 238 O.R.	
		—	Deficient 3 " 79 "	

21st (DIVISIONAL)
SIGNAL COMPANY.
2956.
8 Feby/19

A.P. Ritchie Major R.E.
O.C. 21 Signal Coy.

21st Div'l Signal Company, R.E.

Communications January, 1919

Appendix 1

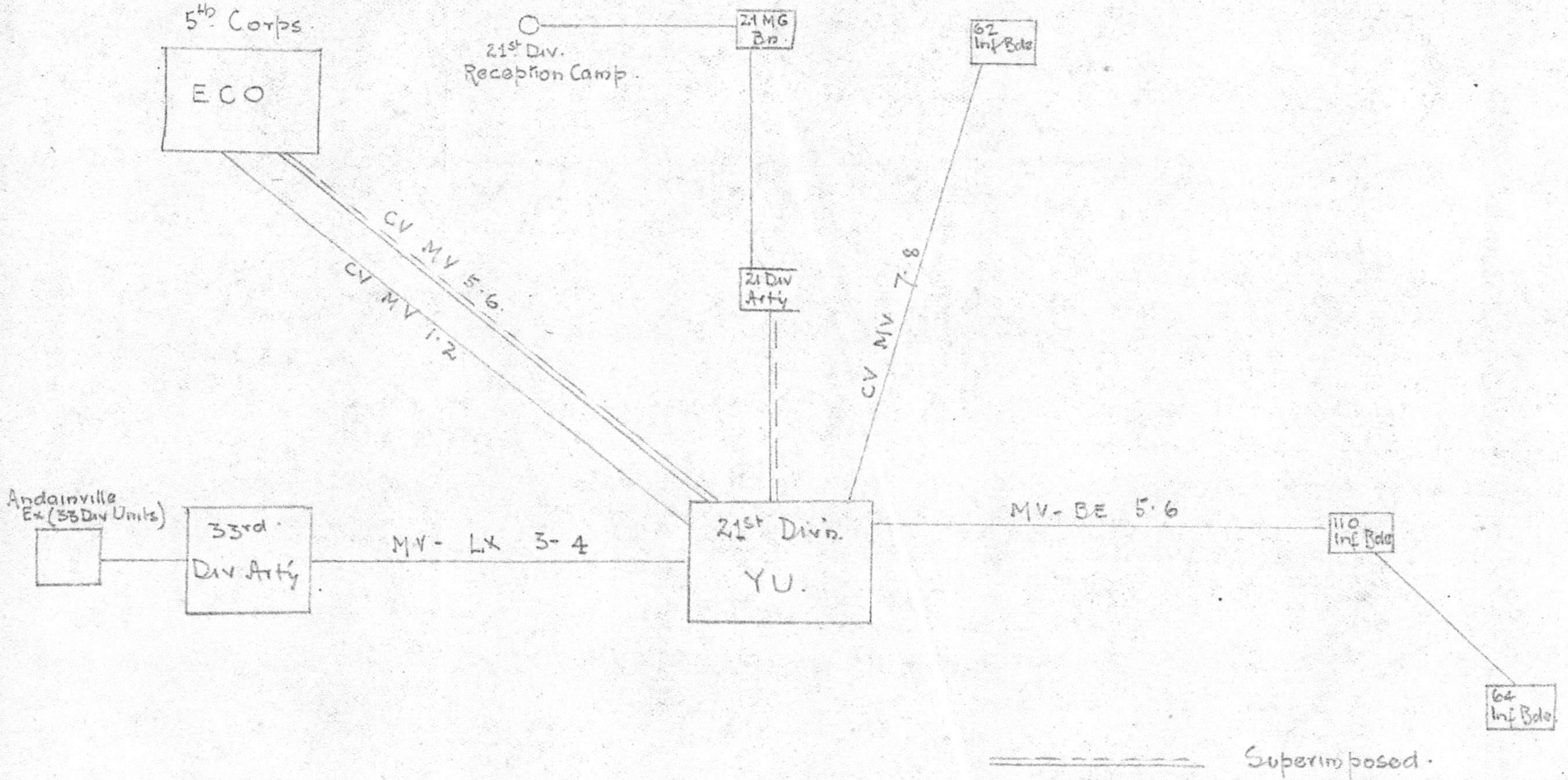

5th Corps.
ECO
21st Div.
Reception Camp.
21 MG Bn.
62 Inf Bde
21 Div Arty
CV MV 5·6.
CV MV 1·2
CV MV 7·8
Andainville
Ex (33 Div Units)
33rd Div Arty
MV - LX 3- 4
21st Divn.
YU.
MV - BE 5·6
110 Inf Bde
64 Inf Bde
Superimposed.

CONFIDENTIAL.
****

WAR DIARY

OF

21st Divl. Signal Coy. R.E.

FROM:- 1st February 1919.   TO:- 28th February, 1919.

Army Form C. 2118.

WAR DIARY
INTELLIGENCE SUMMARY

(Erase heading not required.)

21st Divisional Signal Coy R.E.
February 1919

Instructions regarding War Diaries and Intelligence Summaries are contained in F. S. Regs., Part II. and the Staff Manual respectively. Title pages will be prepared in manuscript.

Place	Date	Hour	Summary of Events and Information	Remarks and references to Appendices
MOLLIENS-VIDAME	1/2/19	—	No change in location of Div. N.Q. or H.Qrs. of Section and Sub-Sections during the month of February 1919. The communications existing throughout the month are as shewn on Appendix I.	
	2/2	—	1 Officer & 1 O.R. rejis. to III Corps Signal Coy.	
	4/2	—	1 O.R. reported from "O" Corps Signal Coy on completion of Electric Wiring Course.	
	4/2	—	Major A.B. Rice-Jones D.S.O, R.E. T.C. posted from 2nd Army Signal School to Command the Unit	
	5/2	—	1 O.R. rejoined from 2nd Army Signal School	
	5/2	—	2 O.R. admitted to Hospital	
	8/2	—	1 O.R. rejoined from -do-	
	12/2	—	1 O.R. admitted to Hospital	
	13/2	—	3 O.R. rejoined from -do-	
	13/2	—	1 O.R. admitted to Hospital	
	17/2	—	1 O.R. rejoined from -do-	
	20/2	—	2 O.R. rejoined from Casualty Coy at LE HAVRE	
	20/2	—	6 O.R. admitted to Hospital	
	24/2	—	Transferred from 38 Division Signal Coy R.E.	
	24/2	—	1 O.R. left for Company ascoris dr. to 517 Bn Signal Coy	
		—	1 Sgt & 1 2nd Cpl. left for 4th Army Signal Coy.	
		—	2 O.R. left for 2nd Army Signal Coy.	
		—	1 O.R. awarded the Military Medal (Late Despatch)	
	23/2	—	1 O.R. left for 4th Army Signal Coy.	
	25/2	—	1 Sgt & 1 O.R. Admitted to Hospital	

Army Form C. 2118.

21st Labour Company R.E.
February 1919.

WAR DIARY
INTELLIGENCE SUMMARY
(Erase heading not required.)

Instructions regarding War Diaries and Intelligence Summaries are contained in F. S. Regs., Part II. and the Staff Manual respectively. Title pages will be prepared in manuscript.

Place	Date	Hour	Summary of Events and Information	Remarks and references to Appendices
MOLLIENS— VIDAME	February 1919	—	2 Sgts & 12 OR unemployed during the month. 11 Riding & 25 Draught Horses disposed of during the month. Strength of Company at end of month:— 8 Offrs. 200 OR 95 " Deposit 4 "	

A.E. Rice ?
Major R.E.
O.C. 21 Labour Coy R.E.

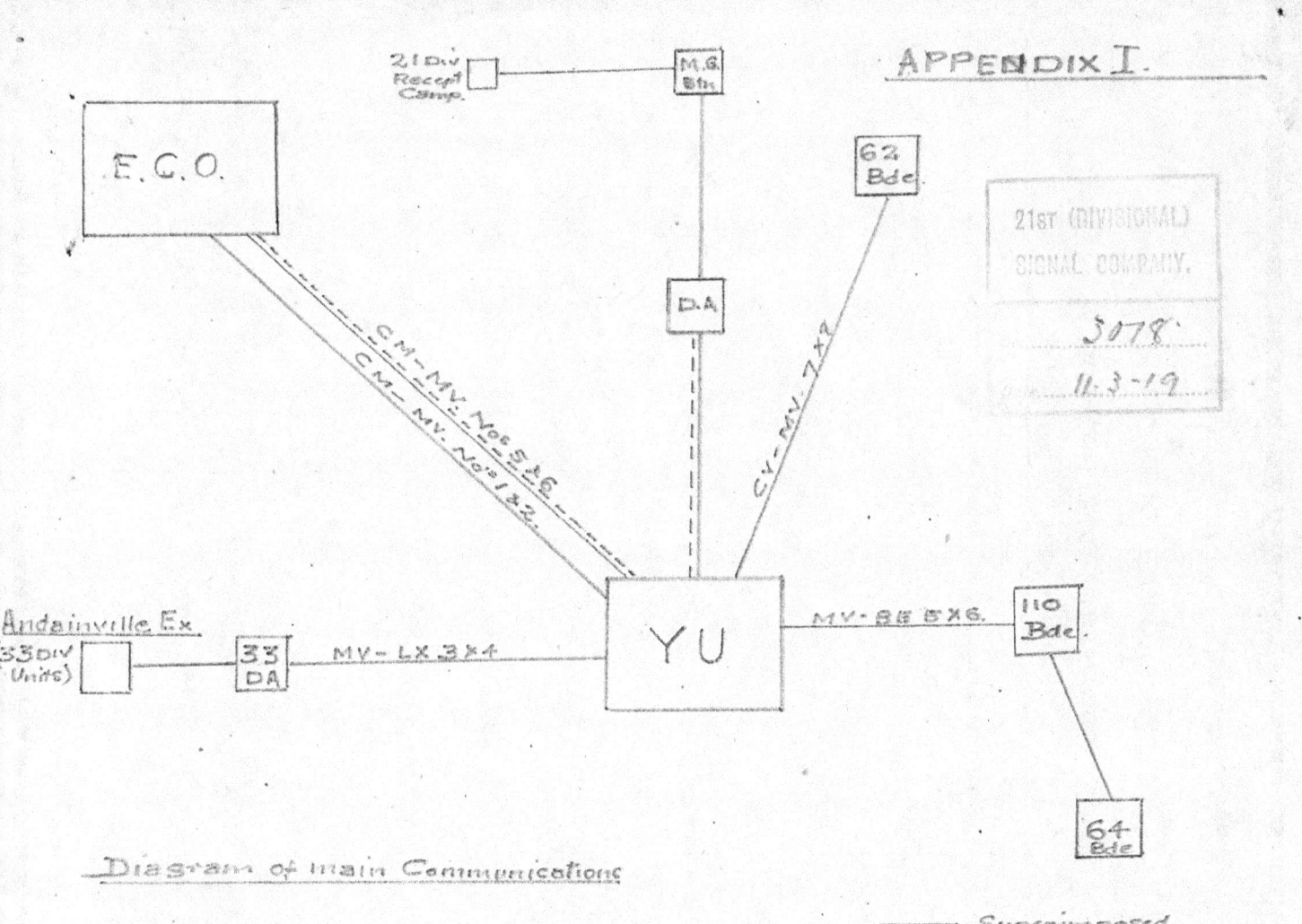

Army Form C. 2118.

WAR DIARY
or
INTELLIGENCE SUMMARY.
(Erase heading not required.)

2nd Signal Company R.E.
War Diary for March 1919

Place	Date	Hour	Summary of Events and Information	Remarks and references to Appendices
MOLLIENS-VIDAME	1-3-19		No change in location of Div.H.Q. or H.Q's of Infantry or Artillery Brigades. The communications existing throughout the month are as shown in appendix	
	3-3-19		1 Sgt. to Hospital	
	7-3-19		2 O.R's rejoined from 3rd Army Signal School	
	8-3-19		1 O.R. Hospital	
			2 OR's Hospital	
	11-3-19		1 O.R. Hospital	
	13-3-19		1 O.R. rejoined from hospital	
	16-3-19		1 O.R. transferred to 3rd Army Signal Corps	
	19-3-19		1 O.R rejoined from hospital	
	23-3-19		1 Officer rejoined from Course (3rd Army Infantry School)	
	30-3-19		1 O.R. Hospital	
			2 Officers 1 Sergeant and 28 O.Rs demobilized during month	
			81 Horses and 2 mules have been disposed of during the month.	
			Strength of Company 6 Officers 212 O.R's	
			Deficient 6 " 105 " (29 O.R. have left for demobilization who are not yet off strength)	

A.P. Ricgman
Major R.E.
O.C. 2nd Signal Coy R.E.

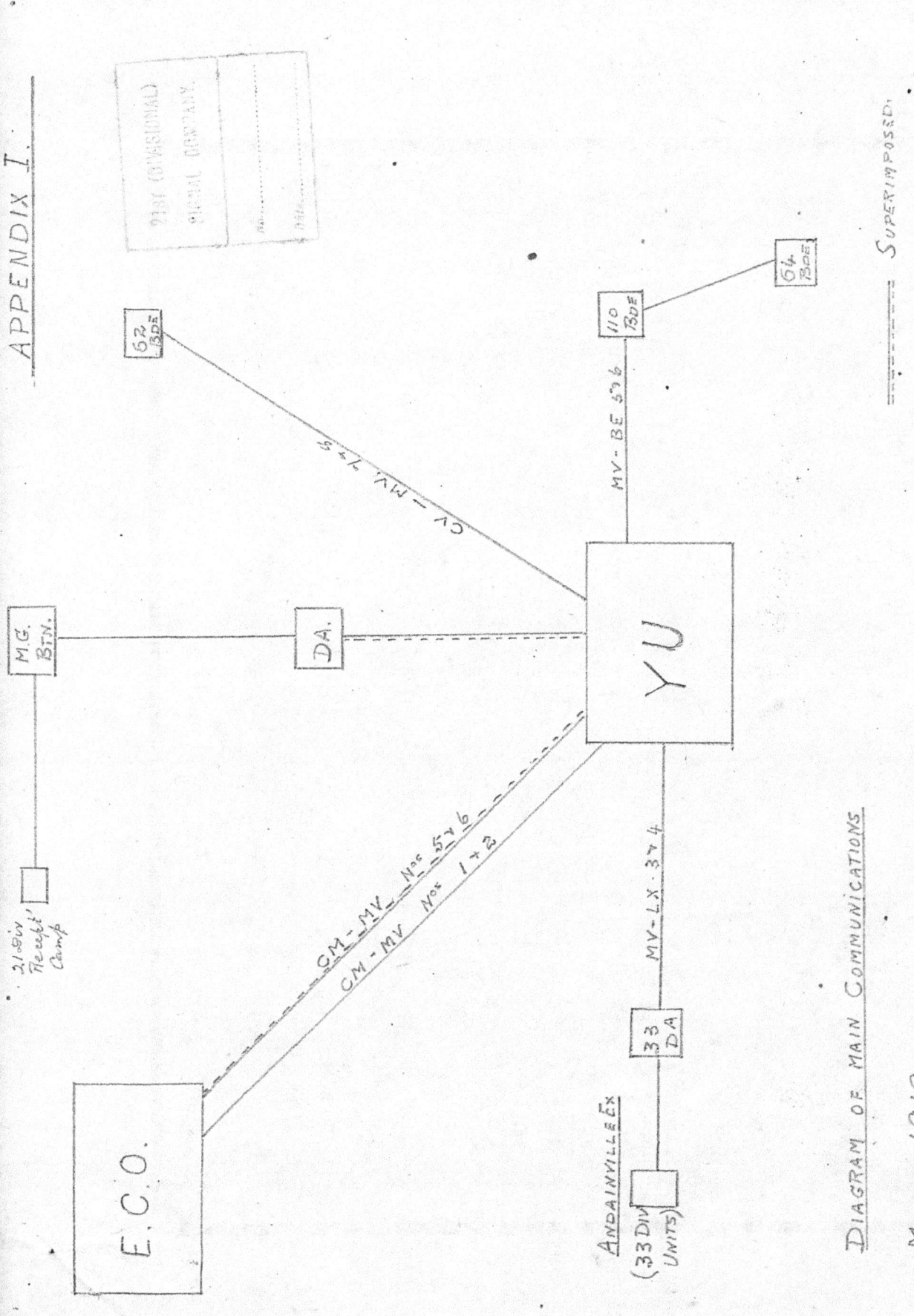

Allanander.
MAJOR, R.E.
Cmdg. 125 Field Co. R.E.

D.A.A.G.(I)

Forwarded

J Hoyle
Maj RE
O/i. R.E. Section

1.5.19

Army Form C. 2118.

WAR DIARY
or
INTELLIGENCE SUMMARY.

(Erase heading not required.)

91st Signal Coy RE
April 1919.

Place	Date	Hour	Summary of Events and Information	Remarks and references to Appendices
Molliens-Vidams	1/4/19		No change in locations of Div. HQ or of HQs of Infantry & Artillery Brigades.	
			No change in main communications.	
Condé-Folie	5/4/19		Div. HQ and HQs. 13th, 12th Inf Bde & 14265 closed at Molliens-Vidame On 7th May and moved to Condé Folie. 5 Div. QR HQ opens day following.	
			Brieulles reported and returned at Condé Folie moved from Dresnou (Telegraph & telephone separated, not long.	
			Diagram of communications on reverse shown on appendix I.	
	6/4/19		1 Fair-Set demobilised	
	7/4/19		9 OR's proceed to Concentration Camp for demobilisation.	
	12/4/19		1 OR rejoined from course with 350th Bn RE.	
	13/4/19		1 OR proceed to Concentration Camp for demobilisation.	
	19/4/19		1 Cpl Sgt Lift Div on 28 days of leave.	
	30/4/19		8 ORs Left for Concentration Camp for demobilisation.	
			88 Horses disposed of during month	
			Total Strength 14 Men 129 ORs	
			3	
			Horses 3	
			53 Other ranks attached and 5 [illegible]	

[signature] Head Qrs
OC 21 Signal Coy RE

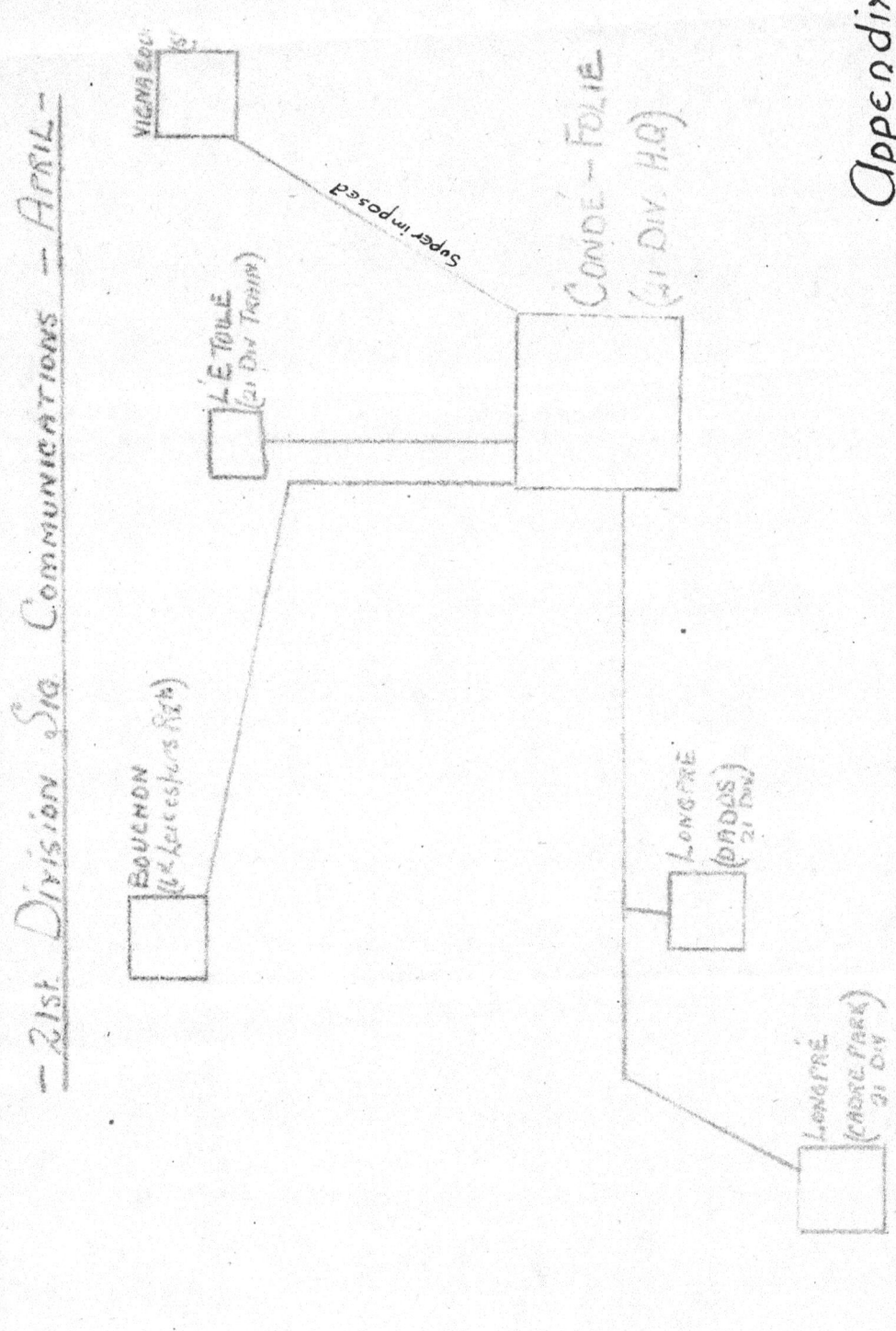

Army Form C. 2118.

WAR DIARY
or
INTELLIGENCE SUMMARY.
(Erase heading not required.)

Instructions regarding War Diaries and Intelligence Summaries are contained in F. S. Regs., Part II. and the Staff Manual respectively. Title pages will be prepared in manuscript.

21 Signal Co RE
May 1919
Vol 4

Place	Date	Hour	Summary of Events and Information	Remarks and references to Appendices
Cose Jolie	1.5.19	-	No change in disposition of Div? HQ and HQ of Bdes. 1, 2, 3 & 7, 10 & 41 Bdes proceed to England during preceding month	
	11.5.19	-	4 ORs demobilized	
	12.5.19	-	OS¹ Lt Wade proceeds to England ※	
	13.5.19	-	2¹ Lt Oac do ※	
	16.5.19	-	1 S OR demobilized	
	17.5.19	-	28 ORs transferred to 5 Corps and 2 OR to 3rd Army Signal Coys	
	18.5.19	-	7 Bn Leic R proceeds to England	
	19.5.19	-	2 Div HQ closed at Corse Jolie – Gear proceeds to Eghin	
			2 DivSupp. HQ opened at L'Etoile. (Communications required with this date to 1 Div (Br to V Corps)	
	21.5.19	-	9 M. Artz Bde proceeds to England (Telephone Exchange provided for this unit those moment closedown 21.5.19)	
L'Etoile	24.5.19	-	1 Bn Innis R & 1 Bn E Yorks R proceed to England Telephone exchange provided for those units at BOUCHON closed down on 25.5.19.	
	25.5.19	-	1 Bn W Yorks R proceeds to England	
			Strength of company 3 officers 55 ORs	

a Statham Capt RE
OC 21 Signal Coy RE

21st (Divisional) Signal Company.
No. 324

21st. DIVISION Group Packet No. A.1276/1.

21st. Division Group Packet Details Camp, L'ETOILE.

1. Owing to the fact that practically all the Cadres of 21st. Div. Units will have proceeded to England by the 25th.inst., it will be necessary to form a Divisional Details Camp, to collect together and to deal with remaining details of units awaiting posting orders, and details returning from leave, etc.

2. This Camp will be established at L'ETOILE, 1500 hrs, 22nd.inst., with H.Q. in the 21st.Div.G.P.office, L'ETOILE. Temporary appointments will be furnished as follows :-

   Off. Commdg.   Capt. HOPPE   1st. Lincs., att 21 Div.H.Q.
   Adjutant.   ?——
   Q.M.& Town   Lt. & Q.M.C.L. FREEMAN 14th.Bn.N.Fus.(P).
   Major.

   The O.C. will be responsible for the organisation and administration of the Camp. Duties for all Officers in the Camp will be detailed by the O.C.

3. Units sending details to this Camp will report the figures of Officers and O.Rs. to O.C.Camp, 24 hours before arrival of details so that billets can be arranged.
   A nominal roll, for each Regiment, on Pro Forma Z attached will be sent with all details to the Camp. This roll will show any details that may arrive from attachments or leave, at later dates.
   It is essential that this Pro Forma be accurately prepared, to avoid any correspondence to Cadres in England.
   The Camp is not to be looked upon as a dumping ground for all oddments and all cases will be cleared up where possible.
   No details from Units that are to be disbanded will be accepted.

4. Rations for the day after arrival at the Camp will be carried, after this date details will be rationed by the Camp.

5. All details will be paid up to a fortnight after arrival, after this date, O.C.Camp will arrange payments.

6. O.C.Camp will arrange direct with S.M.O., 21st.Div. for medical arrangements.

7. Where men have been posted awaiting movement order, or men awaiting demobilization, full and complete documents, and in all cases, A.F.B.122 & A.G.Z.500, will be handed into the O.C.Camp with the nominal rolls.

8. All details returning to the Division by train will be instructed by the R.T.O.LONGPRE to report at Camp H.Q.Office.

                                             Major,
                                    for 21st.Divnl.G.Packet.

20-5-19.

DISTRIBUTION :-

94th.Bde.R.F.A.   222 Emp.Coy.   O.C.Cadre Park.
1st.Bn.Lincs.Rgt.   Div.Train   2.   V Corps G.P.   2.
1st. : Wilts. :   Div.Signals.   R.T.O.LONGPRE.
1st. : E.Yorks: D.A.D.O.S.
98th.Field Coy.RE.   S.M.O., 21 Div. 2.

21st.DIVISION Group Packet Details Camp - L'ETOILE.

Pro Forma Z.

Regiment.

Officers and Other Ranks.			Obtainable, Volunteer or for Demobilization.	With unit at present. (Yes or no)	If on leave, date leave expires	If employed elsewhere name of unit & date returning to Div. if known	If posted name of new unit.	Awaiting posting (Yes or No).	REMARKS
No.	Rank.	Name.							

WAR DIARY
or
INTELLIGENCE SUMMARY.
(Erase heading not required.)

Army Form C. 2118.

Month of June 1919 21st Signal Coy. W.D. 46

Place	Date	Hour	Summary of Events and Information	Remarks and references to Appendices
Condé Folie	1.6.19.		Signal Office at H.Q. H.Q.21E in communication with Corps & Sub Parks	
	3.6.19.		Ordnance stores of the Coy handed in to S.C.S. Longpré, anomaly of gas & equipment had to count	Annex
	4.6.19.	24.O.R.	Proceeded to 4 Corps Concentration Camp for demobilisation	
	6.6.19.	2.O.R.	Transferred to Signals Abbeville. No Transport to Signals tonight time.	
	9.6.19.		P.E.7. Stores despatched to No.2 Base Engineering Stores Depôt. Signal Park Stores despatched by rail to Signal Park Vendroux Calais	
	10.6.19.	8.O.R.	O.R. for XVII Corps concentration Camps for demobilisation	
	13.6.19.	1.O.R.	O.R. for XV Corps Concentration Camps for demobilisation	
	14.6.19.		Signal office at LE TELLE closed & party left Boulogne	
	15.6.19.	1.W.O.R.	Proceeded to XVII Corps Concentration Camp for demobilisation	
		1.O.R.	Attached to 776 Area S. Coy.	
	16.6.19.		2 Motorcycles handed in to No.7 M.T. V.R.D	
	19.6.19.	4.O.R.	Proceeded to XVII Corps Concentration Camp for demobilisation	
			Remainder of M.T. handed in to No.7 M.T. V.R.	
	22.6.19.		2 Officers and 1 O.R. proceeded to XVII Corps Concentration Camp for demobilisation	
		1.O.R.	Transferred to No. 3 Area Signal Coy.	
			The Company in complete disbanded	

Signature G.M.F.E.
O.C. 21 Signal Coy.